Feminist Interventions in Critical Peace and Conflict Studies

This book provides a feminist intervention in Peace and Conflict Studies. It demonstrates why feminist approaches matter to theories and practices of resolving conflict and building peace.

Understanding power inequalities in contexts of armed conflict and peace processes is crucial for identifying the root causes of conflict and opportunities for peaceful transformation. Feminist scholarship offers vital theoretical insights and innovative methods, which can deepen our understanding of power relations in peacebuilding. Yet, all too often feminist research receives token acknowledgement rather than sustained engagement and analysis.

This collection highlights the value of feminist analysis to contemporary Peace and Conflict Studies. Drawing on case studies from around the world – including Croatia, Myanmar, Iceland, Nepal, India, Afghanistan, and Timor-Leste – it demonstrates why paying serious attention to feminist scholarship prompts useful insights for peacebuilding policy, practice, and scholarship.

Feminist theory, epistemology, and methodology provide a rich resource for critically analysing peacebuilding practices. In particular, the chapters highlight the value of feminist reflexivity, the contributions of a feminist corporeal analysis, and the significance of a feminist reading of core concepts in Peace and Conflict Studies – including hybridity, the local, and the everyday.

The chapters in this book were originally published as a special issue of *Peacebuilding*.

Laura McLeod is Lecturer in International Politics at the University of Manchester, UK. Her research focuses on gender, feminism and security concerns in post-conflict contexts. Her current project investigates gender indicators and databases used within UN peacebuilding.

Maria O'Reilly is Senior Lecturer in Politics and International Relations at Leeds Beckett University, UK. Her research focuses on questions of gender and agency in peacebuilding contexts, and she is currently exploring experiences of female ex-combatants in Bosnia & Herzegovina.

Feminist Interventions in Critical Peace and Conflict Studies

Edited by
Laura McLeod and Maria O'Reilly

LONDON AND NEW YORK

First published 2021
by Routledge
2 Park Square, Milton Park, Abingdon, Oxon OX14 4RN

and by Routledge
605 Third Avenue, New York, NY 10158

Routledge is an imprint of the Taylor & Francis Group, an informa business

Introduction, Chapters 1–4 and 6 © 2021 Taylor & Francis
Chapter 5 © 2019 Rachel Julian, Berit Bliesemann de Guevara and Robin Redhead. Originally published as Open Access.

With the exception of Chapter 5, no part of this book may be reprinted or reproduced or utilised in any form or by any electronic, mechanical, or other means, now known or hereafter invented, including photocopying and recording, or in any information storage or retrieval system, without permission in writing from the publishers. For details on the rights for Chapter 5, please see the chapter's Open Access footnote.

Trademark notice: Product or corporate names may be trademarks or registered trademarks, and are used only for identification and explanation without intent to infringe.

British Library Cataloguing in Publication Data
A catalogue record for this book is available from the British Library

ISBN: 978-0-367-77332-8 (hbk)
ISBN: 978-0-367-77334-2 (pbk)
ISBN: 978-1-003-17085-3 (ebk)

Typeset in Minion Pro
by Newgen Publishing UK

Publisher's Note
The publisher accepts responsibility for any inconsistencies that may have arisen during the conversion of this book from journal articles to book chapters, namely the inclusion of journal terminology.

Disclaimer
Every effort has been made to contact copyright holders for their permission to reprint material in this book. The publishers would be grateful to hear from any copyright holder who is not here acknowledged and will undertake to rectify any errors or omissions in future editions of this book.

Contents

	Citation Information	vi
	Notes on Contributors	viii
	Introduction: critical peace and conflict studies: feminist interventions Laura McLeod and Maria O'Reilly	1
1	Mundane peace and the politics of vulnerability: a nonsolid feminist research agenda Tarja Väyrynen	20
2	From power-blind binaries to the intersectionality of peace: connecting feminism and critical peace and conflict studies Stefanie Kappler and Nicolas Lemay-Hébert	34
3	The 'third gender' in Afghanistan: a feminist account of hybridity as a gendered experience Hannah Partis-Jennings	51
4	Care as everyday peacebuilding Tiina Vaittinen, Amanda Donahoe, Rahel Kunz, Silja Bára Ómarsdóttir and Sanam Roohi	67
5	From expert to experiential knowledge: exploring the inclusion of local experiences in understanding violence in conflict Rachel Julian, Berit Bliesemann de Guevara and Robin Redhead	83
6	Veteran masculinities and audiovisual popular music in post-conflict Croatia: a feminist aesthetic approach to the contested everyday peace Catherine Baker	99
	Index	116

Citation Information

The chapters in this book were originally published in *Peacebuilding*, volume 7, issue 2 (June 2019). When citing this material, please use the original page numbering for each article, as follows:

Introduction
Critical peace and conflict studies: feminist interventions
Laura McLeod and Maria O'Reilly
Peacebuilding, volume 7, issue 2 (June 2019), pp. 127–145

Chapter 1
Mundane peace and the politics of vulnerability: a nonsolid feminist research agenda
Tarja Väyrynen
Peacebuilding, volume 7, issue 2 (June 2019), pp. 146–159

Chapter 2
From power-blind binaries to the intersectionality of peace: connecting feminism and critical peace and conflict studies
Stefanie Kappler and Nicolas Lemay-Hébert
Peacebuilding, volume 7, issue 2 (June 2019), pp. 160–177

Chapter 3
The 'third gender' in Afghanistan: a feminist account of hybridity as a gendered experience
Hannah Partis-Jennings
Peacebuilding, volume 7, issue 2 (June 2019), pp. 178–193

Chapter 4
Care as everyday peacebuilding
Tiina Vaittinen, Amanda Donahoe, Rahel Kunz, Silja Bára Ómarsdóttir and Sanam Roohi
Peacebuilding, volume 7, issue 2 (June 2019), pp. 194–209

Chapter 5
From expert to experiential knowledge: exploring the inclusion of local experiences in understanding violence in conflict
Rachel Julian, Berit Bliesemann de Guevara and Robin Redhead
Peacebuilding, volume 7, issue 2 (June 2019), pp. 210–225

Chapter 6
Veteran masculinities and audiovisual popular music in post-conflict Croatia: a feminist aesthetic approach to the contested everyday peace
Catherine Baker
Peacebuilding, volume 7, issue 2 (June 2019), pp. 226–242

For any permission-related enquiries please visit:
www.tandfonline.com/page/help/permissions

Notes on Contributors

Catherine Baker, Department of History, University of Hull, Hull, UK.

Berit Bliesemann de Guevara, Department of International Politics, Aberystwyth University, Penglais, Aberystwyth, UK.

Amanda Donahoe, Peace and Justice Studies, Tufts University, Boston, MA, USA; History and Political Science, Centenary College of Louisiana, Shreveport LA, USA.

Rachel Julian, School of Social Sciences, Leeds Beckett University, City Campus, Leeds, UK.

Stefanie Kappler, School of Government and International Affairs, Durham University, Durham, UK.

Rahel Kunz, Faculty of Social and Political Sciences, University of Lausanne, Lausanne, Switzerland.

Nicolas Lemay-Hébert, Department of International Relations, Coral Bell School, Australian National University, Canberra, Australia.

Laura McLeod, Politics, University of Manchester, Manchester, UK.

Silja Bára Ómarsdóttir, Faculty of Political Science, University of Iceland, Reykjavik, Iceland.

Maria O'Reilly, Leeds School of Social Sciences, Leeds Beckett University, Leeds, UK.

Hannah Partis-Jennings, Politics and International Studies, Loughborough University, Loughborough, UK.

Robin Redhead, School of Social Sciences, Leeds Beckett University, City Campus, Leeds, UK.

Sanam Roohi, Department of Political Science, St. Joseph's College (Autonomous), Bangalore, India; Max Weber Kolleg, University of Erfurt, Germany.

Tiina Vaittinen, Faculty of Social Sciences, University of Tampere, Tampere, Finland.

Tarja Väyrynen, Tampere Peace Research Institute, University of Tampere, Finland.

Introduction

Critical peace and conflict studies: feminist interventions

Laura McLeod and Maria O'Reilly

ABSTRACT

Critical Peace and Conflict Studies (PCS) as a field cares about gender. Yet, feminist work frequently receives token acknowledgement by critical scholars rather than sustained engagement and analysis. This Special Issue demonstrates why critical PCS needs feminist epistemologies, methodologies, and empirical analyses. In this introductory article, we deploy a feminist genealogical analysis of the 'four generations' of PCS and argue that the ghettoization of 'gender issues' marginalises feminist work within academia, policy, and practice. Critical PCS research has taken inspiration from feminist scholars, however there remain opportunities for deeper conversations. Addressing this marginalisation matters if we wish to decolonise PCS and develop a nuanced sensory perception of peace and conflict. Furthermore, engaging with feminist ideas can directly contribute to building more meaningful, sustainable, and equitable forms of peace. In short: feminist insights are crucial to prompting a deeper and more transformative dialogue within the scholarship and practice of critical PCS.

Introduction

What are the connections between critical and feminist approaches to Peace and Conflict Studies (PCS)? What are the similarities and differences, compared to critical research, when feminist scholars study peace? Asking these questions prompts us to consider what feminist PCS research *is*, and to consider the key insights that feminist analysis offers. These questions reoccur throughout this Special Issue, where the authors all showcase the value of feminism to their analysis of key questions and issues currently debated in critical PCS. In this introductory article, we explore our rationale for provoking a feminist intervention in critical PCS and highlight the reasons why a feminist intervention is needed. Our analysis reveals that feminist perspectives are frequently missing and marginalised from critical accounts of peace. We demonstrate that feminist inquiry enables PCS to move away from what Cynthia Enloe calls the 'too-simple explanations'.[1] Initially, our curiosity was provoked by our attendance at conferences and panels claiming an association with critical PCS. At these sessions, we noted the remarkable exclusion or marginalisation of feminist work on peace and conflict. Remarkable, because we felt that the contributions of feminist work were informative, and indeed often formative, of the development of critical perspectives on PCS. What we contend throughout this Special Issue is that feminist approaches, analysis, scholarship, and methods can, should, and already *do*, make significant contributions to critical PCS.

While defining 'feminist PCS research' is contentious, and indeed, there are various ways and extents to which scholarship can be feminist, we take the view that feminist PCS research seeks to develop and apply feminist theory and/or methodology to produce insights about issues of peace and conflict. Feminist approaches, while varied, understand gender as a concept or category that must be unpacked and engaged with to make sense of why conflict emerges and how peace can/should be built. Feminist PCS shares many commonalities with critical PCS scholarship, as we outline below.[2] Both represent alternative approaches to the positivist research agenda that dominates mainstream PCS. Like critical PCS, feminist PCS research aims to achieve positive social change, by critiquing dominant ideologies and methodologies of building peace that (re)produce inequalities of power along lines of gender, race/ethnicity, nationality, class, sexuality, dis/ability, and so on. Both schools tend towards bottom-up methodologies that place lived experience at the centre of the research process. However, unlike critical scholarship, feminist PCS research is characterised by an explicitly feminist commitment, firstly, to identify the androcentric nature of PCS, and, secondly, to challenge the tendency of mainstream and critical PCS researchers to ignore, minimise, or marginalise the perspectives of women, girls, and non-binary people, and/or the category of gender in their analyses. That said, it is impossible to talk of 'critical PCS' and 'feminist PCS' as coherent entities that talk at odds with each other. We do not seek to develop a grand definition of what constitutes feminist or critical PCS – both are very diverse fields, and this is to be celebrated. Acknowledging that there is much slippage, in this Special Issue we aim to illustrate and make this slippage explicit, while demonstrating what is different when feminist scholars intervene in PCS.

This introductory article proceeds in three parts. First, we unpack the key concepts underpinning this Special Issue, making explicit why we feel a feminist intervention is necessary. Second, we chart the connections between critical and feminist approaches to PCS, via an investigation of the 'four generations' of PCS scholarship.[3] Our analysis highlights that: (a) the marginalisation of feminist ideas is a continual thread throughout the development of PCS, and (b) although the 'fourth' generation (critical PCS) has taken some inspiration from feminist scholars, there remain opportunities for deeper conversations. Third, we highlight the three key contributions that a feminist intervention into critical PCS achieves:

---

[1] Cynthia Enloe, *Bananas, Beaches and Bases: Making Feminist Sense of International Politics*, 2nd ed. (Berkeley: University of California Press, 2014), 352.
[2] See: Maria O'Reilly, 'From Gendered War to Gendered Peace? Feminist Perspectives on International Intervention in Sites of Conflict', in *Handbook on Intervention and Statebuilding*, ed. Nicolas Lemay-Hébert (Cheltenham: Edward Elgar Publishing, forthcoming).
[3] Oliver P. Richmond, 'A Genealogy of Peace and Conflict Theory', in *Palgrave Advances in Peacebuilding: Critical Developments and Approaches*, ed. Oliver P. Richmond (London: Palgrave, 2010), 14–38.

(1) Feminist theory, epistemology and methodology is a rich resource, opening way for a less binary, more nuanced approach to PCS.
(2) Feminist analysis encourages a nuanced sensory perception of peace and conflict, following several key feminist insights about the significance of the personal, of embodiment, and of experience.
(3) Efforts to decolonise the modes of knowledge production within PCS cannot be fully realised without incorporating a feminist critique of concepts such as 'the local' and 'the everyday' which are currently at the heart of critical PCS scholarship.

For us, these three reasons begin to address what is different when feminist scholars contend with issues of peace and conflict. These represent three key contributions of a feminist intervention into critical PCS, which is explored further throughout this Special Issue. Finally, the article concludes by outlining suggestions for how to foster a more effective dialogue between these fields.

Key terms: a feminist intervention

Feminism is provocative, and we do not want to pin it – *feminism* – down and define it. Sara Ahmed thinks of feminism as 'homework', because 'we have so much to work out from not being at home in a world' (2017, 7). As feminists, we do not always feel at 'home' within critical PCS. A paper about feminism presented at a conference sometimes leads to an awkward silence. Why? Sara Ahmed's insight that 'when you expose a problem you pose a problem' comes to mind.[4] Or perhaps it is because 'nonfeminist scholars seem convinced that feminist knowledge does not concern them – a feeling reproduced by a common understanding that feminism is only about "identity politics" or "women's stuff"'.[5] This provokes us to wonder if there has been a wilful blindness and marginalisation of the potential and actual contributions of feminist scholarship by many working in critical PCS. As stated, this Special Issue seeks to demonstrate that feminist approaches are vital to achieving a subtle and nuanced analysis of key issues in PCS. Paying serious attention to a wide range of feminist scholarship would highlight useful insights for peacebuilding policy and practice, make stronger efforts to decolonise PCS, and develop a nuanced sensory analysis within PCS scholarship.

It is useful to distinguish between the terms women, gender, and feminism. It might seem obvious, but 'women' relates to a biological sex. 'Gender' typically refers to socially constructed understandings of bodies and how they behave. Gender is a contested and slippery concept. It may be best understood as a 'category developed to explore what counts as "woman" and as "man"'.[6] Gender recognises that masculinity and femininity are culturally and socially constructed and are analytically different to categories such as male/female, boy/girl, which are (problematically) deployed to establish a sexual difference based upon bodily characteristics. Like gender, 'feminism' is tricky to define, and

---

[4]Sara Ahmed, *Living a Feminist Life* (Durham and London: Duke University Press, 2017), 37.
[5]Linda Åhäll, 'Affect as Methodology: Feminism and the Politics of Emotion', *International Political Sociology* 12, no. 1 (2018): 2.
[6]Judith Squires and Jutta Weldes, 'Beyond Being Marginal: Gender and International Relations in Britain', *British Journal of Politics and International Relations* 9, no. 2 (2007): 186.

we do not wish to police what does or does not count as being feminist. Broadly, feminism may be understood as a political orientation and ideological movement geared towards the transformation of gendered power relations. These ideas about transformation are often informed by concepts such as inequality, patriarchy, misogyny, androcentricism, and sexism.

'Intervention' is a word that we use often in PCS. International intervention. Humanitarian intervention. Statebuilding interventions. Intervention can be understood as being intrusive. Marysia Zalewski notes that feminism's presence in International Relations (IR) is an 'explicitly gendered figure', where the shape of arrival is seen as 'an intruder's knowledge', where 'feminism's presence seemingly naturally requires explanation, justification and evaluation'.[7] Our experience is that PCS has been similar. We deliberately chose to title this Special Issue 'Feminist Interventions' because we wanted to intervene into a field stridently, and to point out what needed to be thought about differently. Our intervention is staged because we are concerned that there is a tendency within critical scholarship to engage with many concepts – hybridity, agency, the everyday, friction, the local, participation, and narratives – without paying attention to feminist insights. As the authors in this Special Issue demonstrate, many of these concepts have deep feminist roots, stretching back decades. These roots are rarely acknowledged. Additionally, throughout the Special Issue, authors have sought to demonstrate the ways in which feminist ideas can push us to rethink key concepts, approaches, and methods in contemporary PCS. It is not that feminism is a new approach to PCS, but rather, that the moment is ripe for a sustained feminist intervention, given the increasing use of popular concepts in critical PCS that have feminist roots.

Conceptualising peace and conflict: understanding gendered histories

To explore the ways that PCS rarely acknowledges feminism, we critically engage with Oliver Richmond's 2010 typology of the 'four generations' of PCS,[8] using a feminist genealogical approach to examine both feminist and critical PCS perspectives across each generation. Richmond identifies four generations of theory and practice as constituting the core of PCS scholarship: conflict management, conflict resolution, liberal peacebuilding, and post-liberal peacebuilding. These generations differ fundamentally in their understandings of the causes of conflict, and hold diverging views on whether conflict can be successfully resolved, or else merely managed. This framework is not intended as a strictly chronological narrative of PCS scholarship, and nor is it a linear story of how peacebuilding has evolved in practice. Rather, the generations are categorisations of scholarship which are aligned to different practices of engaging with conflict and conflict transformation. The 'four generations' framework allows us to identify connections between each 'generation' of PCS scholarship and peacebuilding practice and policy. It provides a means of highlighting the entrenched marginalisation of feminist approaches over time. As scholars, we need to 'cast an eye backwards' otherwise 'partial vision, entrenched location, or citational myopia may hinder movement

---

[7]Marysia Zalewski, *Feminist International Relations: Exquisite Corpse* (London: Routledge 2013), 25.
[8]Richmond, 'A Genealogy of Peace and Conflict Theory'.

forwards'.[9] Armed with a better understanding of how the marginalisation of feminism occurs throughout all four generations, we contend that the fourth generation (post-liberal, critical PCS) should recognise the feminist roots of many of the concepts used, and that the failure to acknowledge feminism serves to limit the potential of critical PCS.

There are three points that we wish to make in relation to this analytical move. First, that we seek to build on the 'four generations' framework to highlight gender blind-spots. A feminist gaze could ask how and why this narrative is frequently reproduced or note that, by paying it attention, we are reproducing patriarchal ideas where feminism has been marginalised and excluded from the account. We deploy the 'four generations' framework because it is a reference point for both feminist[10] and critical scholars.[11] It allows us to chart the connections and concerns shared between critical and feminist PCS, whilst demonstrating the entrenched history of feminist marginalisation from thinking about peace and conflict. Despite its rich heritage, feminist work frequently receives token acknowledgement by critical scholars rather than sustained engagement and analysis.[12] This highlights that scholarship is deeply political and deeply saturated in (gendered, racialised, classed) power relations, a point that feminists have long recognised.[13] Using the 'four generations' framework as our starting point for a feminist intervention allows us to be attentive of gender blindness and to develop a more holistic understanding of PCS. There is therefore a political purpose to telling this story.

Second, we believe that the marginalisation of feminist theorising on peace and conflict is reflected within practices of peacebuilding. The citational myopia and other patterns of exclusion faced by feminist scholarship is mirrored in practice, with gender concerns often ghettoised by policymakers and practitioners. For example, the UN's expanding 'Women, Peace and Security' (WPS) Agenda is rarely, if ever, discussed by scholars not typically working within feminist 'camps'. Furthermore, research on gender within the UN Peacebuilding Commission demonstrates that references to WPS are rare within documents produced by the Peacebuilding Commission.[14] Moreover, there is a 'tendency to describe the WPS agenda as a "normative" agenda, and to engage with questions of women's participation as normative questions'.[15] Our article focuses on the marginalisation of scholars who examine the ghettoization of women and/or gender issues in practice. If we are to meaningfully transform the way that gendered and feminist goals are addressed within peacebuilding, then the 'theoretical' and 'academic' space is a productive starting place.

---

[9]Christine Sylvester, *Feminist International Relations: An Unfinished Journey* (Cambridge: Cambridge University Press, 2002), 15.
[10]E.g, Laura J. Shepherd, *Gender, UN Peacebuilding, and the Politics of Space* (Oxford: Oxford University Press, 2017), 29–30.
[11]E.g. Vivienne Jabri, 'Peacebuilding, the Local and the International: A Colonial or a Postcolonial Rationality?' *Peacebuilding* 1, no. 1, (2013): 3–16.
[12]This point emerged during a workshop the editors convened on 'Critical Peacebuilding: Feminist Interventions' in Manchester, 20 June 2016. We thank workshop participants for thoughtful and engaging discussion of these issues.
[13]Lorraine Code, 'Taking Subjectivity into Account', in *Feminist Epistemologies* eds. Linda Alcoff and Elizabeth Potter (New York: Routledge, 1993), 16.
[14]Laura J. Shepherd, 'Victims of Violence or Agents of Change? Representations of Women in UN Peacebuilding Discourse', *Peacebuilding* 4, no. 2 (2016):134.
[15]Ibid., 132.

Finally, this is not to say that feminist and critical PCS scholars should 'merge their perspectives, modes of inquiry, and strategies for action'.[16] We agree with Christine Sylvester's argument that there are 'too many healthy ambiguities within women, and within feminist theories, for there to be any healthy reconciliation of feminist and peace projects'.[17] Rather, we want to realise and acknowledge the ways that feminist scholarship and its heritage is central to critical PCS, and that continuing to marginalise feminist analysis will result in deficiencies and limitations in our analysis of peace and conflict.

First generation approaches: conflict management & achievement of negative peace

Conflict management approaches – associated with international negotiation, mediation, and traditional peacekeeping – are largely inspired by the realist belief in the inevitability of conflict and the impossibility of achieving resolution.[18] These focus narrowly on managing conflict situations and achieving 'negative peace'[19] by halting overt violence. The aim is to reinforce international order and security by 'isolating' and 'containing' conflict.[20]

There is shared agreement between critical and feminist PCS regarding the inadequacies of conflict management approaches for building sustainable peace. Traditional peacekeeping missions, for example, hold a mixed record in limiting armed conflict, and are 'virtually uniform' in their failure to achieve conflict resolution.[21] They rarely created the conditions for peace, and worked largely to 'freeze' rather than resolve conflict.[22] Women and gender issues were largely excluded from traditional peacekeeping missions: for instance, between 1957 and 1989, the number of women participating in the military component of peacekeeping missions was a mere 0.1%.[23] Furthermore, the coercive power wielded by armed peacekeepers is criticised by feminists – for reproducing violent masculinities which (re)create gendered forms of insecurity,[24] and for perpetuating relations of domination which are at the root of violent conflict.[25]

Traditional diplomacy, meanwhile, frequently produced settlements based on 'peace without justice' and often found it difficult to address the rising number of intra-state conflicts due to its state-centric view of conflict.[26] Feminist scholars have documented

---

[16]Betty Reardon, *Sexism and the War System* (New York: Syracuse University Press, 1996),1.
[17]Christine Sylvester, 'Some Dangers in Merging Feminist and Peace Projects', *Alternatives* 12, no. 4 (1987): 494.
[18]Oliver P. Richmond. *Transformation of Peace* (Basingstoke: Palgrave MacMillan, 2005), 89.
[19]Johan Galtung, 'Violence, Peace and Research', *Journal of Peace Research* 6, no. 3, (1969): 167–91.
[20]Oran R. Young, *The Intermediaries: Third Parties in International Crises* (New Jersey: Princeton University Press, 1967), 136–41; and Paul F. Diehl, *International Peacekeeping* (Baltimore: John Hopkins University Press, 1994), 5–13.
[21]Diehl, *International Peacekeeping*, 89–92.
[22]Steven R. Ratner, *The New UN Peacekeeping: Building Peace in Lands of Conflict After the Cold War* (New York: St Martin's Press, 1995).
[23]Louise Olsson, 'Mainstreaming Gender in Multidimensional Peacekeeping: A Field Perspective', *International Peacekeeping* 7, no. 3 (2000): 2.
[24]Paul Higate and Marsha Henry, 'Engendering (In) Security in Peace Support Operations', *Security Dialogue* 35, no. 4 (2004): 481–98.
[25]Diane Francis, 'Culture, Power Asymmetries and Gender in Conflict Transformation', in *Berghof Handbook of Conflict Transformation*, ed. Berghof Research Center for Constructive Conflict Management (Berlin: Berghof Foundation, 2004), 12.
[26]Oliver P. Richmond, *Maintaining Order, Making Peace* (Hampshire: Palgrave, 2002), 77.

the long-standing absence of women from formal peace negotiations.[27] Obstacles include highly gendered norms and practices of diplomacy, which associate negotiations and mediation with men, masculinity, and military affairs.[28] The lack of recognition of women as significant peace-making actors is another factor; as is the priority afforded to high-level political and military actors (usually men), at the expense of women's interests and demands.[29]

From a feminist perspective, conflict management approaches, in theory and in practice, reflect and sustain a 'cult of power' within peace research – one which marginalises the perspectives and contributions of relatively 'powerless' non-state actors, including many women, girls, and non-binary people.[30] Furthermore, the goal of promoting negative peace, is strongly criticised by feminists, who point out that this leaves (gendered) forms of direct violence (e.g. gender-based violence), structural violence (patriarchy), and cultural violence (militarism) unaddressed.[31]

Second generation approaches: conflict resolution & fulfilment of human needs

'Second generation' conflict resolution approaches to ending conflict emerged in response to the limitations of conflict management methodologies, and take the view that conflicts can be resolved rather than merely managed.[32] These approaches aim to create grass-roots mechanisms and processes capable of addressing the complex nature of 'deep-rooted'/'protracted'/'intractable' conflicts.[33] Through problem-solving workshops, third-party facilitation, and project-oriented approaches, bottom-up methods are employed to address the social, psychological, and structural roots of conflict.[34] Feminist scholars and activists have challenged the absence of women, gender, and feminist insights from conflict resolution theory and practice.[35]

Conflict resolution approaches are appealing, given that they engage civil society in peacebuilding, and promote a peace based around mutual agreement and justice.[36] They advocate a shift from official, Track I diplomacy towards the use of unofficial, Track II initiatives. These processes are designed to enable all parties to feel that they

---

[27]Christine Chinkin and Kate Paradine, 'Vision and Reality: Democracy and Citizenship of Women in the Dayton Peace Accords', *Yale Journal of International Law* 26 (2001): 103.
[28]Karin Aggestam and Ann E. Towns, eds, *Gendering Diplomacy and International Negotiation* (Palgrave: London, 2018).
[29]Anne Marie Goetz and Rob Jenkins, 'Agency and Accountability: Promoting Women's Participation in Peacebuilding', *Feminist Economics* 22, no. 1 (2016): 211–36. For an overview of key factors enabling or constraining women's participation in peace negotiations, see: Thania Paffenholz et al., 'Making Women Count – Not Just Counting Women: Assessing Women's Inclusion and Influence on Peace Negotiations', (Geneva: Inclusive Peace and Transition Initiative and UN Women, 2016), https://www.inclusivepeace.org/sites/default/files/IPTI-UN-Women-Report-Making-Women-Count-60-Pages.pdf (accessed September 19, 2018)
[30]Berenice Carroll, 'Peace Research: The Cult of Power', *Journal of Conflict Resolution* 16, no. 4 (1972): 585–616; and Sarai Aharoni, 'The Gender–Culture Double Bind in Israeli–Palestinian Peace Negotiations: A Narrative Approach', *Security Dialogue* 45, no. 4 (2014): 373–90.
[31]Catia Confortini, 'Galtung, Violence and Gender: The Case for a Peace Studies/Feminism Alliance', *Peace and Change* 31, no. 3 (2006): 333–67.
[32]Richmond, *Maintaining Order*, 41.
[33]These terms are deployed by John Burton, Edward Azar and Louis Kriesberg respectively. See M. Hoffman, 'Defining and Evaluating Success: Facilitative Problem-Solving Workshops in an Interconnected Context', *Paradigms* 9, no. 2, (1995): 165.
[34]Richmond, *Maintaining Order*, 75–6.
[35]For an overview, see: Simona Sharoni, 'Conflict Resolution: Feminist Perspectives', in *The International Studies Encyclopedia, Vol. II*, ed. Robert Denemark (Chichester: John Wiley and Sons Ltd, 2010).
[36]Oliver P. Richmond, 'The Dilemmas of Conflict Resolution: A Comparison of Sri Lanka and Cyprus', *Nationalism and Ethnic Politics* 10, no.2 (2004): 185.

have 'won'[37] by satisfying basic needs – to security, recognition, political representation, and economic participation – which are considered the root causes of conflict.[38] Furthermore, the techniques deployed by third-party mediators are designed not to achieve manipulation or control, but rather to assist conflicting parties in processes of self-realisation and immanent transformation,[39] and a true resolution rather than a compromise or settlement.[40] This may unlock possibilities for achieving a self-sustaining peace.[41]

Yet, despite their early promise and innovative techniques, commentators have questioned the efficacy of these methods.[42] Critical PCS scholars highlight that, if undertaken without adequate consideration of the impact of asymmetric power relations and structural constraints, conflict resolution will merely strengthen the stronger party's position and (re)produce conditions of domination, injustice, and inequality.[43] The isolation of peace-making from the social and cultural context in which conflict is embedded is also identified as a major weakness.[44]

Feminist researchers critique the 'gender-blindness' of mainstream theories and practices for excluding women from Track II mediation (as facilitators and participants); and note that problem-solving workshops often fail to consider the significance of gender for conflict analysis and resolution.[45] Without explicit discussion of how gender roles, identities, and structures of power are entangled in conflict and its resolution, Track II initiatives may create the 'impression that conflict and war are genderless phenomena'.[46] To ensure that conflict resolution processes and outcomes are gender-just, feminists identify the need for theorists and practitioners to build theories and methodologies that can identify and address context-specific gender norms, identities, and power structures in sites of conflict, and also recognise the 'practical' and 'strategic' gender interests of women situated in conflicted contexts.[47]

Third generation approaches: the liberal peace

Women, gender, and feminism have historically been relegated to the margins of PCS, as our discussion of the first and second generations illustrates. Yet, from the 1990s onwards, major transformations in peace operations were accompanied by a growing acceptance that

---

[37]A.J.R Groom, 'Problem Solving in International Relations', in *International Conflict Resolution: Theory and Practice*, eds. E. Azar and J. Burton (Sussex: Wheatsheaf Books, 1986), 85.
[38]Edward Azar, *The Management of Protracted Social Conflict: Theory and Cases* (Aldershot: Dartmouth, 1991), 93.
[39]Mark Hoffman, 'Critical Theory and the Inter-Paradigm Debate', *Millennium* 16, no. 2 (1987): 242–3.
[40]John Burton, *Conflict & Communication: The Use of Controlled Communication in International Relations* (London: Macmillan, 1969), 61–2.
[41]Burton, 'The Procedures of Conflict Resolution', in Azar and Burton, eds., *op.cit.* 94.
[42]E.g. Robert C. Schehr and Dragan Milovanovic, 'Conflict Mediation and the Postmodern: Chaos, Catastrophe, and Psychoanalytic Semiotics', *Social Justice* 26, no. 1, (1999): 208–32.
[43]Vivienne Jabri, *Discourses on Violence: Conflict Analysis Reconsidered* (Manchester: Manchester University Press, 1996), 150.
[44]Tarja Väyrynen, *Culture and international conflict resolution: A critical analysis of the work of John Burton* (Manchester: Manchester University Press, 2001), 1–2.
[45]Cordula Reimann, *Gender in Problem-Solving Workshops: A Wolf in Sheep's Clothing?* (Bern: Swiss Peace, 2004), 35.
[46]Maria Hadjipavlou and Cynthia Cockburn, 'Women in Projects of Co-operation for Peace: Methodologies of External Intervention in Cyprus', *Women's Studies International Forum* 29, no. 5 (2006): 524.
[47]Sophie Richter-Devroe, 'Gender, Culture, and Conflict Resolution in Palestine', *Journal of Middle East Women's Studies* 4, no. 2 (2008): 30–59. The distinction between 'practical' versus 'strategic' gender interests was introduced by **Molyneux**. See: Maxine **Molyneux**, 'Mobilization Without Emancipation? Women's Interests, the State, and Revolution in Nicaragua', *Feminist Studies* 11, no. 2 (1985): 227–54.

gender equality is a significant aspect of peacebuilding. After the Cold War, internationally-supported peacebuilding missions were legitimated by the aim of building a 'liberal peace'.[48] Peacebuilding interventions in sites of conflict followed a standardised, top-down model of reconstruction that prioritises Western politico-cultural norms and neo-liberal economics.[49] Liberal peacebuilding combines traditional forms of peacekeeping, mediation, and negotiation, with a range of activities designed to promote democratisation and good governance, respect for human rights and the rule of law, active civil society, and the development of open market economies.[50] Such missions were deployed in Africa (Namibia), Asia (Cambodia), Europe (Croatia), and Latin America (El Salvador), from as early as 1989.[51] In many contexts, the United Nations and other international peacebuilding actors have held extensive mandates to organise elections, reshape military and civil administration, maintain law and order, repatriate and resettle refugees, and rehabilitate infrastructure.[52] What is clear is that conflict management and resolution had moved a long way from simply 'freezing' a conflict.

In parallel with these changes, peacebuilding actors increasingly recognised the gender-specific impact of armed conflict, and the significant role that women play in all aspects of peacebuilding. Significantly, the UN Security Council passed Resolution 1325 on Women, Peace and Security in October 2000, which urged for the integration of a gender perspective across UN peace and security processes. To date, a total of eight WPS resolutions have been adopted.[53] Taken together, these resolutions articulate an agenda to prevent sexual and gender-based violence, encourage the meaningful participation of women in peace and security processes, and to protect women's rights in conflict and post-conflict contexts. The effects of the WPS agenda has been surprisingly pervasive and wide-ranging. It has shaped funding and agendas across the UN system; programmes of national governments and regional organisations[54]; influenced feminist activism across the world[55]; and academic interest in the WPS agenda can be described as 'an industry'.[56]

Feminist scholars and activists have fought hard to integrate women and gender perspectives into peacebuilding. Yet, significant obstacles to gender justice and equality remain. For example, between 1992 and 2011, only 2 percent of chief mediators and 9 percent of negotiators in peace processes were women.[57] And, of

---

[48]Alex J. Bellamy and Paul Williams, 'Introduction: Thinking Anew About Peace Operations', *International Peacekeeping* 11, no.1, (2004): 4–5; and Roland Paris, 'Peacebuilding and the Limits of Liberal Internationalism', *International Security* 22, no.2, (1997): 54–89.

[49]Roger Mac Ginty, 'Reconstructing Post-War Lebanon: A Challenge to the Liberal peace?' *Conflict, Security & Development* 7, no. 3 (2007): 457.

[50]Roger Mac Ginty and Oliver P. Richmond, 'Myth or Reality: Opposing Views on the Liberal Peace and Post-War Reconstruction', *Global Society* 21, no.4 (2007): 491.

[51]Roland Paris, *At Wars End: Building Peace After Civil Conflict* (Cambridge: Cambridge University Press, 2004).

[52]For an example, see Mandate of the United Nations Transitional Authority in Cambodia (UNTAC), http://www.un.org/en/peacekeeping/missions/past/untac.htm.

[53]These resolutions are UNSCR 1325 (2000); 1820 (2008); 1888 (2009); 1889 (2009); 1960 (2010); 2106 (2013); 2122 (2013); and 2242 (2015).

[54]For an overview of the 'localisation' of WPS agenda through national (and in some cases regional) action plans, see Special Issue of *International Political Studies Review* on 'Women, Peace and Security: Exploring the implementation and integration of UNSCR 1325' 37, no. 3.

[55]E.g Laura McLeod, *Gender Politics and Security Discourse: Personal-Political Imaginations and Feminism in 'Post-conflict' Serbia* (London: Routledge, 2015).

[56]Laura McLeod Interview with NGO activist, New York, USA 26 August 2016.

[57]UN Women, *Women's Participation in Peace Negotiations: Connections Between Presence and Influence* (2012), 3, http://www.unwomen.org/~/media/Headquarters/Media/Publications/en/03AWomenPeaceNeg.pdf (accessed September 19, 2018).

585 peace agreements signed between 1990 and 2010, only 16 percent contained any references to women and/or gender.[58] Post-conflict peacebuilding initiatives frequently (re-)produce a 'patriarchal gender order'.[59] There is an ongoing need to challenge masculinist visions of peace as a process which excludes women, and as an outcome which fails to tackle gender-based violence and provide for gender justice and equality.[60]

Liberal peacebuilding interventions have been roundly critiqued by both critical and feminist PCS scholarship. Both 'camps' have, for example, highlighted the gulf that exists between the normative agenda espoused by liberal peacebuilding actors and the everyday realities of those groups and communities affected by peace and conflict.[61] Both approaches have examined the unequal encounters, narratives and interactions between 'local' and 'international' actors in conflicted and post-conflict settings.[62] They note the tendency for peace and security interventions to reinforce, rather than disrupt, hierarchical structures and relations of power,[63] and have examined the differential capacities of peacebuilding subjects to respond in agential and resistant ways.[64] In particular, critical PCS has questioned the failure to engage with the everyday needs, voices, and interests of 'local' stakeholders.[65] Peacebuilding, they argue, has been captured by hegemonic interests and neo-colonial agendas, and the liberal vision of peace is fatally undermined by cultural insensitivity, technocratic rationality, exclusion, and coercion.[66] Feminist scholars point to the significant gaps between international rhetoric on WPS, and the reality of implementation.[67] They highlight the propensity of liberal peacebuilding actors to articulate essentialist notions of gender and (re)produce gendered hierarchies of power in (post-) conflict environments.[68]

As the above discussion highlights, there is much that is shared between critical and feminist analyses of peacebuilding. Both have articulated important questions about the effectiveness and the legitimacy of the liberal peace. However, as we outline below, feminist

---

[58]Christine Bell and Catherine O'Rourke, 'Peace Agreements or Pieces of Paper? The Impact of UNSC Resolution 1325 on Peace Processes and their Agreements', *International and Comparative Law Quarterly* 59, no. 4, (2010): 941–80.

[59]Maria-Adriana Deiana, *Gender and Citizenship: Promises of Peace in Post-Dayton Bosnia-Herzegovina* (London, Springer 2018), 200.

[60]For an overview see: Maria O'Reilly, 'Gender and Peacebuilding', in *Routledge Handbook of Peacebuilding*, ed. Roger Mac Ginty (London: Routledge, 2013), 72–83.

[61]Louise Olsson and Theodora-Ismene Gizelis, eds., *Gender, Peace and Security: Implementing UN Security Council Resolution 1325* (London: Routledge, 2015); and Séverine Autesserre, *Peaceland: Conflict Resolution and the Everyday Politics of International Intervention* (Cambridge: Cambridge University Press, 2014).

[62]Oliver P. Richmond, *Liberal Peace Transitions: Between Statebuilding and Peacebuilding* (Edinburgh: Edinburgh University Press, 2009); and Laura McLeod, 'A Feminist Approach to Hybridity: Understanding Local and International Interactions in Producing Post-Conflict Gender Security', *Journal of Intervention and Statebuilding* 9, no. 1 (2015): 48–69.

[63]Michael Pugh, Neil Cooper, and Mandy Turner, eds., *Whose peace? Critical Perspectives on the Political Economy of Peacebuilding* (London: Palgrave, 2016); and Nicola Pratt 'Reconceptualizing Gender, Reinscribing Racial–Sexual Boundaries in International Security: The Case of UN Security Council Resolution 1325 on "women, peace and security"', *International Studies Quarterly* 57, no. 4 (2013): 772–83.

[64]Stefanie Kappler, *Local Agency and Peacebuilding: EU and International Engagement in Bosnia-Herzegovina, Cyprus and South Africa* (London: Palgrave, 2014); and Maria O'Reilly, *Gendered Agency in War and Peace* (London: Palgrave, 2018).

[65]Timothy Donais, *Peacebuilding and Local Ownership: Post-Conflict Consensus-Building* (Abingdon: Routledge, 2012).

[66]Oliver P. Richmond and Roger Mac Ginty, 'Where now for the Critique of the Liberal Peace?' *Cooperation and Conflict* 50, no. 2 (2015): 171–89.

[67]Nicole George and Laura J. Shepherd, 'Women, Peace and Security: Exploring the implementation and integration of UNSCR 1325', *International Political Science Review* 37, no. 3, (2016): 297–306.

[68]Tarya Väyrynen, 'Gender and UN Peace Operations: The Confines of Modernity', *International Peacekeeping* 11, no.1, (2004): 126, 139.

work frequently receives token acknowledgement by critical scholars rather than sustained engagement and analysis. Despite potential connections, the synergies between critical and feminist approaches remain under-explored.

Fourth generation approaches: post-liberal peace

Fourth generation approaches move away from the critiques of the liberal peace. They suggest that the argument which claims that international institutions and actors are imposing an agenda onto the local context is one which 'tend towards caricatures', imagining a monolithic and 'all powerful liberal internationalism'.[69] Such approaches recognise agency, noticing ways that local actors 'subvert, exhaust, renegotiate and resist the liberal peace'.[70] Using conceptual tools such as hybridity,[71] the local,[72] friction,[73] agency,[74] and resistance,[75] critical PCS scholars seek to develop sophisticated and attuned analysis of the functioning of post-conflict interventions.

'Post-liberal' peace approaches have a high level of affinity with feminist goals, insights, concepts, and methods. Both critical and feminist approaches, as noted above, share the normative aim of achieving social change. Both focus on examining everyday peace work,[76] so often undertaken 'out of sight and mind' by women in the private sphere.[77] They also both work to identify hidden narratives, networks and 'cultures of peace'.[78] Both also employ similar methodological approaches, such as the use of fieldwork, ethnography, narrative methods, and a desire to build in personal experiences of war and peace. The possibilities for meaningful synergy are countless, and indeed, some researchers have started to push in this direction. This is notable, for example, in discussions about hybrid interactions in peace interventions, with feminist insights drawing attention to the value of gendered power relations[79] and embodiment[80] in shaping the process of hybridity.[81] It is also notable in explorations of the assumed tension between the goals of gender equality and local ownership.[82] Feminist research has provided important concepts such as

---

[69]Roger Mac Ginty, 'Hybrid Peace: The Interaction Between Top-Down and Bottom-Up Peace', *Security Dialogue* 41, no. 4 (2010): 391.
[70]Roger Mac Ginty, *International Peacebuilding and Local Resistance* (London: Palgrave, 2011), 6–7.
[71]Oliver P. Richmond and Audra Mitchell, eds., *Hybrid Forms of Peace: From Everyday Agency to Post-Liberalism* (Basingstoke: Palgrave Macmillan, 2012).
[72]Joakim Öjendal, Isabell Schierenbeck, Caroline Hughes, eds., *The 'Local Turn' in Peacebuilding: The Liberal Peace Challenged* (London: Routledge, 2017).
[73]Annika Björkdahl and Kristine Höglund, 'Precarious Peacebuilding: Friction in Global–Local Encounters', *Peacebuilding* 1, no.3 (2013): 289–99.
[74]Kappler, *Local Agency*.
[75]Mac Ginty, *International Peacebuilding and Local Resistance*.
[76]Roger Mac Ginty, 'Everyday Peace: Bottom-up and Local Agency in Conflict-Affected Societies', *Security Dialogue* 45, no. 6 (2014): 548–64.
[77]Elise Boulding, *The Underside of History: A View of Women Through Time (Vols. 1–2)* (Newbury Park, CA: Sage, 1992), 16.
[78]Elise Boulding, *Cultures of peace: The hidden side of history* (New York: Syracuse University Press, 2000); and Oliver P. Richmond, *Peace Formation and Political Order* (Oxford: OUP, 2016).
[79]McLeod, 'A Feminist Approach to Hybridity'.
[80]Hannah Partis-Jennings, 'The (in)security of Gender in Afghanistan's Peacebuilding Project: Hybridity and Affect', *International Feminist Journal of Politics* 19, no.4 (2017): 411–25.
[81]See also Nicole George, 'Policing "Conjugal Order": Gender, Hybridity and Vernacular Security in Fiji', *International Feminist Journal of Politics* 19, no. 1 (2017): 55–70.
[82]Eleanor Gordon, Anthony Cleland Welch, and Emmicki Roos, 'Security Sector Reform and the Paradoxical Tension between Local Ownership and Gender Equality', *Stability: International Journal of Security and Development* 4, no. 1, (2015): 1–23.

'empathetic cooperation',[83] significant empirical insights such as those derived from war ethnography,[84] and innovative methods such as institutional ethnography,[85] which have inspired fourth generation debates on the 'local turn' within critical scholarship.[86]

Despite these connections and potential for positive synergies to emerge, it is both striking and puzzling as to why feminist research continues to be marginalised by the fourth generation of critical PCS scholarship. To illustrate this, we conducted a systematic review of the journal *Peacebuilding*, examining all articles included in the five complete volumes published by the time of writing (summer 2018). Our results show that although 66% of all articles do include reference(s) to women, gender and/or feminism, 67% contain no *references* to feminist scholars in PCS/IR. This is disappointing given the feminist insight that violent masculinities and gendered inequalities of power are crucial for understanding the emergence of armed conflict, the continuum of violence that spans war and peace, and ultimately the success or failure of peacebuilding initiatives.[87]

Furthermore, the articles in this Special Issue demonstrate that, when drawing upon concepts such as hybridity, the everyday, or when discussing 'the local turn', the rich heritage of feminist peace research continues to be ignored by critical PCS. As we outline below, feminist scholarship is uncited at the peril of much research in critical PCS, particularly since feminist ideas are rooted in the everyday, bottom-up, and complex relationships between actors.

Introducing the special issue: what is different when feminists do peace and conflict studies?

Taken together, the articles in this Special Issue demonstrate the relevance of drawing upon feminist perspectives when exploring issues in PCS. All contributors draw on feminist theory or undertake careful gender analysis to better explore international interventions in peacebuilding. The contributions of these articles are threefold. Firstly, they demonstrate the methodological, theoretical, and epistemological value of feminist perspectives to PCS. Secondly, they highlight how feminist ideas about embodiment, experience, and sensory perceptions can strengthen critical analyses of peacebuilding. Finally, they show that feminist analyses can further the project of decolonising PCS. Overall, the Special Issue spotlights the centrality of feminist scholarship to critical PCS, showcasing the implications of dislodging the boundaries between these fields.

---

[83]Christine Sylvester, 'Empathetic Cooperation: A Feminist Method for IR', *Millennium* 23, no. 2 (1994): 315–34. This concept has been deployed by critical scholars to conceptualise 'post-liberal' or 'hybrid' forms of peace. See e.g. Richmond and Mitchell, *Hybrid Forms of Peace*.
[84]Carolyn Nordstrom, *A Different Kind of War Story* (Philadelphia: University of Pennsylvania Press, 1997). Nordstrom's work was cited by 10% of all articles published in the first five complete volumes of *Peacebuilding*, according to our systematic review of the journal.
[85]Dorothy E. Smith, *Institutional Ethnography: A Sociology for People* (London: Rowman & Littlefield, 2005). Smith's influence on PCS is highlighted in: Mike Klein, 'Institutional Ethnography as Peace Research', in *Ethnographic Peace Research*, ed. Gearoid Millar (Cham: Palgrave Macmillan, 2018), 65–87.
[86]For an overview of the local turn, see Roger Mac Ginty and Oliver P. Richmond, 'The Local Turn in Peace Building: A Critical Agenda for Peace', *Third World Quarterly* 34, no. 5 (2013): 763–83.
[87]Cynthia Cockburn, 'Gender Relations as Causal in Militarization and War: A Feminist Standpoint', *International Feminist Journal of Politics* 12, no. 2 (2014): 139–57; and Gordon et. al., 'Security Sector Reform'.

Feminist theory, epistemology and methodology as rich resource for PCS

Critical PCS comes under fire for reinforcing binaries – such as local/international; everyday/exceptional; male/female – and for perpetuating hierarchies between lay/expert forms of knowledge. The articles in this special issue of *Peacebuilding* all draw on feminist theory, epistemology, and/or methodology to highlight their implications for how we might critically analyse and reflect upon peacebuilding practice. One key insight is that feminist approaches open the way for a less binary, more nuanced approach to PCS. Stefanie Kappler and Nicolas Lemay-Hébert explore this in relation to hybridity, the everyday, and narratives – key areas of PCS research which may reaffirm binaries and power hierarchies if approached without care. Kappler and Lemay-Hébert introduce an 'intersectionality of peace' approach to prompt a broader understanding of power relations as they are lived and experienced on the ground by a variety of actors (including researchers and peacebuilding interveners). They show that feminist understandings of intersectionality, firstly, enable an exploration of hybrid identities without (re)producing common dichotomies; secondly, allow the complex power dynamics operating within everyday dimensions of peacebuilding interventions to be unpacked; and, finally, support an approach to narrative analysis which identifies structural inequalities. This has implications for how we analyse peace in theory and practice, pushing us to overcome rigid binaries (such as local/international, us/them, male/female), and to challenge discursive and material structures of domination which pervade (post-)conflict settings.

One reason that feminist perceptions help to destabilise binary boundaries the emphasis of feminist research practice upon reflexivity.[88] Feminist researchers recognise that 'the selection of research questions and ... the development of (new) research practices' are among the areas 'where feminist insights can make their biggest impact'.[89] In this Special Issue, Catherine Baker explores how young people engage with popular music in Croatia, Rachel Julian, Berit Bliesemann de Guevara and Robin Redhead examine artistic expressions of silenced voices in Myanmar, and Hannah Partis-Jennings asks questions about the manifestations of the 'third-gender' in Afghanistan. These articles, and others in this Special Issue, emphasise emancipatory and participatory forms of research across a range of very different post-conflict contexts. Such approaches allow researchers to break down barriers between private and public aspects of peace. They enable scholars to tap into voices, culture and community that often remain hidden or unappreciated by existing approaches to PCS, and can introduce everyday experiences of conflict and peace that are not frequently captured. By re-centring on ideas about emancipation and participation, feminist methodologies can be deployed to subvert and address gendered power relations shaping the practice of research in PCS.

Key to the self-reflexivity of feminist research is to raise 'new ethical and political dilemmas that expand methodological inquiry'.[90] Again, all the articles in the Special

---

[88]Brooke A. Ackerly, Maria Stern and Jacqui True, 'Feminist Methodologies for International Relations', in *Feminist Methodologies for International Relations*, eds. Brooke A. Ackerly, Maria Stern and Jacqui True (Cambridge: Cambridge University Press, 2006), 4; and Annick T. R. Wibben, 'Introduction: Feminists Study War', in *Researching War: Feminist Methods, Ethics and Politics*, ed. Annick T. R. Wibben (London: Routledge, 2016), 7.
[89]Wibben, 'Introduction', 7.
[90]Ackerly et. al., 'Feminist Methodologies for International Relations', 5.

Issue do this in one way or another. In particular, Julian *et al* explore the effects of methodological choice in their investigation of the 'Raising Silent Voices' project in Myanmar. They note that feminist epistemology prompted them to foreground the experiential knowledge of 'ordinary people' in conflict situations. Such knowledge, they contend, is essential for understanding the social world and should be placed at centre of analysis. The authors demonstrate how experiential knowledge can be gathered with arts-based methodologies. In doing so, they highlight the importance of knowledge about conflict/peace being produced from standpoint of women and marginalised others whose experiences are so often written out. They argue that this involves re-working and contesting hierarchical power relations between 'researched' and 'researcher'. In recognising that knowledge is produced intersubjectively, the authors note the importance of 'raising silent voices' (and indeed of the silence) of those who have experienced war. In doing so, they make a compelling case for the value of feminist insights for PCS research.

Embodiment, experience and sensory perceptions

Feminism has much to offer in terms of understanding that spaces between conflict and peace are all lived, embodied experiences. A key contribution of feminism to critical PCS is the nuanced sensory perception that feminist analysis offers. This arises out of several key feminist insights about the personal, about bodies, and about experience. While not all feminist work *explicitly* refers to senses, sensory perceptions shape feminist research, analysis and writing. This is because making sense of the human social experience requires us to draw on bodily senses. We cannot know about the world without seeing, hearing, touching, smelling or tasting. Senses are crucial data for perceiving the world, and how you use your senses affects how you interact and make sense of the world. Realising that senses are data is a powerful realisation: data are bits of information that we put together – but how do we access that information? Through our senses. Likewise, processes of conflict and peace are encountered/perceived through the senses – indeed, the common phrases used to describe war refer to senses, e.g. the cry for war/peace; sight of suffering; touch of violence/care; smell of death/disease; the taste of victory (sweet) or defeat (bitter). This means that developing a nuanced sensory perception of the world is crucial to better understanding the processes and practice of international peacebuilding.

Catherine Baker, in this Special Issue, explores how young people engage with (listen to, sing) popular music in post-conflict Croatia to provide insights into how understandings of everyday peace are contested. By exploring how gendered and racialised constructs are attached to and detached from material bodies within audio-visual media, she shows how feminist and aesthetic approaches can help critical PCS reach a deeper understanding of the affective politics of post-conflict masculinities. Sensory explorations are a powerful reminder of how the personal is political: apparently personal, private, 'merely' social aspects of daily life (such as popular music heard and listened to by teenagers) are 'in fact infused with power' and so are intensely political.[91] There are important connections to be made between sensory perceptions,

---
[91] Enloe, *Bananas, Beaches and Bases*, 348 .

bodies and experience, which may open the way for a more nuanced analysis within PCS.

Feminist scholars make gendered bodies and corporeality central to critical PCS. This begins from the premise that it is necessary to avoid adding 'women' as an essentialised category to analyses of peace and conflict. Rather, as noted earlier, gender as an analytical category needs to be contextualised, conceptualised and analysed in all its messy, glorious complexity. The contributions in this Special Issue do this in various ways. Tarja Väyrynen argues against abstract and theoretical understandings of peace, pointing to the significance of vulnerability and corporeality in comprehending how peace is expressed through situated, embodied encounters. Tiina Vaittinen, Amanda Donahoe, Rahel Kunz, Silja Bára Ómarsdóttir and Sanam Roohi suggest that placing feminist understandings of care and of everyday peace at the forefront of critical PCS debates on the 'local turn' would significantly expand understandings of how peace emerges in theory and practice. Vaittinen et al spotlight the vital contributions offered by gendered relations of care and of caring towards the construction of everyday peace. As they show, these relations are invaluable, yet are frequently neglected by critical analyses of peace. The articles by Väyrynen and by Vaittinen et al demonstrate that corporeality can give greater texture and depth to the role that gendered power relations play in the shift towards 'post-liberal peace'.

The feminist interest in corporeality has no doubt emerged out of a wariness 'of any attempts to link women's subjectivities and social positions to the specifics of their bodies'.[92] As noted earlier in this introduction, critical PCS tends to view gender as a problem, or an issue to solve (rather than a critical lens on the world). A feminist perspective about corporeality enables us to think about how bodies have an ability to 'extend the frameworks which contain them'.[93] The ramifications of this insight is powerfully made in this Special Issue by Hannah Partis-Jennings, who explores the use of the 'third gender' by international peacebuilders working in Afghanistan. By developing a framework of gendered hybridity, Partis-Jennings demonstrates how bodies and performances of female internationals adopting and/or assigned the category of the third gender, is central to understanding how actors perform and shape peace promotion at the everyday level. This article is a valuable addition to a growing body of scholarship on hybridity – which highlights how a feminist perspective can prompt a more complex set of questions about the gendered dynamics between local and international actors and how that shapes and produces gender in the practice and process of post-conflict reconstruction.[94]

Decolonising the concepts and methods of PCS

Critical scholarship has been criticised for its propensity to recreate rather than adequately challenge the hierarchies, binaries, and exclusions of mainstream

---

[92]Elizabeth Grosz, *Volatile Bodies: Towards a Corporeal Feminism* (Bloomington: Indiana University Press, 1994), x.
[93]Ibid., xi.
[94]McLeod, 'A Feminist Approach to Hybridity'; Partis-Jennings, 'The (in)security of Gender in Afghanistan's Peacebuilding Project'; Caitlin Ryan and Helen Basini, 'UNSC Resolution 1325 National Action Plans in Liberia and Sierra Leone: An Analysis of Gendered Power Relations in Hybrid Peacebuilding', *Journal of Intervention and Statebuilding* 11, no. 2 (2017): 186–206; George, 'Policing "Conjugal Order"'; and Maria Martin de Almagro, 'Hybrid Clubs: A Feminist Approach to Peacebuilding in the Democratic Republic of Congo', *Journal of Intervention and Statebuilding* Online First (2018).

scholarship.[95] Bennett and Watson, for example, note 'a lack of real engagement' with local stakeholders plus a failure of 'white middle class Western researchers' to reflect on their positionality and privilege and its impact on relationships with research participants.[96] Sabaratnam highlights a tendency to disregard or downplay the agency and subjectivity of societies and communities targeted by liberal interventionism, despite critical scholars claiming to search for 'local', 'everyday', or 'subaltern' understandings of peace.[97] There is an urgent need to decolonise PCS research by challenging neo-colonial modes of knowledge production.

We do not claim that feminist scholarship has entirely escaped Eurocentric assumptions. We acknowledge that the authors in this Special Issue are in the main white scholars situated in the Global North. Furthermore, as Heidi Hudson points out, 'the exploration of gender and decoloniality in relation to peacebuilding remains underrepresented and undertheorised, with the literature focussed on gender and coloniality generally'.[98] Nevertheless, we contend that feminist scholarship is an invaluable source for critical scholars engaging with many of the difficult theoretical issues, methodological challenges, and ethical dilemmas involved in undertaking 'decolonial' research. Feminist research aims to build 'non-exploitative relationships within research' by paying attention to the significance of gender whilst attending to the intersections between sexism, racism, heteronormativity, classism, and so on.[99] Central to this is the understanding that research relationships are shot through with dynamic, shifting, yet hierarchical relations of power.[100]

Thinking about the complexity of power relations in relation to gender and decoloniality is crucial for thinking about 'local' and 'everyday' in analyses of peacebuilding. Making sense of how to use global peacebuilding architectures (such as the WPS resolutions) in local contexts requires us to draw upon feminist ideas about the local, the everyday, and lived experience.[101] Feminists have long argued that 'gender analysis offers a bottom-up foundational logic' which may counter the ways that liberal peacebuilding projects masks disparities between a range of civil society actors.[102] Building on these ideas, in this Special Issue, Tarja Väyrynen draws on a long heritage of feminist peace research about everyday embodied experiences to develop a construct of 'eventness'. Through 'eventness' she highlights how to bring peace back to the lives of ordinary people, seeking to expose the radical potential embedded in the everyday by recognising the spectacular within the ordinary.

---

[95]Suthaharan Nadarajah and David Rampton, 'The Limits of Hybridity and the Crisis of Liberal Peace', *Review of International Studies* 41, no. 1 (2015): 49–72.
[96]Bennett Collins and Alison Watson, 'The Impetus for Peace Studies to Make a Collaborative Turn: Towards Community Collaborative Research' in *Ethnographic Peace Research*, ed. Gearoid Millar (Basingstoke: Palgrave MacMillan, 2018), 96.
[97]Meera Sabaratnam, 'Avatars of Eurocentrism in the Critique of the Liberal Peace' *Security Dialogue* 44, no.3 (2013): 259–78.
[98]Heidi Hudson, 'Decolonising Gender and Peacebuilding: Feminist Frontiers and Border Thinking in Africa', *Peacebuilding* 4, no. 2 (2016): 195.
[99]Gayle Letherby, *Feminist Research in Theory and Practice* (Buckingham: Open University Press, 2003), 73.
[100]Sabine Grenz, 'Intersections of Sex and Power in Research on Prostitutes: A Female Researcher', *Signs: Journal of Women in Culture and Society* 30, no. 4 (2005): 2091–113.
[101]Shweta Singh, 'Gender, Conflict and Security: Perspectives from South Asia', *Journal of Asian Security* 4, no. 2 (2017): 150, 153.
[102]Heidi Hudson, 'Decolonising Gender and Peacebuilding: Feminist Frontiers and Border Thinking in Africa', *Peacebuilding* 4, no. 2 (2016): 205.

Part of decolonising PCS includes considering the ways that scholarship and research practices continue to perpetuate the colonial and Eurocentric nature of academia itself.[103] This awareness was especially heightened around the 'Sapphire Series' panels at the International Studies Association (ISA) annual conference in 2015, where the showpiece panels created by ISA were all-white scholars situated in the Global North.[104] Feminist approaches to research and scholarship can support decolonising the academy. To achieve this, researchers often 'engage creative strategies and a range of traditional and contemporary media as resources through which the subaltern speaks in varied social and community contexts'.[105] In this Special Issue, the articles by Julian *et al*, Väyrynen, and Baker all do this via making use of the visual arts to 'raise silent voices', personal vignettes to highlight the significance of the mundane, and audio-visual media taken from a video-sharing website to problematise masculinities.

As noted, the very practice of academic scholarship also needs decolonising. Feminists have sought to address this. One article in this Special Issue – by Vaittinen *et al* – was the product of Feminist Peace Research Network meetings organised by the Universities of Tampere, Lund and Tromsø during 2016–17.[106] This international, interdisciplinary network brings together feminist PCS researchers from both Global South and North, as well as from academic and practitioner backgrounds. One of the network's innovative practices was to group participants with similar research interests from across the Global North and South to develop a co-authored paper.[107] The impetus behind this was to build a research network celebrating diverse lived experiences and to strengthen collaborations across research communities. Both critical and feminist PCS scholars might develop similar collaborative research practices in order to democratise knowledge production within PCS and challenge institutions and practices that maintain injustice.

Conclusions: action manifesto

Taken together, the articles open up the possibility of a much more gendered critical PCS by spotlighting the potential for feminist theories, concepts, methods, and empirical insights to push the boundaries of critical PCS. We believe that the articles themselves prise open the theoretical and methodological significance of breaking down boundaries between Feminist and Critical PCS. Productive dialogue can unleash positive synergies between these fields. We contend that if critical PCS scholars continue to use concepts such as 'everyday peace' or methods such as institutional ethnography without acknowledging the feminist heritage of these tools, this will indicate the persistence of a wilful blindness and marginalisation of the potential and actual contributions of feminist

---

[103]In the UK, much of this debate was initially prompted by the student-led campaign 'Why is my curriculum white?'. See https://www.nus.org.uk/en/news/why-is-my-curriculum-white/ (accessed September 11, 2018).
[104]Cynthia Weber, 'ISA's Sapphire Series – Is Blue the New White?' (2015), http://duckofminerva.com/2015/02/isas-sapphire-series-is-blue-the-new-white.html (accessed September 11, 2018).
[105]M. Brinton Lykes and Rachel M. Hershberg, 'Participatory Action Research and Feminisms', in *Handbook of feminist research: Theory and praxis*, ed. Sharlene Janice Hesse-Biber (London: Sage, 2007), 342.
[106]Feminist Peace Research Network, 'Feminist Peace Research Network' (2016), http://www.uta.fi/yky/en/feministpeaceresearch/index.html (accessed September 12, 2018).
[107]See also: Annick T.R. Wibben et al., 'Collective Discussion: Piecing-Up Feminist Peace Research', *International Political Sociology*, oly034 (2018), online first.

scholarship within PCS. Thus, we conclude not on an ending, but with an action manifesto[108] for scholars to develop potential connections within the field:

(1) *Critical PCS scholars should identify and challenge misconceptions they may hold about feminist PCS scholarship, and explore the useful insights that may be gained from feminist approaches.* Feminist research is not only relevant for studying women and gender in war and peace. Rather, as this Special Issue spotlights, feminist concepts, methods, and empirical insights are significant for a wide range of issues in PCS. When examining, for example, everyday aspects of conflict and peacebuilding, attention to feminist insights into the significance of the family/private sphere could avoid the danger of reinventing the wheel.

(2) *Seek out ways of making the curricula and teaching of PCS inclusive.* As this article has highlighted, dominant PCS epistemologies and methodologies remain rooted in colonialist, masculinist worldviews and traditions. Placing feminist research, in particular research emanating from the Global South, at the centre of PCS learning, teaching, and scholarship, can help to challenge these entrenched Eurocentric and androcentric biases. This requires ensuring students can access feminist PCS scholarship, by including feminist PCS scholarship within curricula and ordering relevant books/journals into university libraries. It is worth considering if the syllabus would benefit from feminist research appearing throughout teaching modules instead of being ghettoised into 'the week on gender'.

(3) *Seek out ways of making the scholarship and research of PCS inclusive.* Awareness that all-male and all-white panels serve to reinforce the structural inequalities of our discipline is on the increase.[109] Conference organisers could take steps to discourage such panels by insisting that panels should be diverse, and that this diversity does not only happen simply by appointing women and people of colour as panel chairs or discussants. Editorial discretion remains a significant factor in publication and citations. Journal editors can put in place a written policy identifying that citation gaps remain and giving guidance to editors, authors, and reviewers on how they could play a part in addressing this citation gap.[110] The use of feminist Special Issues and Special Sections is helpful in focussing attention on the insights that the various debates within feminist PCS provide. Yet, it is also crucial that authors and editors view feminist scholarship as integrally connected to core concepts and debates at the heart PCS, rather than separating out feminist perspectives, and thereby relegating them to the margins of PCS. We all must work hard to continue to identify gaps. For example, there is a need for all of us to promote feminist PCS scholarship

---

[108]Inspired by Ahmed, *Living a Feminist Life*, 251–68.
[109]The Feminist Collective, 'Feminist labour at the ISA: White manels, the Politics of Citation and Mundane Productions of Disciplinary Sexism and Racism', https://thedisorderofthings.com/2018/06/26/feminist-labour-at-the-isa-white-manels-the-politics-of-citation-and-mundane-productions-of-disciplinary-sexism-and-racism/; Saara Särmä, 'Congrats, You Have an All-Male Panel!' *International Feminist Journal of Politics* 18, no. 3 (2016): 470–76; and Marysia Zalewski, '#AllMalePanels...but...but...but...' *International Feminist Journal of Politics* 18, no. 3 (2016): 492–95; and Cai Wilkinson et al., 'Responding to #AllMalePanels: A Collage', *International Feminist Journal of Politics* 18, no. 3 (2016): 477–91.
[110]International Studies Quarterly asks all involved to consider citations: International Studies Quarterly, 'Guidelines and Policy' (2015), https://www.isanet.org/Publications/ISQ/Guidelines-and-Policy (accessed September 19, 2018).

from the Global South: this exploration would serve to provide an even more intersectional picture of PCS.

Disclosure statement

No potential conflict of interest was reported by the authors.

Funding

The co-authoring of the article was made possible by grants from the British International Studies Association [Research Workshop in International Studies grant], University of Manchester [School of Social Sciences small grant], Goldsmiths University of London [Research Development Fund grant], and the Joint Committee for Nordic research councils in the Humanities and Social Sciences (NOS-HS) [Workshop Grant number 2015-00127, for the establishment of the Feminist Peace Research Network]. In addition, Maria O'Reilly's research was supported by a PaCCS Innovation Award from the UK Arts & Humanities Research Council [grant number AH/N00848/1].

ORCID

Laura McLeod http://orcid.org/0000-0001-7424-9106
Maria O'Reilly http://orcid.org/0000-0001-7633-120X

Mundane peace and the politics of vulnerability: a nonsolid feminist research agenda

Tarja Väyrynen

ABSTRACT
This article draws on critical feminist theorising and post-colonial theories of the body, relatedness, vulnerability and the everyday to offer an alternative framing of peace and suggest a new research agenda. Although there are multiple ontologies in feminist peace theory, the concern for marginalisation and the understanding of the relational and vulnerable nature of human existence are the key contributions that enable a new take on mundane practices of peace. The article argues that traditional ways of thinking about peace ignore the notion that peace is best studied as an event that arises within mundane and corporeal encounters. Furthermore, the article provides a novel take on eventness that centers peace in the lives of ordinary people, and develops the concept of *choreography* as a means to grasp the richness and fluidity of the everyday techniques of interaction that are relevant for peace.

Introduction

In this article, I draw on critical feminist theorising of the body, relatedness, vulnerability and the everyday to offer an alternative framing of peace and suggest a new research agenda. Furthermore, I provide a novel construct of eventness by which I center peace in the lives of ordinary people. I also introduce the concept of *choreography* to grasp the richness and fluidity of the everyday techniques of interaction that are relevant for peace. Ultimately, I propose a critical research agenda whose ambition is to *re-theorise peace by locating it within social and political contexts and examining the practices and eventness of mundane peace, thereby defying the dominant non-situated and abstract conceptions of peace*. This proposal is a critical response to the abstract and ontologically solid nature of peace approaches in general, as well as to the limited way in which critical peace approaches seek to theorise the local as an antidote to abstractions.

My aim is to demonstrate that the microsociology of corporeality, vulnerability and relatedness enables a renewed grasp of the study of peace. The research agenda I suggest departs radically company from the mainstream – in which peace is conceptualised as abstract, solid or the 'opposite of violence' – by locating the substantial and situated nature of peace within social and political life. Ultimately, the agenda seeks to cultivate – in the spirit of non-representational theory, which goes beyond representation and focuses on embodied experience – an affinity for the analysis of 'events, practices, assemblages, structures of feeling, and the backgrounds of everyday life against which relations unfold in their myriad potentials'.[1] To accomplish this, I introduce a phenomenological register that moves away from totalising perspectives towards microsociological approaches and an examination of the mundane practices where lived experience offers a rich fabric of corporeal presence, relationality and affect. I argue that the radical and transformative aspects of everyday life can be examined by exposing the extraordinary in the seemingly ordinary and therewith the transformative potential embedded in the everyday.

Studying peace as a mundane practice

In philosophy, international relations, and peace and conflict studies, peace has seldom been theorised in ways that would contextualise it – which is to say, socially and politically situate it. Nor has peace been discussed without it becoming an auxiliary concept of war or conflict. Peace often seems to be an elusive concept, which is deployed to 'bludgeon humanity with its extraordinariness, forever out of reach, illusive by definition, a dream too flatteringly sweet to be substantial', as described by Rose Mary Shinko,[2] or a concept so ontologically solid and attached to war that no debate beyond theorising violence is required, as Oliver Richmond[3] argues. It is this perceived extraordinariness and ontological solidness of peace, as well as its coupling with war and violence, that my article seeks to challenge. In my view, not even the Galtungian-inspired conceptualisations of positive and negative peace break fully with solidity and bring peace and its myriad forms back to the sphere of everyday life.[4] I seek to contest the views in which peace is removed from its corporeality, experienced qualities and everydayness – and therefore from its mundane visibility.

I establish the foundations of my argument not only on the phenomenological orientation (which is discussed further below), but also on feminist peace and conflict studies, which emphasise the relationality of human existence. To elaborate the importance of the body and its relationality for the study of peace, this article draws from those strains of feminist and post-colonial theorising[5] that are marked by a strong

---

[1]Philip Vannini, 'Non-Representational Ethnography: New Ways of Animating Lifeworlds', *Cultural Geographies* 22, no. 2 (2015): 317. See also Hanna Partis-Jennings in this issue.
[2]Rose Mary Shinko, 'Agonistic Peace: A Postmodern Reading', *Millennium – Journal of International Studies* 36, no. 3 (2008): 489.
[3]Oliver Richmond, *The Transformation of Peace* (London, New York: Palgrave Macmillan, 2005), 5.
[4]Johan Galtung, 'Twenty-Five Years of Peace Research: Ten Challenges and Some Responses', *Journal of Peace Research* 22, no. 2 (1985): 141–158.
[5]See, for example, Bibi Bakare-Yusuf, 'The Economy of Violence: Black Bodies and the Unspeakable Terror', in *Gender and Catastrophe*, ed. Ronit Lentin (London and New York: Zed Books, 1997), 171–85; Urvashi Butalia, 'A Necessary Journey: A Story of Friendship and Reconciliation', *Alternatives* 27, no. 2 (2002): 147–64; Parin Dossa, 'The Body Remembers: A Migratory Tale of Social Suffering and Witnessing', *International Journal of Mental Health* 3, no. 3 (2003): 50–73; Kavita Daiya, '"Honourable Resolutions": Gendered Violence, Ethnicity, and the Nation', *Alternatives* 27, no. 2 (2002): 219–47; Veena Das, *Life and Words: Violence and the Descent into the Ordinary* (Berkeley, Los Angeles, London: University of California Press, 2007); Prasenjit Duara, *Rescuing History from the Nation: Questioning Narratives of Modern China* (Chicago: University of Chicago Press, 1995); Ranjarit Guha, 'The Small Voices of History', in *Subaltern Studies IX, Writings on South Asian History and Society*, eds. Amin Shahid and Dipesh Chakrabarty (New Delhi: Oxford University Press, 1999), 1–12; Hirofumi Hayashi, 'Disputes in Japan over the Japanese "Comfort Women" System and Its Perception in History', *The Annals of the Academy of the American Political and Social Science* 617, no. 1 (2008): 123–32; Jaspir Puar, *Terrorist Assemblages. Homonationalism in Queer Times* (Durham and London: Duke University

commitment to both corporeality and to the everyday. I argue that the mainstream theorising of peace, particularly as presented in the gatekeeper journals the *Journal of Peace Research* and the *Journal of Conflict Resolution*, has dismissed this tradition and hardly ever acknowledged feminist or post-colonial knowledge claims.[6] By drawing from early feminist peace and conflict studies, post-colonial theory, feminist theorising on vulnerability and critical theorising on the everyday, the proposed agenda brings forth the sensuous, embodied, non-cognitive, pre-intentional and common-sensical nature of everyday life as well as the lived experience of conflict, violence, peace and peacebuilding. In sum, I will argue that peace is an event that comes into being through mundane and corporeal encounters.

The everyday life that I suggest be studied is the world of shared typifications and cultural material. It is also a world in which the subject has a living presence through and in her body. In the phenomenological tradition, Edmund Husserl considered the body the zero point of our orientation, the point around which our world is centred.[7] Maurice Merleau-Ponty, on the other hand, emphasised that we gain access to the world through the body, and hence our experience of the everyday depends upon a 'lived body'.[8] In this vein of thought, the symbolic order is constituted through the body, as the body's being-in-the-world is at once mediated through both physical embodied presence and cultural meanings.[9] Both our living presence as sentient beings and our apprehension of the symbolic actualises in our bodies – or rather, in our relational bodies, as the body is always already in relation to other bodies.

The study of the relational body and the mundane practices of peace require, in my view, research approaches and designs that appreciate the complexity of corporeal existence and encounters. In order to understand the workings of power, institutions and bodies, I use a methodology of *diffractive reading*, in which new insights are built by carefully reading for differences that matter, while recognising that at the core of the analysis is ethics.[10] Diffractive reading enables the reader to determine where problematic reductions and assimilations of difference have taken place. By using a diffractive reading strategy, the researcher can engage with different disciplinary practices and blur the boundaries between different disciplines and theories. In addition to its emphasis on difference, the diffractive method also implies a 'curiosity'[11] on the part of the researcher: it requires *cura* – that is, care, concern and attention to detail. Curiosity calls for immersing oneself in a variety of research material, including interviews, life

---

Press, 2017); Nthabiseng Motsemme, 'The Mute Always Speak: On Women's Silence at the Truth and Reconciliation Commission', *Current Sociology* 52, no. 5 (2007): 909–932.

[6]Matti Jutila, Samu Pehkonen and Tarja Väyrynen, 'Resuscitating a Discipline: An Agenda for Critical Peace Research', *Millennium: Journal of International Studies* 36, no. 3 (2008): 623–40; Tiina Vaittinen, *The Global Biopolitical Economy of Needs: Transnational Entanglements between Ageing Finland and the Global Nurses Reserve of the Philippines* (Tampere: Tampere Peace Research Institute, 2017).

[7]Edmund Husserl, *Grundprobleme der Phänomenologie* (Hamburg: Felix Meiner Verlag, 1992), 20.

[8]Maurice Merleau-Ponty, *Phenomenology of perception* (London: Routledge & Kegan Paul, 1962), 88–92.

[9]For a summary see Nick Crossley, 'Merleau-Ponty, the Elusive Body and Carnal Sociology' *Body and Society* 1, no. 1 (1995): 44–5.

[10]Karen Barad, *Meeting the Universe Halfway: Quantum Physics and the Entanglement of Matter and Meaning* (Durham and London: Duke University Press, 2007), 93. Donna Haraway, *Modest_Witness@Second_Millenium. FemaleMan©_Meets_OncoMouse™: Feminism and Technoscience* (New York: Routledge, 1997), 273.

[11]Cynthia Enloe, *The Curious Feminist, Searching for Women in a New Age of Empire* (Berkeley, Los Angeles, London: University of California Press, 2004). For a similar point on curiosity and the usage of a variety of research material see Catherine Baker in this issue.

stories, visual materials and faithful descriptive works. The curious interest in the details of how individuals and groups interact allows researchers, as Robert Latham writes, to examine 'how institutions function and operate, … how belief and ethos bring the world to movement, and … how the materiality of the world is profoundly bound up with these affective elements'.[12]

Diffractive reading can also provoke new thoughts and theories and allow the researcher to examine how such thoughts and theories can be made or remade so that they matter more towards inclusion than towards exclusion and the creation or maintenance of boundaries. Since active engagement with the world has always been a part of the ethos of peace and conflict studies, diffractive reading is well suited to the field: seeing, thinking and researching diffractively implies a self-accountable, critical and responsible entanglement with the world.

To exemplify the study of mundane events of peace and to provide responsible entanglement with the world, I will present narratives that I have collected and examined in my earlier research. It is important to note that while I use narratives as empirical material when employing diffractive methodology, the narratives as such do not form the data of my study in that I would seek to produce knowledge claims on their truthfulness or accuracy. Rather, the narratives and the vignettes I have written about them are embodied data in the sense that they bear witness to the affective and corporeal elements of the cases and events examined.[13] The original empirical material collected for the vignettes is audiovisual (e.g. documentaries, images) and textual (e.g. narratives in media, interviews) and was collected from a variety of sources.

Spatialising the 'local' and producing the distant 'other'

Although the scholars of the so-called local turn in peacebuilding are also critical of ontological solidness and the lack of context in theorising peace, their position on the everyday and the local is still too restricted for my agenda. In general, local turn scholarship engages with the peace implications of neo-liberal governance, which according to many scholars writing in this tradition, seeks to reproduce and impose Western models and to reconstruct Westphalian frameworks of state sovereignty. The liberal framework of individual rights, winner-takes-all elections and neoliberal free market economic programmes are seen to be at the core of such models.[14] With their critique of Westphalian frameworks, local turn scholars aim at dismantling the Western bias in both theorising and practicing peace. In order to elaborate the problems of liberal peace, Roger Mac Ginty and Oliver Richmond argue that peace is simply not as neo-liberal as neo-liberal institutions would like it to be. Rather, peace is always hybrid where the local meets the international, and furthermore, it is often contested, since the form of peace implemented through the practices of neo-liberal governance is moulded in local contexts in ways that challenge the neo-liberal aspirations outlined above. In short, according to Mac Ginty and Richmond, the imposition of the Western peacebuilding and peace model is doomed to fail in non-Western contexts.[15]

---

[12]Alan Latham, 'Guest Editorial', *Environment and Planning* 35 (2003): 1904.
[13]Cf. Valerie Walkerdine, 'Communal Beingness and Affect: An Exploration of Trauma in an Ex-Industrial Community', *Body & Society* 16, no. 1 (2010): 91–116.
[14]David Chandler, 'The Uncritical Critique of "Liberal Peace"', *Review of International Studies* 36, no. S1 (2010): 137–55.
[15]Roger Mac Ginty and Oliver P Richmond, 'The Local Turn in Peace Building: a critical agenda for peace', *Third World Quarterly* 34, no. 5 (2013): 764.

Subaltern views of peace are important for local turn scholarship since subaltern actors possess everyday agency in either promoting peace or resisting top-down neoliberal peacebuilding attempts. The everyday is fundamental for this branch of thinking, as the 'pursuit of everyday tasks may allow individuals and communities in villages, valleys and city neighborhoods to develop common bonds with members of other ethnic or religious groups, to demystify "the other" and to reconstruct contextual legitimacy'.[16] Given the agency that the subaltern exercises, the local turn responds by focusing on everyday life and the forms of transversal solidarity and grassroots mobilisation that enable peacebuilding. In other words, the assumption is that a vibrant civil society and an everyday solidarity cutting across ethnic and religious affiliations is the guarantee of peace. The local turn argues that the promoters of liberal peace fail to recognise this type of agency and solidarity in their focus on elite-lead and top-down approaches to peacebuilding and thereby miss the opportunity for sustainable and local peace.[17]

Although the local turn functions as an important critique of neoliberal governance and peace, for my research agenda, where the aim is to capture the corporeality and eventness of mundane peace, the discussion and understanding of the everyday offered by local turn scholarship is limited. The everyday implies for me more than the resilience and resistant potential of the 'local' and of 'ordinary people' in the face of neo-liberal peacebuilding, as it is largely understood within local turn scholarship. From my perspective, the local turn's interest in the everyday is too narrow, as it has not been translated into a sustained consideration of the productiveness of mundane practices.

Where I most radically depart company from local turn scholarship is in its tendency to define the everyday with reference to the subaltern's spatiality – namely, through the spatial location where the subaltern is assumed to reside and through the forms of everyday life that are thought to characterise her.[18] In the local turn, the subaltern and her everyday life are projected to be somewhere 'out there': in a distant location of

---

[16]Ibid., 769.

[17]See e.g. Roger Mac Ginty, 'Indigenous Peace-Making versus the Liberal Peace', *Cooperation and Conflict* 43, no. 2 (2008): 139–63; Roger Mac Ginty, *International Peacebuilding and Local Resistance* (Basingstoke: Palgrave, 2011); Mac Ginty and Richmond, 'The Local Turn'; Oliver Richmond, 'A post-liberal peace: Eirenism and everyday', *Review of International Studies*, 35, no. 3 (2009): 557–80; Oliver Richmond, 'The Romanticisation of the Local: Welfare, Culture and Peacebuilding', *International Spectator* 44, no. 1 (2009): 149–69; Oliver Richmond, 'Beyond Local: Ownership and Participation in the Architecture of International Peacebuilding', *Ethnopolitics*, no. 4 (2012): 354–75. For works that summarise and/or criticise the local turn, see Séverine Autesserre, 'Going Micro: Emerging and Future Peacekeeping Research', *International Peacekeeping* 21, no. 4 (2014): 492–500; Annica Björkdahl and Kristine Höglund, 'Precarious peacebuilding: friction in global–local encounters', *Peacebuilding* 1, no. 3 (2013): 289–99; Tanja Hohe, 'Clash of Paradigms: International Administrational Local Political Legitimacy in East Timor', *Contemporary Southeast Asia* 24, no. 3 (2002), 569–89; Hanna Leonardsson, 'The "Local Turn" in Peacebuilding: A Literature Review of Effective and Emancipatory Local Peacebuilding', *Third World Quarterly* 36, no. 5 (2015): 825–39; Gearoid Millar, *An Ethnographic Approach to Peacebuilding: Understanding Local Experiences in Transitional States* (London: Routledge, 2014); Gearoid Millar, J. van der Lijn and W. Verkoren 'Peacebuilding Plans and Local Reconfigurations: Frictions Between Imported Processes and Indigenous Practices', *International Peacekeeping* 20, no. 2 (2013): 137–43.

[18]Although Roger Mac Ginty suggests that there is need to move away from the overtly territorial understanding of peace, he does not develop the idea further. He writes that 'if we understand the local as de-territorialised, networked and constituted by people and activity rather than place, then standard meanings of peace require reappraisal'. Roger Mac Ginty, 'Where is the Local? Critical Localism and Peacebuilding', *Third World Quarterly* 36, no. 5 (2015): 840–56. What is implied in the quote is that the local is synonymous with networked activity and transversal solidarity, rather than spatial location. As will be argued later in the article, this does not yet capture the everydayness and eventness of peace that are central to my feminist agenda. For feminist scholarship that explores transversal activism and/or practices of solidarity in contexts of conflict or peacebuilding, see Cynthia Cockburn, *The Space Between Us: Negotiating Gender and National Identities in Conflict* (London: Zed Books, 1998); Maja Korac, 'Women Organizing Against Ethnic Nationalism and War in the Post-Yugoslav States,' in *Feminists Under Fire: Exchanges Across Warzones*, eds. Wenona Giles, Malathi de Alwis, Edith Klein and Neluka Silva (Toronto: Between the Lines, 2003), 25–33; Maria O'Reilly, *Gendered Agency in War and Peace: Gender Justice and Women's Activism in Bosnia-Herzegovina* (London: Palgrave MacMillan, 2018).

violent political conflict or far-away post-conflict zone. This is, in my view, a traditional Orientalist projection, in which the spatially projected 'local' world and its everyday are conceived of as radically different from our own.[19] In this projection, the local and the subaltern are constructed as distant 'others', whose emancipatory potential the Western and male local turn scholar is concerned with. This is a reminder of the colonial condition, in which white men seek to save 'brown women from brown men'.[20] To avoid this, it is important to recognise that the everyday and the ordinary are constituted through enactments – that is, they are corporeal rather than spatial and not necessarily the 'subaltern' in the Orientalist sense, with its implication of non-Western populations. The focus on embodied enactments enables us to retain the local whilst distancing ourselves from the spatial hegemony of the distant 'other'.

Feminist peace and conflict studies

As noted earlier, feminist theorising has a strong commitment to corporeality and the everyday (in a non-territorial sense) and therefore functions as a starting point for my agenda. Furthermore, this corpus of thinking establishes a strong connection between corporeal ontology and peace epistemology. Radical feminist scholarship is instrumental, in my view, when investigating the body, the ordinary and the everyday.[21] There are multiple ontologies in feminist peace theory, but the concern for marginalization and the understanding of the corporeal and relational nature of human existence are the key contributions that enable a new take on the corporeality of peace.[22]

Particularly important for my proposed nonsolid feminist research agenda is the theorising of Elise Boulding and Sara Ruddick. Boulding's focus on peace as a daily process situates peace within the ordinary and its corporeal rhythms. Her work emphasises the personal and interpersonal promotion of peace, which for her involves shaping and reshaping understandings and behaviours to adapt to a constantly

---

[19]On 'othering', see also Thania Paffenholz, 'International Peacebuilding goes Local: Analysing Lederach's Conflict Transformation Theory and its Ambivalent Encounter with 20 Years of Practice', *Peacebuilding* 2, no. 1 (2014): 11–27; Thania Paffenholz, 'Unpacking the Local Turn in Peacebuilding: a Critical Assessment Towards an Agenda for Future Research', *Third World Quarterly* 36, no. 5 (2015): 857–74; Jan Nederveen Pieterse, *Development Theory*, (London: SAGE, 2010).
[20]Gayatri Spivak, 'Can the Subaltern Speak?' in *Marxism and the Interpretation of Culture*, eds. Cary Nelson and Lawrence Grossberg (Chicago: University of Illinois Press, 1994), 93.
[21]For recent alternative research agendas see, for example, Catia Confortini, 'Galtung, Violence, and Gender: The Case for a Peace Studies/Feminism Alliance' *Peace & Change* 33, no. 3 (2006): 333–67; Catia Confortini and Abigail Ruane, 'Sara Ruddick's *Maternal Thinking* as Weaving Epistemology for Justpeace', *Journal of International Political Theory* 10, no. 1 (2013): 70–93; Vaittinen, *Global Biopolitical*. See also Rachel Julian et al. in this issue.
[22]See e.g. Elise Boulding, *Building a Global Civic Culture: Education for an Interdependent World* (Syracuse, NY: Syracuse University Press, 1990); Elise Boulding, 'Peace Behaviours in Various Societies', in *From a Culture of Violence to a Culture of Peace* (Paris: Unesco, 1996), 31–53; Birgit Brock-Utne, *Feminist Perspectives on Peace and Peace Education*. (New York: Pergamon Press, 1989); Cynthia Enloe, 'Margins, Silences and Bottom Rungs: How to Overcome the Underestimation of Power in the Study of International Relations', in *International Theory: Positivism and Beyond*, eds. Steve Smith, Ken Booth and Marysia Zalewski (New York: Cambridge University Press, 2004), 186–202; Tony Jenkins and Betty Reardon, 'Gender and Peace: Towards a Gender-inclusive and Holistic Perspective', in *Handbook of Peace and Conflict Studies*, eds. Charles Webel and Johan Galtung (New York: Routledge, 2007), 209–31; Sara Ruddick, 'The Rationality of Care', in *Women, Militarism, and War: Essays in History, Politics, and Social Theory*, eds. JB Elshtain and S Tobias (Lanham, MD: Rowman & Littlefield 1990), 229–54; Sara Ruddick, 'New Feminist Work on Knowledge, Reason and Objectivity'. *Hypatia* 8, no. 4 (1993): 140–149; Sara Ruddick, *Maternal Thinking: Toward a Politics of Peace* (Boston, MA: Beacon Press, 1995); Sara Ruddick, 'Making Connections Between Parenting and Peace', *Journal of the Association for Research on Mothering* 3, no. 2 (2001): 7–20.

changing world and sustain well-being for all.²³ Boulding's theory is instructive for my agenda as it emphasises the praxis of peace, in which the daily 'doing' of peace is fundamental. In addition, Boulding's views concur with the critical and phenomenological thinking on the everyday, which argues that our existence in the world and our everyday life is embodied and relational – that is, human existence is based on our dependency on others and is hence always multiple. Her view resonates with Merleau-Ponty's notions of intercorporality and carnal intersubjectivity, which denote a primordial carnal bond between human beings.²⁴ According to this view, we are always open to each other, and always with others. In my view, Boulding's theorising provides a new opening for a radical theory of peace that does not limit itself to civil society and its resistant and emancipatory potential. Rather, radical theory such as Boulding's is 'attuned to all facets of human existence: the poetic, irrational, corporeal, ethical and affective'.²⁵

In the following vignette, I will demonstrate how the war reveals the relational nature of being in the world. My colleague Eeva Puumala had interviewed her grandmother about her life on the homefront during the Second World War. We wrote about the experience:

VIGNETTE 1

At many points, Nan's story takes up acts of solidarity. Although the actual battles took place far from her home, there were prison camps for Soviet prisoners of war also in the Western-most Finland. Nan tells: 'My elder sister Eeva was a maid in Köyliö in the Kepola mansion, which was located near a camp for Soviet prisoners of war. The prisoners were kept within barbed wire fences, and they hadn't much to eat. Eeva told that when she passed by the camp, the prisoners used to ask for bread, liepuska. A couple of times she took bread to them, but Eeva was always afraid of being caught. She stole the bread from the house where she worked'. After describing her sister's act, Nan exclaims 'But it is terrible for the prisoners also!' Then she elaborates: 'And they were innocent, just like the Finnish men who were merely told to go and fight. They had no choice, either one'.²⁶

The vignette demonstrates the relational nature of being in the world and the radical potential that can emerge from it – namely, the daily practices of peace. The encounter between Nan's sister and the Soviet prisoner of war is ultimately an event of acknowledgement and recognition: she recognises him and feels accountable. An affect of 'response-ability',²⁷ an instantaneous accountability, emerges. The vignette shows that peaceful relationality and response-ability can emerge in the midst of enmity, and as such supports Ruddick's observation that peace is a matter of creating relationships in which people feel that they are respected. At the core of Ruddick's observation is her conception of motherly care as the opposite of the practices of violence and war. Care, according to Ruddick, is always a relation, and as such it is also a foundation for knowing the world: we come to know the world through corporeal, mundane and relational practices – by being an embodied part of the world. For Ruddick, the

---

[23]Boulding, 'Peace Behaviours', 31–53. On corporeal rhythms, see also Tarja Väyrynen and Eeva Puumala, 'Bodies of War, the Past Continuous, and (Ar)rhytmic Experiences', *Alternatives: Global, Local, Political* 40, no. 3–4 (2015): 237–250.
[24]Merleau-Ponty, *Phenomenology of Perception*, 19, 173; Crossley, 'Merleau-Ponty, the Elusive Body'.
[25]Michael Gardiner, *Critiques of Everyday Life* (New York and London: Routledge, 2000), 19.
[26]Väyrynen and Puumala, 'Bodies of War', 242.
[27]Karen Barad, 'On Touching – The Inhuman That Therefore I Am.'. *Differences* 23, no. 3 (2012): 208.

relational practices of mothering can generate advance peacemaking through the practices and knowledge.[28]

In connecting care and ways of knowing, Ruddick establishes a link between corporeal ontology and epistemology. Catia Confortini and Abigail Ruane expand upon Ruddick's thinking on practices of care and knowledge production by arguing that mothering and the knowledge generated through it engage us in the practices of de-centering ourselves. De-centering implies both locating oneself within a situation and, at the same time, stepping out of it. This double move allows us to hold someone else in personhood. Confortini and Ruane write that we need 'participatory epistemology, or an understanding of how actors develop knowledge through their practices of engagement with others'.[29] Knowing, in this view, is not a skill possessed by a detached, unembodied observer, but grows from interactions between multiple beings and bodies living and acting together in a world that is in a constant process of becoming.[30]

In addition to care as a motherly practice, I also view care as an 'intercarnal relation', a practice of engagement with a corporeal other. I concur with Michael Gardiner who argues that care – like Nan's sister surreptitiously giving bread to the Soviet prisoners of war – is ultimately an ordinary gesture of the everyday, an unspoken desire of the body and a 'microscopic' expression of solidarity 'where the pre-emptive promise of the everyday continues to persist, in the interstices of more formal social relations and organizational structures'.[31] However, the everyday is not solely the realm of solidarity, but also involves the distribution of violence, torture and massacres, practices which haunt and shape the everyday and its relations.[32] By drawing from the feminist peace studies literature and by paying attention to the sensuous, embodied, non-cognitive, pre-intentional and common-sensical nature of everyday life and lived experience – which are also elaborated in post-colonial literature[33] – we can uncover the epistemological potential of thinking through the everyday.[34]

Complementing the feminist agenda

As outlined above, early feminist peace and conflict researchers, such as Elise Boulding and Sara Ruddick, insisted on the importance of the relational body when studying peace. I also argued above that local turn scholarship is limited in its understanding of the everyday and mundane practices of peace. In my view, both the relational body and mundane practices require a more nuanced reading of power, governance and the vulnerabilities that practices of power produce, since the body is always both 'active

---

[28]Ruddick, *Maternal Thinking*, 219.
[29]Confortini and Ruane, 'Sara Ruddick's Maternal', 71.
[30]Ibid., 80–97.
[31]Gardiner, *Critiques of Everyday Life*, 17. See also Tiina Vaittinen's Concept 'Care as a Corporeal Relation' in Tiina Vaittinen, 'The Power of the Vulnerable Body: A New Political Understanding of Care', *International Feminist Journal of Politics* 17, no. 1 (2015): 100–18; Vaittinen, *The Global Biopolitical*. See also Tiina Vaittinen et al. in this issue.
[32]Das, *Life and Words*.
[33]See note 5 above.
[34]Cf. J.D. Dewsbury, 'Performative, Non-Representational and Affect Based Research: Seven Injuctions' in *The SAGE Handbook of Qualitative Geography*, eds. Dydia DeLyser, Steve Herbert, Stuart Aitken, Mike Crang and Linda McDowell (London: SAGE, 2010): 31–54; Vannini, 'Non-Representational Ethnography', 319.

and acted upon'.³⁵ In short, practices of governance that are targeted at the body also produce the body.³⁶ Yet the fleshy living body also has agency, which makes it an 'engaged body-subject'.³⁷ In other words, the body is never a passive target of practices of governance: it also has a capacity to escape these practices.³⁸

Eighty-year-old Kaisu told her story in a Finnish documentary film in 2010.³⁹ She was among the Finnish women accused of having fraternised with German soldiers during the Second World War. She moved to Germany with the withdrawing German troops and was repatriated to Finland after the war. The following is my description of Kaisu's narrative:

VIGNETTE 2

Kaisu was among the women whose bodies were securitised and transferred to the camp immediately on their arrival on the Finnish soil. She calls it the 'quarantine camp' as if there had been something contagious in her body that needed purification. Hence medicalisation also takes hold of her body even in her most intimate memories. Her young body had been securitised and medicalised as it was seen to constitute the contagious risk of knowing too much. In the documentary, her body is stiff, but strong when she sits on the porch of the barracks, in which she thinks she was incarcerated sixty years ago. She is smoking a cigarette with a firm hand. Her body and her solemn voice convey her strength. Kaisu recalls how the Security Police had suspected her of being a German mole. She is very proud of the fact that she did not cry during the interrogations: 'In front of Hautojärvi [the interrogation officer] I did not cry'. In the narrative, her resistance is not just geared towards the interrogation officer, but also towards the Finnish state, whose security apparatus suspected and humiliated her. In her upright body, she resists the forces that sought to silence her.⁴⁰

When considering mundane peace, Judith Butler's observation that one way of managing populations is to distribute vulnerability among people unequally is crucial.⁴¹ Biopower – power that is about managing the births, deaths, reproduction and illnesses of a population and which is ultimately utilised by the state ostensibly in the protection of life – establishes a norm that allows for measurement, evaluation and hierarchical

---

[35] Crossley. 'Merleau-Ponty and the Elusive', 51. For a similar argument see Nicolas Lemay-Hebert and Stefanie Kappler in this issue.
[36] Michel Foucault's early work shows how the body and its operations have been broken down by the many historical regimes that produced disciplinary inscriptions upon the body. Complex and historical social practices, i.e. technologies of power, have been at work on the human body, moulding and forcing the body in ways that make it subject to disciplinary forms of conduct. In his later work, Foucault complements his view of the 'body infused with power' with a consideration of power in terms of populations, namely, in terms of biopower. Biopower is ultimately utilized ostensibly in the protection of life. He writes that biopower is 'an explosion of numerous and diverse techniques for achieving the subjugations of bodies and the control of populations'. Michel Foucault, *History of Sexuality*, Vol. I, (New York: Vintage Books, 1990), 140; Michel Foucault, 'Nietzsche, Genealogy, History', in *Language, Counter-Memory, Practice: Selected Essays and Interviews*, ed. D. F. Bouchard (Ithaca: Cornell University Press, 1977), 139–64.
[37] Crossley. 'Merleau-Ponty and the Elusive', 101.
[38] Eeva Puumala, Tarja Väyrynen, Anitta Kynsilehto and Samu Pehkonen, 'Events of the Body Politic: A Nancian Reading of Asylum Seekers' Bodily Choreographies and Resistance', *Body & Society* 17, no. 4 (2011): 83–104; Tarja Väyrynen, Eeva Puumala, Samu Pehkonen, Anitta Kynsilehto and Tiina Vaittinen, *Choreographies of Resistance: Mobile Bodies and Relational Politics* (London, New York: Rowman and Littlefield, 2017).
[39] Virpi Suutari, *Auf Wiedersehen Finnland*, CD, (Helsinki: For Real Productions, 2010).
[40] Tarja Väyrynen, 'Muted National Memory: When the "Hitler's Brides" Speak the Truth', *International Feminist Journal of Politics*, 16, no. 2 (2014): 227.
[41] Judith Butler, *Frames of War* (London, New York: Verso, 2009). Feminist security studies have also recognized vulnerability as characterising human existence and rendering it insecure on many occasions. See e.g. Annick Wibben, *Feminist Security Studies: A Narrative Approach* (Abingdon, New York: Routledge, 2011).

ranking. As such, it constitutes a mechanism of control and distributes vulnerability and invulnerability among the population.[42] In Kaisu's case, her body was rendered vulnerable – shaped as that of an outcast – through the mechanisms of governance in the post-war Finnish national order. The vignette demonstrates that power is multiple and relational, as it establishes socio-historical relationships that render some bodies more vulnerable than others. Biopower increases efficiency and capacity at the level of individual bodies and whole populations, yet it also distributes vulnerability and invulnerability. This is particularly acute during times of economic, social and political transformation, such as peacebuilding and reconstruction, when social relations must be re-imagined and re-structured.

Butler theorises peace and argues that peace is a way of indicating one's dependency on others and being acknowledged. She not only theorises peace as individual vulnerability but says that it needs to be institutionalised:

> I think that peace is the active and difficult resistance to the temptation of war; it is the prerogative and the obligation of the injured. Peace is something that has to be vigilantly maintained; it is a vigilance, and it involves temptation, and it does not mean we as human beings are not aggressive. It does not mean that we do not have murderous impulses. This is a mistaken way of understanding non-violence. … Peace is a certain resistance to the terrible satisfactions of war. It's a commitment to living with a certain kind of vulnerability to others and susceptibility to being wounded that actually gives our individual lives meaning… I think it needs to be institutionalised. It needs to be part of a community ethos. I think in fact it needs to be part of an entire foreign policy.[43]

For Butler, therefore, the recognition of vulnerability can lead to more adequate, peaceful responses to different forms of violence and can counter the tendency to react to violence with more violence.[44] Alyson Cole has noted that Butler's view on vulnerability paves the way to 'nonviolent interaffectivity'.[45] Vulnerability does not, in this view, imply weakness or inferiority; rather, it is a human condition, 'a basic kind of openness to being affected and affecting in both positive and negative ways, which can take diverse forms in different social situations (for example, bodily, psychological, economic, emotional, and legal vulnerabilities)', as Erin Gilson summarises Butler's views.[46] Understanding oneself as vulnerable involves an understanding of the self as shaped by its relationships to others, the world, power and its environs. This has, in my view, implications for the everyday, as our embodiment and vulnerability are embedded in the everyday – in its historicity, forms of power, materiality and concreteness.

Vulnerability is not just a way of referring to the capacity to be wounded, however. It is also a 'way of indicating one's dependency on another, a set of institutions, or a circumambient world to be well, to be safe, to be acknowledged', argues Butler, in the

---

[42] In addition to the governance-induced vulnerability that emerges from being embedded in specific structures of power, there is also another type of vulnerability: the vulnerability that is a basic condition of life. Judith Butler, *Precarious Life: The Power of Mourning and Violence* (London, New York: Verso, 2004); Butler, *Frames of War*, 30.
[43] Judith Butler, 'Interview with Jill Stauffer', *Believer*, May 2003, http://www.believermag.com/issues/200305/?read=interview_butler .
[44] Butler, *Precarious life*, 28–9.
[45] Alyson Cole, 'All of Us Are Vulnerable, But Some Are More Vulnerable than Others: The Political Ambiguity of Vulnerability Studies, an Ambivalent Critique', *Critical Horizons* 17, no. 2 (2016): 262.
[46] Erin Gilson, 'Vulnerability, Ignorance, and Oppression', *Hypatia* 26, no. 2 (2011), 310.

spirit of early feminist peace and conflict researchers' work.⁴⁷ While the vulnerable body is often thought to be private and non-political, when in contact with other bodies, *the politics of vulnerability* comes to the fore – firstly, in the form of the unequal distribution of vulnerabilities, and secondly, in the form of accountability, recognition and acknowledgement. In other words, the way in which vulnerability is recognised, accounted for, acknowledged and responded to is at the core of the political. 'The political' is hence an existential relation that we all live out, on a daily basis, in ways that create, re-produce, transcend and challenge differences, hierarchies, discriminations and vulnerabilities between subjectivities and political positions. Furthermore, vulnerable bodies are agentic, as receptivity, accountability and vulnerability are actually the presuppositions of agency, not its opposites.⁴⁸ In short, vulnerability is enabling for our being in the world; that is, vulnerability is a 'condition of potential that makes possible other conditions',⁴⁹ including peace. It can be argued that Kaisu's bold appearance in the documentary film was a political event of claiming back her silenced body and evoking recognition of the existence of the bodies of her kind. Her vulnerable body thereby carried an agentic capacity capable of challenging the existing hierarchies, discriminations and differences.

Although vulnerability can be seen as a shared human condition, it is lived and experienced in different ways, as well as distributed unequally, as argued above. The ways in which we live and are affected can be understood only in light of the particularity of embodied, social and mundane experiences. It is in this way that feminist and critical theorising of the body, the everyday and vulnerability open up new pathways to re-theorise peace. Peace is something that becomes expressed and takes place through acts and points of everyday contact between variously situated and variously vulnerable bodies – namely, in corporeal events where accountability, response-ability, recognition and acknowledgement emerge. The pluralistic and critical approaches indicated in my agenda are more sensitive to the changing patterns and dynamics of peace than many abstract, ontologically solid or violence-dependent approaches.

The eventness of peace

The research agenda developed in this article calls for the analysis of events in which recognition and acknowledgement have an emergent potential. As Latham says, social scientists are 'recognising the need to acknowledge the event-ness of world, along with the profound importance of affect in the unfolding of this event-ness'.⁵⁰ In thinking about peace, paying attention to the eventness of the world is useful because it suggests that research should focus on the rhythms and textures of everyday life. In short, everyday life comes into being through events and engages the human being in practical doing.⁵¹ As the self and the other co-mingle in the event of being, the

---

⁴⁷Judith Butler, 'Confessing a Passionate state – Judith Butler im Interview', *Feministische Studien* 2 (2011): 200.
⁴⁸Cf. Cole, 'All of Us Are Vulnerable', 268–71.
⁴⁹Gilson, 'Vulnerability, Ignorance', 310.
⁵⁰Latham, 'Guest editorial', 1902.
⁵¹Cf. Boulding, 'Peace behaviours'.

eventness of the world is relational; the self and other remain, however, distinctly 'incarnated'.[52]

I find it revealing how Kaisu recalls the suffering of the Jewish population she saw when she was in Germany and how the event of co-being emerged. She describes in detail how the Jews were contained in small underground bunkers, and how their bodies were malformed as a result. I interpret Kaisu's experience in the following manner:

VIGNETTE 3

'I and some other Finnish girls encountered a Jewish woman who wore a yellow patch with the Jewish star. Her eyes were full of anguish and they were begging us to notice that she was indeed wearing the patch'. She wonders what kind of suffering has caused such timidity in a fellow human being. Her voice becomes low and husky when she reminisces the suffering of the others. Her own hardship in war-torn and ravaged Germany seems to have only minor importance compared to the suffering of the Jewish population. When Kaisu mourns the suffering of the others, a splitting of the subject as well as temporality takes place. She is not Kaisu located here and now, but young Kaisu who glimpsed into the void of human existence. She loses her notion of herself as an autonomous subject and in control.[53]

As the vignette of Kaisu retelling her experience in war-torn Germany attests, the event of co-being can have relatively vague temporal and spatial boundaries as they can cross temporal and spatial boundaries.

My notion of 'event' in this article bears similarities with Alain Badiou's: for him, events are gateways to future possibilities and reconfigurings and enable novel modes of being-in-the-world.[54] But while Badiou limits events to rare revolutionary and spectacular moments in history, for me, events are everyday occurrences that open up novel ways of being-in-the-world, just as Kaisu's encounter with the suffering and vulnerability of the other did for her. More generally, thinking through eventness can, in my view, point peace and conflict studies towards the fleshy and carnal existence from which mundane practices of peace can potentially emerge. By attending to the specifics of particular events and paying attention to detail, the researcher can come to appreciate when and why such mundane activities and encounters matter for peacebuilding, reconciliation and peace.

If the starting point for research is the assumption that peace emerges from *everyday contacts between variously situated and variously vulnerable bodies*, it is necessary to further conceptualise these contacts. My colleagues and I have introduced the notion of choreography to capture the corporeal eventness of everyday contacts. Through the notion of choreography we have sought to capture the affective potential of everyday encounters as they articulate a body's capacity to communicate and integrate with other bodies. In this sense, bodies coming together form everyday choreographies that are always social and connecting. Because of its common association with dance, choreography is often understood primarily to signify composing and arranging movement in

---

[52]Gardiner, *Critiques of Everyday Life*, 47.
[53]Tarja Väyrynen, 'Re-thinking National Temporal Orders: The Subaltern Presence and Enactment of the Political', *Review of International Studies* 42, no. 4 (2016): 607–608.
[54]Alan Badiou, *Being and Event* (London: Continuum, 2005).

advance. However, there is another etymology for *choreo*: 'being in, passing, entering into or holding space'. In our use, choreography indicates practices of being corporeally in space and inhabiting space.[55]

Elsewhere, we have summarised the idea of choreography as follows:

> Through choreographies, we examine the oscillation of bodies as lived, experienced, and material configurations, which are simultaneously extremely personal, shared, and relational. The body is always partially marked and already-made-visible, yet simultaneously always in the process of becoming, with other bodies in particular, historically contingent choreographies.[56]

Choreographies do not happen in a vacuum: they are enacted in the corporeal practices people deploy in the everyday to form and maintain movement within practices of power. For the actors, then, choreographies are always partially pre-given, already planned and presented as fixed lines to be followed – yet the interactional resources of bodies can be used to remould the situation, as my vignettes demonstrate. Looking closer at these everyday techniques of interaction reveals that choreographies are in fact open to surprises and even disturbances, and tend to produce extraordinary acts out of the ordinary.[57]

Because the everyday is made and remade thorough the changing positions and relations of bodies, choreographies are always situationally enacted in events. As such, choreography allows, in my view, the study of embodied micro-practices of peace. In short, the immediacy of the everyday and its encounters, as well as their relevance for peace, calls for the analysis of events and their corporeal choreographies where acknowledgement and recognition emerge. This 'corporeal turn' in peace thinking points research towards events and processes that are marked by their mundaneness and ordinariness – their everydayness – as well as towards embodied data collected from multiple sources.

Conclusions

In this article, I have advocated for the value of bringing the body, everydayness and ordinary people to the study of peace. The research agenda I have suggested offers a heightened sensitivity to the fleshy realities of the human body. Taking the body seriously introduces phenomenological registers that prioritise the relational and vulnerable elements of human existence and thereby prioritise mundane practices, including mundane practices of peace. My research agenda and its ontological commitment to corporeality and vulnerability do not precede or escape politics, but rather have a politics of their own: a politics of the reality that takes shape when bodies are rendered vulnerable or invulnerable.

The ontology of being vulnerable and connected guides the suggested research agenda towards new ways of thinking about community and practices of peace.

---

[55] Samu Pehkonen, 'Choreographing the Performance-Audience Interaction', *Journal of Contemporary Ethnography* 46, no. 6 (2016): 699–722; Eeva Puumala and Samu Pehkonen, 'Corporeal Choreographies Between Politics and the Political: Failed Asylum-Seekers Moving from Body Politics to Bodyspaces', *International Political Sociology* 4, no. 1 (2010): 50–65; Väyrynen et al., *Choreographies*.
[56] Väyrynen et al., *Choreographies*, 11.
[57] Cf. E. Laurier, 'Youtube: Fragments of a Video-Tropic Atlas', *Area*, January 23, 2015.

Encountering vulnerability creates moments of accountability, recognition and acknowledgement in which the peace ethos of the community is created. Being wounded and being susceptible to vulnerability constitute a rupture in the smooth ordering of political space and hence is of vital importance for the peace ethos. The commitment to living with a certain kind of vulnerability to others and a susceptibility to being wounded is in this research agenda the litmus test of peace.

In short, I have sought to demonstrate that feminist and post-colonial theorising on the body offers a new bodily ontology that bears relevance for peace. This is an ontology and politics that is attuned to the nonviolent realisation of mutual dependence and exposure, as it is from those instances that mundane practices of peace emerge.[58] My understanding of peace hence bears some resemblance to the theorising of the local turn. Yet it differs greatly in the sense that this alternative agenda is based on embodied data, diffractive methodology and a corporeal analysis that brings together affect, emotions and the somatic and provides an understanding of the body as both the subject and object of discourses, materialities and practices and policies of peace.

Disclosure statement

No potential conflict of interest was reported by the author.

Funding

This research was made possible by the Academy of Finland grant number 297053.

---

[58]Cf. Ann Murphy, *Violence and the Philosophical Imaginary* (Albany, NY: SUNY Press, 2012).

From power-blind binaries to the intersectionality of peace: connecting feminism and critical peace and conflict studies

Stefanie Kappler and Nicolas Lemay-Hébert

ABSTRACT
Critical Peace and Conflict Studies scholars have increasingly sought to overcome binary approaches to engage more fully the ways in which peacebuilding missions are designed, implemented and contested. In doing so, scholars have tried to understand 'the local' and mobilised three different concepts to do so – hybridity, the everyday and narratives. However, this shift has failed to translate into fully convincing research transcending the old binaries of 'international' and 'local'. The use of the 'everyday' sees power everywhere, hybridity approaches fall into the same binary trap scholars want to avoid in the first place, and narrative approaches tend to focus on very personal stories, removing structural power from the equation. We suggest that a fruitful interaction with Feminist approaches and methodologies, and especially the scholarship on intersectionality, can help shed a new light on the power imbalances and inequalities within peacebuilding missions. We highlight the possible contribution of the concept of intersectionality to Critical Peace and Conflict Studies through an *intersectionality of peace* approach, which allows for a better understanding of multiple and complex identities of researchers and researchees. We illustrate this argument through a discussion of intersectional narratives centred around the space of the 'guesthouse' of South Africa.

Introduction: the pervasive power of dichotomies

In a context where the demise of the 'liberal peace' agenda is now almost consensual, critical peacebuilding research has slowly turned its gaze towards 'how best to access all other narratives so far silenced.'[1] Moving away from the critique of the top-down, technocratic, 'Western' or 'Northern' agenda, critical peace and conflict research is increasingly focusing on local, alternative paradigms of the 'everyday'. This (re)discovering of the 'local' has quickly been labelled the 'local turn' in the discipline,[2] with the 'local' becoming a 'new object, a new domain or field for policy intervention.'[3] This

---

[1] Elisa Randazzo, 'The Paradoxes of the "Everyday": Scrutinising the Local Turn in Peace Building', *Third World Quarterly* 37, no. 8 (2016): 1353.
[2] Roger Mac Ginty and Oliver P. Richmond, 'The Local Turn in Peace Building: A Critical Agenda for Peace', *Third World Quarterly* 34, no. 5 (2013): 763–783.
[3] David Chandler, *Resilience: The Governance of Complexity* (London: Routledge, 2014), 82.

agenda has taken different forms. On the one hand, some of the critical peacebuilding research has rested on the traditional fault-line of the 'international' versus the 'local', even if this time focusing on the local side of the equation.[4] On the other hand, for scholars wanting to emancipate themselves from the international-local dichotomy, this semantic move has so far held dubious results, with the same dichotomy creeping back in in many studies.[5] One has to say that this is true for the proponents of the 'local turn', but also their critiques to a certain extent, who end up most of the time disaggregating the 'local' category into 'national' and 'local' categories and the international with 'regional' and 'transnational' categories; hence replacing a simple dichotomy with a set of slightly more complex dichotomies. As Julian et al show, these categories are based on hierarchical imaginations of local-international identities.[6]

One way to move this debate forward is not to reinvent the wheel, as Peace & Conflict Studies (PCS) scholars have been known to often do, but to open up to other subfields and highlight the possible connections between the epistemological debates in the different subfields. In line with the theoretical starting point presented in the introduction of this special issue, we posit here that feminist methodologies[7] can help us apprehend the complexity of power relations, and help shed a new light on the old debates in PCS. A specific focus will be put on the concept of intersectionality in this article. Despite its potential in terms of understanding the complexity of power relations, the concept of intersectionality has mainly been used by feminist thinkers and has only sporadically found its way into other subfields. We argue that the concept of intersectionality can help inform the debates about binaries in the subfield of PCS and, in fact, provide a language which precisely avoids the reinforcement of such rhetorically-created binaries. What is more, an *intersectionality of peace* approach does not deny the hybridity of experience and allows to integrate research on the everyday and the narratives that emerge therein, yet without being blind to the power relations that shape the formation of identities in peacebuilding contexts. It is an approach that enables us to unpack the complex stacking of privilege or, to the contrary, discrimination, exclusion, marginalisation and inequalities, both for researchees and researchers.[8]

---

[4]Annika Björkdahl and Kristine Höglund, 'Precarious Peacebuilding: Friction in Global-Local Encounters', *Peacebuilding* 1, no. 3 (2013): 289–299; Nicolas Lemay-Hébert, 'The Bifurcation of the Two Worlds: Assessing the Gap Between Internationals and Locals in State-Building Processes', *Third World Quarterly* 32, no. 10 (2011): 1823–1841; Nicolas Lemay-Hébert and Stefanie Kappler, 'What Attachment to Peace? Exploring the Normative and Material Dimensions of Local Ownership in Peacebuilding', *Review of International Studies* 42, no. 5 (2016): 895–914.; and Kristoffer Lidén, 'Building Peace Between Global and Local Politics: The Cosmopolitan Ethics of Liberal Peacebuilding', *International Peacekeeping* 16, no. 5 (2009): 616–634.

[5]For an overview of this critique, see: Shahar Hameiri and Lee Jones, 'Beyond Hybridity to the Politics of Scale: International Intervention and "Local" Politics', *Development and Change* 48, no. 1 (2017): 56–59; John Heathershaw, 'Towards Better Theories of Peacebuilding: Beyond the Liberal Peace Debate', *Peacebuilding* 1, no. 2 (2013): 275–282; Andreas T. Hirblinger and Claudia Simons, 'The Good, the Bad, and the Powerful: Representations of the "Local" in Peacebuilding', *Security Dialogue* 46, no. 5 (2015): 422–439; Charles T. Hunt, 'Beyond the Binaries: Towards a Relational Approach to Peacebuilding', *Global Change, Peace & Security* 29, no. 3 (2017): 209–227; Randazzo, 'The Paradoxes of the "Everyday"'.

[6]Julian et al., this volume.

[7]There is not a single feminist methodology, but multiple ones. See: Barbara Ann Cole, 'Gender, Narratives and Intersectionality: Can Personal Experience Approaches to Research Contribute to "Undoing Gender"?', *International Review of Education*, 55 (2009): 563; Fionnuala Ni Aolain, Dina Francesca Haynes and Naomi Cahn, *On the Frontlines: Gender, War, and the Post-Conflict Process* (Oxford: Oxford University Press, 2011).

[8]A good example of an intersectionality approach in practice can be found in: Bina D'Costa, 'Marginalized identity: new frontiers of research for IR?' in: Brooke A. Ackerly, Maria Stern and Jacqui True (eds) *Feminist Methodologies for International Relations* (Cambridge: CUP, 2006), 129–152.

In other words, the *intersectionality of peace* approach enables us to unpack power dynamics at play in PCS, analysing the compounded privileges and inequalities (or discrimination) experienced and lived by all parties, researchers included. It should be emphasised that this intersectionality is not simply a reflection of identities and representations, but also emerges from, and has ramifications in, the material conditions specific to the complex assemblage of privilege and exclusion. These connections, which can be considered as different forms of *attachment* or *detachment*,[9] help shape the socio-material world we live in, conditioning the social constellations we are situated in. They can 'place us' in closer proximity to some rather than to other actors, thus helping us to make sense of complex stories of inclusion and exclusion and underlining the power differentials at play in each of these stories. Hence, the *intersectionality of peace* approach contributes to our understanding of why specific voices are marginalised and silenced, when others are privileged and considered authoritative. Maybe more importantly, it also helps us to grapple with all the situations falling 'in between' these two extremes; situations that PCS have been struggling so far to conceptualise.

This article is a personal journey for the authors. We are two scholars whose work is generally associated with PCS, with a long-standing interest to fight the compartmentalisation and disciplinisation of our subfield, whether it is through a renewed engagement with scholarship located in international law, sociology and anthropology, or political geography. We have followed debates in the feminist literature from afar, without feeling comfortable enough to engage directly with the debates. Understanding that this de facto position reinforces the actual division between the two subfields, we have decided to seize the opportunity offered to us by the guest editors and move outside of our comfort zone by engaging with feminist debates in order to highlight the bridges that exist between Critical PCS and Gender Studies. It is also important to underline the modest scope of this article. The main audience for this piece is not necessarily the feminist community of scholars, but our PCS colleagues who are maybe not familiar with this vibrant body of literature. Having said that, we think the article does offer a contribution to the field by highlighting the possible research avenues resulting from the interconnections between PCS and feminist methodologies. We suggest one such tangible avenue through *the intersectionality of peace* approach.

This article is divided in three sections. In the first section, we look at three specific lenses or approaches dominantly used in PCS to overcome the binaries often used by researchers to make sense of local processes: the everyday, hybridity, and narrative studies. In doing so, we connect the scholarship on these three approaches with recent work done by feminist scholars. The second section looks at the intersectionality approach and connects it with PCS preoccupations, especially identity formation, power imbalances, and the move beyond the 'local' versus 'international' binary. The third section illustrates the usefulness of the intersectionality concept by discussing one of the author's own fieldwork in South Africa by zooming in on the micro-space of the 'guesthouse'. Methodologically, this move allows us to challenge the primacy of the public sphere, as we observe it in PCS. Instead, through a small-scale dialogical analysis of two narratives, we show that the

---

[9]Lemay-Hébert and Kappler, 'What Attachment to Peace?'.

intersectionality that can be observed in our case study in narrative terms highlights the ways in which inequalities overlap both public and private life and makes the distinction between those almost impossible. In that sense, the guest house as a meeting point between public activities (tourism) and private experiences (as they relate to guests and staff) helps us complicate simplified narratives of segregation in South Africa.

Hybridity, everyday, narrative: using feminist approaches to challenge dichotomies

This section will cover three main areas of research in the PCS community: hybridity, the everyday and Narrative Studies. Looking at each approach's answer to the dichotomy debate, we make three interconnected arguments: 1) the use of the concept of hybridity has not enabled scholars to fully emancipate themselves from the 'local' versus 'international' dichotomy; 2) the use of the concept of 'everyday' has diffused power relations to the extent that it becomes difficult to make a substantial analysis of the interplay of actors on the ground; and 3) Narrative Studies have similarly risked to end up in many cases depoliticising the interplay of actors, individualising experiences to the extent that it becomes difficult to analyse and apprehend structural/collective power relations through them. We argue here that feminist approaches can help us bring back power considerations into our analysis and understanding of the 'local'; something that will also be further explored in the next section on intersectionality.

Hybridity

Hybridity has emerged as one of the all-purpose theoretical lenses, meant to reflect the everyday complexity of world politics. Migrating from the cultural and postcolonial fields, the hybridity lens has now permeated many disciplines, including IR and PCS. Fundamentally, hybridity theorists question the binaries often mobilised by researchers, such as the human-nature distinction, understanding it instead as hybrid networks of human and non-human elements,[10] but also question other binaries such as 'modern-traditional', 'Western-Non-Western'. 'international-local', 'centre-periphery', 'internal-external' or 'us-them'.

In PCS, two main and complementary strands of hybridity scholarship have emerged in the past few years.[11] The first one focuses on the interplay between international and local practices, norms and institutions as a way to emphasise local agency in its interaction with outside forces, and/or to engage with local actors beyond the nation-state.[12] The second strand of scholarship is more focused on transcending universalising theories to include the plurality of social

---

[10] Based on the work of Bruno Latour. See for instance: Anders Blok and Torben Elgaard Jensen, *Bruno Latour: Hybrid Thoughts in a Hybrid World* (London: Routledge, 2011).
[11] Nicolas Lemay-Hébert and Rosa Freedman, 'Critical Hybridity: Exploring Cultural, Legal and Political Pluralism', in: N. Lemay-Hébert and R. Freedman (eds) *Hybridity: Law, Culture, and Development* (London: Routledge, 2017), 3–14.
[12] Roberto Belloni, 'Hybrid Peace Governance: Its Emergence and Significance', *Global Governance* 18 (2012): 21–38; Oliver P. Richmond and Audra Mitchell, 'Introduction – Towards a Post-Liberal Peace: Exploring Hybridity Via Everyday Forms of Resistance, Agency and Autonomy', in: O. Richmond and A. Mitchell (eds) *Hybrid Forms of Peace: From*

orders.[13] The first approach is a direct challenge to liberal institutionalism and suggests looking at the complex creations that emerge out of interventions. The second approach challenges (neo-)Weberian notions of the state as a lens through which we generate knowledge about post-colonial and post-conflict societies.[14] As discussed above, this scholarship has faced an 'anti-hybridity backlash' in the discipline, with authors questioning the bundling of local actors together, or the quiet return to the old dichotomies that were meant to be overcome.[15] It reflects to a certain extent the blatant absence of power considerations, which has led to overlook the power differentials behind the 'hybridisation' processes.[16] In that sense, hybridity has tended to assume a mix of things. It has done so without problematizing the underlying power relations that shape such mixing and often implicitly assumed that such power relations are evened out in the process of hybridisation.

In that context, the call to develop a feminist approach to hybridity seems particularly relevant. As Laura McLeod notes, the concept of hybridity echoes many elements of feminist scholarship on post-conflict, to the extent that the two literatures are almost 'mirror images'.[17] McLeod notes that the concept of hybridity can allow to analyse the diversity of 'locals and internationals,'[18] even if in practice, and as discussed before, it tends to be stuck in this binary thinking. It can also highlight the interconnection between the personal, the political and the international, which is crucial to move beyond the unhelpful local-international binary.[19] Furthermore, as Nicole George and Lia Kent also argue, a feminist approach to hybridity highlights the fact that 'the gendered restrictions of liberal peacebuilding are not easily overcome or minimised when local structures of authority or local governance practices are deliberately incorporated into peacebuilding interventions.'[20] Linked to this point, a feminist perspective on hybridity can help us to question how local actors are portrayed, especially through a 'feminised' portrayal of 'local' actors in certain cases.[21] Finally, it can help put emphasis on the 'affective and relational dimensions of peace'[22] and especially the

---

Everyday Agency to Post-Liberalism (Basingstoke: Palgrave, 2012), 1–38; and Roger Mac Ginty, 'Hybrid Peace: The Interaction Between Top-Down and Bottom-Up Peace', *Security Dialogue* 41, no. 4 (2010): 391–412.

[13]Volker Boege et al., 'On Hybrid Political Orders and Emerging States: What is Failing – States in the Global South or Research and Politics in the West?' *Berghof Handbook Dialogue Series* no. 8 (2009): 15–35; and Peter Albrecht and Louise Wiuff Moe, 'The Simultaneity of Authority in Hybrid Orders', *Peacebuilding* 3, no.1 (2015): 1–16.

[14]Philipp Lottholz and N. Lemay-Hébert, 'Re-reading Weber, Redefining State-Building? From Neo-Weberian to Post-Weberian Approaches to State, Legitimacy, and State-Building', *Cambridge Review of International Affairs* 29, no. 4 (2016): 1467–1485.

[15]Hameiri and Jones, 'Beyond Hybridity to the Politics of Scale'.

[16]For an overview of this argument, see: Jenny Peterson, 'A Conceptual Unpacking of Hybridity: Accounting for Notions of Power, Politics and Progress in Analyses of Aid-Driven Interfaces', *Journal of Peacebuilding and Development* 7, no. 2 (2012): 9–22. 48–69.

[17]Laura McLeod, 'A Feminist Approach to Hybridity: Understanding Local and International Interactions in Producing Post-Conflict Gender Security', *Journal of Intervention and Statebuilding* 9, no. 1 (2015): 49.

[18]McLeod, 'A Feminist Approach to Hybridity', 51.

[19]Cynthia Enloe, *Bananas, Beaches and Bases: Making Feminist Sense of International Politics*. Berkeley: University of California Press, 348; and Laura McLeod, 'Gender and Post-Conflict Reconstruction', in: Laura Shepherd, Laura Sjoberg and Caron Gentry (eds), *Handbook of Gender and Security* (London: Routledge, 2018).

[20]Nicole George and Lia Kent, 'Sexual violence and hybrid peacebuilding: how does silence "speak"?' *Third World Thematics* 2, no. 4 (2017): 519. See also: Annika Björkdahl and Johanna Mannergren Selimovic, 'Gendering Agency in Transitional Justice', *Security Dialogue* 46, no. 2 (2015): 165–182; and Nicole George, 'Light, Heat and Shadows: Women's Reflections on Peacebuilding in Post-Conflict Bougainville', *Peacebuilding* 4, no. 2 (2016): 166–179.

personal aspect of encounters between different actors, encompassed in affective notions linked to hybridity.[23] These works offer a substantial contribution to PCS by problematizing the construction of the 'local' and 'international' categories. However, the hybridity framework, even when power relations are brought back in through a critical approach,[24] is still arguably mired in this unhelpful dichotomisation, which we hope the *intersectionality of peace* approach can overcome.

The everyday

Whilst hybridity dealt with the more general ways of framing and dealing with post-conflict identities, it still struggles to state what that would mean concretely for the ways in which intervention is perceived, interpreted, complied with or resisted on the part of its respective host society. Hence, as part of IR's and PCS's attempt to engage with the lived realities of politics, we have seen an increasing focus on the 'everyday' sphere of intervention. There is a strong acknowledgement that intervention is no longer just a matter of high politics, but instead translates explicitly into everyday life.[25] At the same time, such debates have not just been limited to PCS, but have for some time also been picked up in IR more broadly.[26] Much of this work on the everyday goes back to Henri Lefebvre's suggestion that the everyday can serve as a critique of politics, connecting 'the particular and the universal, the local and the global.'[27] Such concepts rarely speak of power as they assume that the location of power at the elite levels of society is a result of social assumptions, and when we start acknowledging the power located in the everyday, this will be a form of empowerment in itself in terms of shifting attention to the agency located within everyday practices and discourses.[28] The recognition of local capacity and agency is the outcome of such processes.[29]

Feminist scholars such as Elise Boulding or Sara Ruddick have investigated 'daily social transactions'[30] as well as the power inequalities inherent in the 'private' realm of the family.[31] We therefore need to acknowledge that feminist thought has managed to

---

[21]Caitlin Ryan and Helen Basini, 'UNSC Resolution 1325 national action plans in Liberia and Sierra Leone: An analysis of gendered power relations in hybrid peacebuilding', *Journal of Intervention and Statebuilding* 11, no. 2 (2017): 186–206.

[22]Laura Shepherd, "The road to (and from) 'recovery': a multidisciplinary feminist approach to peacekeeping and peacebuilding', in: Gina Heathcote and Dianne Otto (eds), *Rethinking Peacekeeping, Gender Equality and Collective Security* (London: Routledge), 112; and McLeod, 'Gender and Post-Conflict Reconstruction'.

[23]Hannah Partis-Jennings, 'The (in)security of gender in Afghanistan's peacebuilding project: hybridity and affect', *International Feminist Journal of Politics* 19, no. 4 (2017): 411–425; and Nina Wilén, 'Security sector reform, gender and local narratives in Burundi', *Conflict, Security & Development* 14, no. 3 (2014): 33–354. See also Partis-Jennings, this volume.

[24]Lemay-Hébert and Freedman, 'Critical Hybridity'.

[25]Séverine Autesserre, *Peaceland: Conflict Resolution and the Everyday Politics of International Intervention* (Cambridge: Cambridge University Press, 2014).

[26]Matt Davies and Michael Niemann (2002) 'The Everyday Spaces of Global Politics: Work, Leisure, Family', *New Political Science* 24, no. 4 (2002): 557–577; Matt Davies and Michael Niemann, *International Relations and Everyday Life* (London: Routledge, 2004).

[27]Henri Lefebvre, *Critique of Everyday Life vol.3*; translated by G. Elliott (London: Verso, 2008), 16.

[28]Stefanie Kappler, *Local Agency and Peacebuilding. EU and International Engagement in Bosnia-Herzegovina, Cyprus and South Africa* (Basingstoke: Palgrave, 2014). See also: Marta Iñiguez de Heredia, 'The Conspicuous Absence of Class and Privilege in the Study of Resistance in Peacebuilding Contexts', *International Peacekeeping* (2018; online first).

[29]Julian et al, this volume.

[30]Elise Boulding, *Cultures of peace: The hidden side of history* (Syracuse, NY: Syracuse University Press, 2000), 147.

[31]Sara Ruddick, 'Maternal Thinking', *Feminist Studies* 6, no. 2 (1980): 342–367. See also: Väyrynen, this volume; and Vaittinen, this volume.

cast light on the artificial binary between the public and the private, suggesting that the everyday work in the private scene is clearly shaped by power asymmetries.[32] Susan Gal, for instance, points out that social relations and identities can never be situated in one of these spheres, but always transcend them.[33] Gal argues that the dichotomy between public and private is not just a rhetorical one but has actual impact upon everyday lives.[34] Ruth Lister goes further suggesting that this binary notion has framed our understandings of citizenship to the detriment of female notions of citizenship.[35] In that sense, the understanding of the public has tended to be considered a male domain, while women tended to be associated with the private domain. This was linked to an assumption that 'intervention', as a public, political phenomenon, could mainly be discussed in the public sphere, whilst its implications for individuals was given less attention – not least owed to the fact that the emotional effects of war and peace were side-lined from such debates.[36] However, through the work of feminists such as Christine Sylvester, there has been an increasing emphasis on the connection between public and private phenomena – war as an experience rather than merely a matter of top-down decision-making.[37] Taking the experiential side of politics into account also means acknowledging the relevance of private experience for public phenomena (or war, in this case). Politics is thus no longer assumed to be limited to the public and collective, but also has its roots in the individual, private experience of it.

What feminist thought has managed to bring to the debate of the everyday is an account of the implicit power structures inherent in the ways politics is understood and conceptualised. Whilst the more traditional debates around the 'everyday' have managed to overcome some of the binaries (the local vs the international or global), they have, much like the hybridity debates, tended to become blind to power politics. There is an implicit assumption that power in the everyday is so dispersed that it can be found everywhere and has therefore almost become meaningless as an analytical category. This assumption risks projecting the illusion of equality (all actors are equalised as being situated in their own everyday) where there is inequality (where different everyday lives are privileged in different ways). Feminist thought as cited above, however, can be said to have challenged binary thinking whilst retaining the focus on power inequalities. There is recognition that, even in the merging between categories, subtle power structures remain active and translate into the gendered practices that conceptualise spaces across private and public spheres.

In this, feminist research has acknowledged the interplay between the symbolic and material dimensions of space. Nightingale, for instance, points to the ways in which the symbolic interactions within the space of nature are conditioned by its material, ecological properties.[38] By taking an intersectional perspective, she proposes to explore 'the production of difference through the everyday movement of bodies in space to

---

[32]Ibid.
[33]Susan Gal, 'A Semiotics of the Public/Private Distinction', *Differences: A Journal of Feminist Cultural Studies* 13, no. 1 (2002): 77–95.
[34]Gal, 'A Semiotics of the Public/Private Distinction', 87.
[35]Ruth Lister, 'Citizenship and gender', in: Kate Nash and Alan Scott (eds), *The Wiley-Blackwell companion to political sociology* (London: Wiley, 2001), 323–31.
[36]Väyrynen, this volume.
[37]Christine Sylvester, *War as Experience: Contributions from International Relations and Feminist Analysis* (London: Routledge, 2013).
[38]Andrea J. Nightingale, 'Bounding difference: Intersectionality and the material production of gender, caste, class and environment in Nepal', *Geoforum* 42 (2011): 153–162.

show how subjectivities are produced out of the multiple and intersecting exercise of power within socio-natural networks'.[39] In that sense, spaces materially *and* symbolically reproduce power differentials and therefore act as platforms on which inequalities can be read. The ways in which peacebuilding practices play out in people's everyday lives is therefore spatially performed and expressed, as feminist geographers have shown particularly well.[40] We will elaborate in further detail below how a focus on the spatial dimensions of intersectionality can benefit PCS as a way to reposition the researcher in relation to the researchee.

Narratives

As we have argued above, dominant approaches in both IR and PCS have fallen into the trap of either dichotomising categories (local vs international) or, alternatively, downplaying the power differentials between different actors in the post-conflict landscape. Similarly, the concept of 'narrative' has become increasingly popular among scholars in the field over the past two decades, but this has not always and necessarily been accompanied by an active and critical engagement with its full ontological, epistemological and methodological implications.[41] PCS scholars are increasingly interested in how narratives (or stories) as a 'basic human strategy for coming to terms with time, process, and change'[42] can help us understand local reality on the ground. The process of narration is necessarily selective, because there is always more than one story to tell. These are primarily afforded by our multiple social identities (e.g. white, male, female, disabled) and the public narratives of the communities in which they are embedded (e.g. family, ethnic group, nation).[43]

A focus on individual narratives can help us distract our gaze from our preconceived categories of 'local' vs 'international' and instead allow us to read intervention from the eyes of those experiencing it. Narratives can therefore act as gazes into the everyday of international relations in their ability to connect space, time and emotions in a grounded way.[44] This is so because, instead of theorising peace and conflict as abstract concepts, narratives situate them in a given time, in a given space. They make those concepts graspable and relevant to the host societies as they connect to their subjective realities and contexts. The narrative approach to peace, recently promoted by researchers including Molly Andrews, Jenny Edkins, Naeem Inayatullah and Elizabeth Dauphinee appears to us as essential in accessing humane expressions of post-conflict identity formation.[45] Yet, there is a risk that narrative research may individualise an experience that is collective or

---

[39]Ibid., p.153.
[40]Cf. Gülsüm Baydar, 'Sexualised productions of space', *Gender, Place & Culture*, 19, no. 6) (2012): 699–706.
[41]Josefin Graef, Raquel da Silva and Nicolas Lemay-Hébert, 'Narrative, Political Violence, and Social Change', *Studies in Conflict and Terrorism* 43, no. 6 (online first).
[42]David Herman, 'Introduction,' in David Herman, ed., *The Cambridge Companion to Narrative* (Cambridge: Cambridge University Press, 2007), 3.
[43]Molly Andrews, *Shaping History: Narratives of Political Change* (Cambridge: Cambridge University Press, 2007), 206; Margaret R. Somers, 'The Narrative Constitution of Identity: A Relational and Network Approach', *Theory and Society* 23 (1994): 619.
[44]See: Solomon and Steele, 'Micro-Moves in International Relations Theory'.
[45]Andrews, *Shaping History*; Jenny Edkins, 'Novel Writing in International Relations: Openings for a Creative Practice', *Security Dialogue* 44, no. 4 (2013): 281–297; Naeem Inayatullah and Elizabeth Dauphinee, *Narrative Global Politics: Theory, History and the Personal in International Relations* (London: Routledge, 2016).

structural in nature. If oppression is perceived as a 'one-off' experience, a deviation from normalcy, it is easier to write it off as an exception. Narrative research can indeed be said to have made it possible to gaze at a collective experience through the lens of an individual, yet this can only happen when a narrative is presented and contextualised in a way that de-essentialises and de-individualises the experience by looking at the structural factors that helped the narrative emerge. It is at this stage where feminist approaches inspire us to not stop at the individual (private) experience and instead look at the ways in which this is co-produced by politics and economics. Feminist approaches that investigate the securitisation of narratives that are often constructed vis-à-vis groups of women have pointed to the inherent power structures within these narratives and their associated 'grammars of insecurity' as well as discursive representations of danger.[46] In this vein, Wibben reminds us of the importance of language when it comes to understanding the ways in which security discourses are constituted, shaken and challenged.[47] Furthermore, as the work done by Maria Stern with Guatemalan women revealed, women and members of marginalised ethnic groups experience (multiple) forms of insecurity that do not neatly fit into prevailing security discourses,[48] constraining the possibilities of discursive practices of and on (in)security.

Having outlined the value and shortcomings of 'hybridity', the 'everyday' and 'narratives', we now turn to the concept of 'intersectionality' to investigate the ways in which the concepts above can be revisited in a meaningful way, attentive to power inequalities and therefore of key relevance to PCS.

Using feminist approaches to investigate intersectionalities

Whilst feminism has made a range of contributions to the social sciences as highlighted above, one of its very important ones is the concept of *intersectionality*. Leslie McCall even suggests that '[o]ne could even say that intersectionality is the most important theoretical contribution that women's studies, in conjunction with related fields, has made so far.'[49] Coined by Kimberlé Crenshaw and based on the insight that different women are affected differently by multiple forms of discrimination and inequality, *intersectionality* opposes the reduction of identity categories to a single one (e.g. gender or race).[50] Instead, the concept denotes the complex ways in which people are affected by power structures based on their multiple identities, without automatically privileging one over another. In that sense, power is seen as differentiated not only between, but also within identity groups, that is for Crenshaw, not all women are equally oppressed, and not all black people are in the very same societal position. Instead, inequalities are understood to be differentiated along multiple lines, presented in different forms and modes.[51]

---

[46]Maria Stern, '"We" the Subject: The Power and Failure of (In)Security', *Security Dialogue* 37, no. 2 (2006): 187–205.
[47]Annick Wibben, *Feminist Security Studies: A Narrative Approach* (London and New York: Routledge, 2011).
[48]Maria Stern, 'Racism, sexism, classism, and much more: reading security-identity in marginalized sites', in: Brooke A. Ackerly, Maria Stern and Jacqui True (eds) *Feminist Methodologies for International Relations* (Cambridge: CUP, 2006), 177.
[49]Leslie McCall, 'The Complexity of Intersectionality', *Signs: Journal of Women in Culture and Society*, 30, no. 3 (2005): 1771.
[50]Kimberlé Crenshaw, 'Demarginalizing the Intersection of Race and Sex: A Black Feminist Critique of Antidiscrimination Doctrine, Feminist Theory and Antiracist Politics', *University of Chicago Legal Forum* 1989, 138–67.
[51]Heidi Safia Mirza, '"A second skin": Embodied intersectionality, transnationalism and narratives of identity and belonging among Muslim women in Britain', *Women's Studies International Forum* 36 (2013): 6.

Therefore, intersectionality allows for multiple levels of analysis[52] and an understanding of inequalities as embedded in the interplay between different power systems. Intersectionality brings together a number of 'intersections' (race, class and gender are most often cited in this context) to investigate their mutual interaction whilst supporting 'the deconstruction of binaries, normalisation theories and homogenising categories.'[53] We therefore suggest that intersectionality challenges identity politics, group essentialism and assumptions of in-group uniformity.[54]

There have been initial efforts to explore intersectionality in transitional justice, for instance by investigating the effects of peace agreements and transitions on poor women.[55] Such studies remain close to the early questions that Crenshaw posed with the introduction of the concept. From a legal context, she had shown how Black women's everyday lives are shaped by the way they are represented (both in culture and politics and law) and how this influences how they can interact within and outside their community.[56] At the same time, it is important to be aware that the concept of intersectionality does not just refer to gender and race (although they seem to be addressed most often), but includes many more facets of identity and difference, such as class, nationality, disability, sexuality and so forth – or, to speak in Butler's terms, the 'etc' that she reads as a 'sign of exhaustion as well as of the illimitable process of signification itself'.[57] On the other hand, of course, keeping the list inconclusive also allows for the integration of multiple identity categories as they become salient over the course of time, and thus avoids fixating or privileging some identity categories over others indefinitely.

We argue that, based on the previously outlined critique of 'hybridity', 'the everyday' and 'narratives', a refocusing of these three concepts with an intersectionality lens enables us to address their shortcomings. Our proposed intersectionality of peace approach means that we can 1) understand hybrid identities without dichotomising them; 2) read the everyday yet with a clear intention of understanding power differentials therein; and 3) understand narratives not as individualised experiences, but instead as ways of accessing larger structural inequalities.

What we suggest in this article is what Baukje Prins calls the British approach to intersectionality, that is, to treat intersectionality as a social construction.[58] This does by no means signify a demotion of intersectionality as 'not real' or only imagined, but instead as part of everyone's identity in relation to the societal constellations in which such intersectional oppressions are continuously produced and reproduced.

---

[52]Nira Yuval-Davis, 'Intersectionality and Feminist Politics', *European Journal of Women's Studies*, 13, no. 3 (2006): 197.
[53]Cole, 'Gender, Narratives and Intersectionality', 566.
[54]Ange-Marie Hancock, 'When Multiplication Doesn't Equal Quick Addition: Examining Intersectionality as a Research Paradigm', *Perspectives on Politics* 5, no. 1 (2007): 65.
[55]Fionnuala Ní Aoláin and Eilish Rooney, 'Underenforcement and Intersectionality: Gendered Aspects of Transition for Women', *The International Journal of Transitional Justice* 1 (2007): 338–354; Eilish Rooney, 'Engendering transitional justice: questions of absence and silence', *International Journal of Law in Context* 3, no. 2 (2007): 173–187; Paul Gready and Simon Robins, 'From Transitional to Transformative Justice: A New Agenda for Practice', *International Journal of Transitional Justice* 8, no. 3 (2014): 339–361.
[56]Kimberlé Crenshaw, 'Mapping the Margins: Intersectionality, Identity Politics, and Violence against Women of Color', *Stanford Law Review* 43, no. 6 (1991): 1241–1299.
[57]Judith Butler, *Gender Trouble: Feminism and the Subversion of Identity* (New York: Routledge, 1990), 143.
[58]Baukje Prins, 'Narrative Accounts of Origins: A Blind Spot in the Intersectional Approach?', *European Journal of Women's Studies* 13, no. 3 (2006): 280.

In this, the intersectionality approach as such does not prescribe a set methodology as it can be studied in different ways, quantitatively and qualitatively. At the same time, some feminists interested in intersectionality have taken an interest in narrative studies to explore the complexity of identities.[59] And whilst intersectionality approaches can resort to a variety of methodologies,[60] both quantitative and qualitative, they often start from a narrative angle. Personal narratives investigated through an intersectionality lens allow us to view the individual experience as a specific translation of wider structures of disadvantage and privilege. They consider the experience not as anatomised one, but instead as a peephole through which the 'worlds' of violence and peace can be explored.[61]

It is specifically the multi-layered and complex nature of inequality that arises out of intersectional (rather than binary representations of) identity that can be accessed through narratives as the latter tend to allow for complexity – as opposed to the reductionism of other forms of data collection. At the same time, relying on narratives to understand intersectionality allows us to not only account for *structures* of domination, but at the same time also for the narrator's *agency* in dealing with and resisting them on an everyday basis:

> According to the constructionist perspective [...] the processes by which individuals become subjects do not merely involve 'being subjected to', in the sense of being subordinated to a sovereign power or anonymous system. It also implies that the individual is 'becoming a subject', i.e. made into a source of his or her own thinking and acting."[62]

Put in dialogue with the socio-economic and political contexts in which they emerge, expressions of intersectionality can shed light on where different intersectional processes produce multiple layers of oppression or privilege. They can show how the layering of different identities represents more than the sum of their layers. Actually, these different identities, whether they are linked to gender, class and social provenance, being considered 'disabled', one's citizenship or national 'affiliation', the colour of one's skin, or the language one speaks more fluently, 'stack up' or are compounded in complex assemblages, constituting a mix of different forms of privilege or exclusion. In a field like PCS, where identity-formation has long been seen as a binary phenomenon, focusing on the ways in which intersectionality is narrated can provide a constructive challenge to an otherwise black-and-white representation of conflict and peace alike. Putting the findings of an intersectional focus on narratives in the context of the material structures of inequality from which they emerge allows for a power-aware gaze on a political scenario. This process can cast light on the hybridity of the experience of war and peace, whilst avoiding the flattening out of power inequalities. We will therefore now zoom in on the space of the South African guest house as a way of engaging with intersectional power relations as they emerge in its material and symbolic dimensions. We will show how an intersectional reading of post-conflict

---

[59]Cole, 'Gender, Narratives and Intersectionality'; McCall, 'The Complexity of Intersectionality', 1783; Mirza, '"A second skin"'.
[60]Lisa Bowleg, 'When Black + Lesbian + Woman ≠ Black Lesbian Woman: The Methodological Challenges of Qualitative and Quantitative Intersectionality Research', *Sex Roles* 59 (2008): 312–325.
[61]Cf. Audra Mitchell, *Lost in Transformation: Violent Peace and Peaceful Conflict in Northern Ireland* (Basingstoke: Palgrave, 2011).
[62]Prins, 'Narrative Accounts of Origins', 280.

violence helps us understand the ongoing challenges that South Africans face, more than twenty years after the transition from apartheid to democracy. It also helps us understand questions of disadvantage and privilege as they emerge from the research process itself.

The intersectionality of peace: a conversation around the South African guest house

Let us now turn to investigate how the *intersectionality of peace approach* can help highlight the power dynamics in a specific context, where matters of gender, race and class have continued to play a major role in the ways in which transitional justice and peacebuilding discourses play out. Indeed, South Africa has long been shaped by multi-dimensional inequalities and has not always, but often been reduced to a black vs white binary when it came to understanding society or, when taking the intersection of race and class into account, inadvertently subordinating gender divisions to a third, lesser rank.[63] It is important to understand that the multiple dividing lines that shape South African society are key to understanding its systems of inequality and, therefore, also the complex manifestations of violence that are still at play over twenty years after the formal end of the apartheid state.

However, despite the hope that had been placed into the transition to democracy in 1994, the post-apartheid state has failed to reduce or deal with those multiple inequalities, as they specifically affect black women from economically deprived backgrounds. Certainly, women have meanwhile gained almost equal representation in government positions as well as parliament and the Black Economic Empowerment laws, which incentivise the recruitment of black South Africans into the labour force, have, albeit only to a small extent, generated hope for a less unequal future for the most disadvantaged South Africans.[64] The image of the 'rainbow nation' indeed instils the vision of a diverse and peaceful society where everyone enjoys equal rights. At the same time, the realities of everyday life hold very different prospects for many: high levels of unemployment, a lack of housing for the economically deprived, inequalities in land distribution as well as skyrocketing levels of crime continue to impede prosperity for the majority of South Africans.[65] Certainly, the latter must be seen in connection to such intersectional inequalities.

So, if we, as researchers, are to find a 'local' South African experience, what would that be? The experience of a white owner of a guest house in Cape Town? Or that of a township inhabitant without access to running water and electricity? Or instead of a miner who works for little money in one of the mines on the outskirts of Johannesburg?

---

[63]Paul Gordon Lauren, *Power And Prejudice. The Politics and Diplomacy Of Racial Discrimination* (New York, Routledge, 1996); Shula Marks and Stanley Trapido (eds.), *The politics of race, class and nationalism in twentieth-century South Africa* (Abingdon; New York: Routledge, 2014); Jeremy Seekings, 'Just deserts': Race, class and distributive justice in post-apartheid South Africa', *Journal of Southern African Studies* 34, no. 1 (2008): 39–60; Jeremy Seekings and Nicoli Nattrass, *Class, race and inequality in South Africa* (New Haven, CT: Yale University Press, 2005).
[64]Cf. Bill Freund, 'South Africa: The End of Apartheid & the Emergence of the "BEE Elite"', *Review of African Political Economy*, 34, no. 114 (2007): 661–678.
[65]Cf. Bernadette Atuahene, 'South Africa's Land Reform Crisis: Eliminating the Legacy of Apartheid', *Foreign Affairs*, 90, no. 4 (2011): 121–129; Gregory D. Breetzke, Karina Landman & Ellen G. Cohn, 'Is it safer behind the gates? Crime and gated communities in South Africa', *Journal of Housing and the Built Environment*, 29, no. 1 (2014): 123–139.

Or would we be interested in the lived experience of a migrant worker from Zimbabwe who just earns enough money to send back a little to their family abroad?

There is a huge degree of differentiation between those different locals and the ways in which they go about their everyday lives. This diversity would be impossible to capture through a hybridity lens in which we look at the ways in which these experiences hybridise with each other. How would that help us understand why the township inhabitant may have never set foot into a city centre, or why the guesthouse owner may never have seen one of the many South African townships? We can clearly identify the huge differences in those peoples' everyday lives, but how can we make sense of them to understand the ways in which economic, political and social inequalities impact upon their social relations and identities? Here, the *intersectionality of peace* approach can help us not only to grasp the multiple dividing lines that shape the manifestation of violence in South Africa, but it can also zoom in on the intersectional inequality between researcher and researchee. It is important to be aware of one's own privilege as part of the research project. Our positionality is not outside the field that we research, but instead part and parcel of the research process. It shapes our gaze on what we consider relevant as object of inquiry on the one hand. On the other hand, it reflects the extent to which the experience of the researcher intersects with those we interact with and places our position within wider unequal power structures. Especially in PCS, where we are always at the search of local and global identities, the *intersectionality of peace* approach will be particularly helpful in shedding light of the nuanced and multi-dimensional inequalities that are at the core of our research process within a broader social context.

Through a conversation between the field notes of one of the authors, a white female researcher (WFR), as well as a published narrative account of a black, male South African, we look at the ways in which a focus on the 'guest house' can complicate our understanding of the 'local' and its everyday experience vis-à-vis the researcher. The South African tourism sector itself is a representation of power differentials and, in letting narratives speak to each other, we understand the intersections of race, class and gender in this particular sector as they become salient in the field research process – in a way, a form of academic tourism.[66]

The WFR has noticed throughout various research trips to South Africa that it is indeed the norm to see white guests in guest houses and that cleaning and the provision of breakfast as well as night shifts tend to be done by black female housekeepers. She writes in her 2017 research diary:

> It feels weird to be a white researcher from abroad, writing about the detrimental effects of colonialism and social inequality, and at the same time sitting at the breakfast table of a guest house, being served by a black housekeeper who tells me that she has not seen her children in months as they are in Zimbabwe. I checked out later and made sure the white, male owner of the guest house has received the money from my research budget.

Mvuselelo Ngcoya in his account of being a tourist, writes of his experience as a tourist in South Africa in 1983: 'We always stepped aside when a white person appeared. [...] Tourists were white and I was black.'[67] Ngcoya goes on to show how what he

---

[66] Cf. Marcus Breen, 'Privileged migration: American undergraduates, study abroad, academic tourism', *Critical Arts* 26, no. 1 (2012): 82–102.
[67] Mvuselelo Ngcoya, 'Hyperapartheid', *Journal of Narrative Politics*, 2, no. 1 (2015): 38.

experienced in 1983 had not changed at all in 2014, when he was a tourist in his own country again and witnessed how a B&B owner referred to the housekeepers as 'my girls'.[68] This certainly has both a gender component (being possessive of women) as well as a class component that is inextricably linked to skin colour – it is indeed proportionally more common for white South Africans to own property than for Black South Africans. Ngcoya confirms that 'success is often equated with whiteness. At the petrol station for example, I cringe when the attendant refers to me as mlungu wami (my white man).'[69]

The WFR was regularly told by white South Africans, male and female, to watch out and not walk around on her own. Many times, the black housekeepers of the guest house, when asked, said that they were not so worried, not least as they are exposed to a very different set of dangers when walking around. Those who do not live at the guest house where they work are confronted with a lack of public transport, which is often too expensive in relation to the little money that they earn.[70] This creates a particular infrastructure of threat narratives, held by people in relation to their own exposure to threat levels. From the diary of the WFR:

> Today, we [a white local student and myself] booked a walking tour through the inner city of Johannesburg. After quite a few people came up to us and told us it was not safe to walk around there as white women, the student asked our [black] guide why people kept telling us this specifically in relation to us being white. Was it more unsafe for us to walk around than for black women? The guide responded that we were more likely to become victims of theft and robbery, but black women in other parts of the city faced the constant danger of being abducted and trafficked.

That of course tells us not only about the different effects that urban geographies have on individuals, but also about the implications of the failing public transport system and the low salary of housekeepers (who will not be able to afford a car as most white people do) on those black women's lives. Whilst the threat of being mugged is something publicly articulated to white women, black women in other parts of the city who are at risk of being abducted will rarely be warned. Instead, the elevated level of danger to them is accepted as part of their daily lives.

It becomes clear that the location of the South African tourist guest house provides a glimpse onto a space in which we can read intersectionality: through the pressures imposed on black female housekeepers, through the ownership of property, usually by white owners, as well as of the complicity or a white female researcher in a colonial-style system of inequality that she is trying to resist. The everyday lives of the housekeepers are a particular 'local' that emerges from the political economy of the guest house and from the intersection between different categories of oppression. Theirs is a completely different local experience than that of the guest house owner, who will in fact spend the best part of every day in the same location. The housekeeper's everyday life maybe shaped by the hybridity of identities that surrounds her work, but can only be understood in the light of the multi-faceted power relations that intersect her life – usually in dependence on an insecure job, exposed to increased levels of danger and without regular contact with

---

[68]Ngcoya, 'Hyperapartheid', 39.
[69]Ngcoya, 'Hyperapartheid', 42.
[70]Ngcoya, 'Hyperapartheid', 41.

her family. This inequality is not merely a matter of representation, but is engraved in the material substructures of a larger system of inequality. In the interplay between the material underpinnings of the guest house – expressed in ownership and physical location – as well as the symbolic transactions that take place within it, the space of the guest house becomes a sphere in which we can understand intersectional inequality.

Building on this conversation, we would like to suggest that the *intersectionality of peace* approach can present useful research avenues for PCS scholars. For one, it helps desegregate the pervasive binaries present in many analyses by focusing on lived experiences of different actors on the ground – from precarity to privilege, or from insecurity to safety. As such, we agree with Marta Iñiguez de Heredia about the general 'absence of class and privilege' in peacebuilding studies,[71] and we believe that the concept of intersectionality can contribute to redress this. In the conversation above, we hint at how the everyday lies at the intersection of categories of oppression (gendered, racial, economic, political), but also categories of privilege, and how these different categories can intersect. A WFR is, for instance, a very good example of an intersection between privilege (the intersection between whiteness and the social and economic capital coming with UK-based higher education) as well as femininity, associated with 'weakness' and the perceived need to be protected as well as the lived experience of insecurity.

Whilst this discussion is based on a personal, lived experience, it is not meant to simply reflect the general tendency in the literature for constant self-reflection; we believe that the *intersectionality of peace* approach can help us broaden our understanding of the material power relations as they are lived and experienced on the ground by a variety of actors, including researchers and interveners. The concept hence intends to highlight these dynamics in a way that *hybrid orders* or *hybrid forms of peace* didn't manage to completely achieve, at least in the way that the concepts were used in the PCS community. The *intersectionality of peace approach* instead helps underline the fact that categories such as race, class and gender structure social relationships in South Africa, and power relations lie at the intersection of multiple identities. The recent history of South Africa is a series of well-known attempts from multiple actors to overcome institutionalised racial discrimination, before and after the apartheid regime, but less known is the fact that some of these attempts have resulted in the bolstering of patriarchal power relations.[72] As Beth Glodblatt and Sheila Meintjes argue, 'patriarchy was embedded within the social fabric of apartheid in particular ways and meant that women and men from different racial, class and cultural backgrounds experienced life very differently.'[73] At the same time, a mono-dimensional focus on race or gender as analytical categories only disguises the extent to which the transition from apartheid to democracy has further complicated oppressions. Whilst the abolishment of formal segregation was certainly to be welcomed, there are continuing power inequalities that derive not only from racial, but also gendered and economic discrimination. As researchers, we find ourselves in the midst of and complicit with such inequalities.

---

[71]Marta Iñiguez de Heredia, 'The Conspicuous Absence of Class and Privilege in the Study of Resistance in Peacebuilding Contexts', *International Peacekeeping* 25, no. 3 (2018): 325–348.

[72]Beth Goldblatt and Sheila Meintjes, 'South African Women Demand the Truth', in: Meredeth Turshen and Clotide Twagiramariya (eds.) *What Women Do in Wartime* (London: Zed Books, 1998), 29.

[73]Goldblatt and Meintjes, 'South African Women Demand the Truth', 30.

Intersectionality, as an analytical tool, can help unveil those categories of oppression that tend to be overlaid and disguised by simplified binary explanations that place the origins of oppression within a single identity category. It thus serves as a lens to identify structures of inequality – which can be seen as a key issue for the ongoing manifestations of violence on different levels in South African society.[74] Investigating the ways in which inequalities intersect thus allows for a more nuanced understanding of the multiple factors that shape people's everyday lives, impact upon the research process, organise the manifestation of violence in society, and eventually, the ways in which peacebuilding often fails to address underlying and intersectional discrimination.

Conclusion

This article tried to shed new light on the heated debate regarding the use of, and the attempt to overcome, dichotomies in PCS. By doing this, we have noted the limits of three recent strands in the PCS literature, focusing on the everyday, hybridity, and narratives. The three approaches, each in their own ways, tend to either reproduce binary logics they attempt to overcome, or risk glossing over power considerations. Hence, this article is an attempt to (re)connect the PCS scholarship with the feminist literature, which has been discussing and debating these issues for quite some time. We have particularly highlighted the potential of the concept of intersectionality to bring a fresh perspective on this debate. An intersectional analysis of narratives, we argue, can reap the benefits that narrative approaches have brought into PCS whilst casting light on the politicised nature of identities that emerge from those. In that sense, narratives are no longer seen as individualised, exceptional experiences, but as products and co-producers of systems of inequality. To investigate this process, we have provided an illustration of the potential of intersectionality as an analytical tool by putting in conversation one of the author's field notes from South Africa with a published narrative on the power relations within South Africa's tourism sector. Our small-scale case study shows that the complication of conflict narratives is necessary to understand the different effects that structural inequality has on the reproduction of violence in the everyday of public and private arenas.

It is important to note that the *intersectionality of peace* approach allows one to argue the relative importance of one source of privilege or discrimination over others when trying to understand specific phenomena – the key here is to acknowledge, understand and analyse these various sources rather than simply imply that one is more important than the other. As such, it would be unfair to criticise interdisciplinarity scholarship on the ground that it does not allow one to argue for the pre-eminence of a source of privilege and discrimination over other sources. What seems important here is to note that the *intersectionality of peace* does not run against these approaches. We want to bring power back in the conversation, and we believe that intersectionality does contribute, along with other approaches, to take a hard look at power dynamics at play in the (re)production of social structures.

---

[74] John Gaventa and Carin Runciman, 'Untangling economic and political inequality: The case of South Africa', in: ISSC, IDS and UNESCO (eds) *Challenging Inequalities: Pathways to a Just World, World Social Science Report 2016*, (Paris: UNESCO Publishing, 2016): 70–73.

We therefore aim to highlight the need to go beyond the 'self-reflective' move, which tends to be associated with a very self-centred, auto-ethnography approach, to discuss what the complexity of categories means for actors on the ground, but also for us researchers. This is a call to discuss the various forms of privilege – in its 'local' and 'international' components as much as along the lines of gender, race, class, disability and other forms of social differentiation – and to highlight the complexity of the dynamics associated with this privilege. Inequality in power status is thus no longer assumed to eventually be evened out, or hybridised as some scholars would postulate, but as perpetuated through social practices and discourses. It is indeed surprising that the notion of 'privilege' has long been used in different feminist research traditions, yet has rarely been used in Peace and Conflict Studies. If one was cynical, one could raise the question about the researchers' complicity and power relations and the associated reluctance to dismantle systems of power that have kept the discipline in an alleged position of superiority. Feminist approaches can provide the language and tools to open up such Pandora's boxes to address questions of complicity, not only in the realm of identity-formation in (post-)conflict zones, but also on the part of the researchers of the discipline. They help us zoom in on the social systems that reproduce unequal power relations and are swept aside in traditional PCS, which often focuses on the hybridisation of two oppositional identity categories. Drawing on the feminist approach of intersectionality helps us understand identities not as oppositional, but as transversal and multi-directional, at the same time viewing gender not as the only, but as one of several categories of differentiation. A more nuanced understanding of the social settings in which violence is exercised between social groups can thus be crucial for peace-building to capture the multi-faceted nature of conflict and violence.

Acknowledgments

A draft version of this article has been presented at the ISA Annual Conference in San Francisco, April 2018. The authors would like to thank Laura McLeod, Maria O'Reilly, Tarja Väyrynen, Nina Wilén, and two anonymous reviewers for exceptionally constructive comments on earlier drafts. We would also like to thank Marsha Henry for her keynote presentation at the Conflict Research Society conference in Birmingham in September 2018, where she has further convinced us of the merits of linking intersectionality with Peace and Conflict Studies. All mistakes – including omissions – remain our own.

Disclosure statement

No potential conflict of interest was reported by the authors.

The 'third gender' in Afghanistan: a feminist account of hybridity as a gendered experience

Hannah Partis-Jennings

ABSTRACT
This article offers a significant contribution to critical peace studies and feminist peace studies by exploring an undertheorized manifestation of hybridity and friction in Afghanistan from a feminist perspective. It focuses on female international humanitarian actors, their use of the term 'third gender' to describe their perceived position, and their experiences of performing their gender in hybridised ways. Using original interview data, it argues that the particularly gendered experiences of these actors are key to recognising the gendered nature of peacebuilding and the intersections between feminist approaches and critical peace concepts.

Introduction

The purpose of this article is to explore the manifestation of the critical peace studies (CPS) concepts hybridity and friction in Afghanistan from a feminist perspective. It will do so by focusing on female international humanitarian actors,[1] their use of the term 'third gender' to describe their perceived position and their experiences of performing their gender in hybridised ways. While the focus on international humanitarian actors as sites of hybridity and friction in-and-of themselves is unusual and under-theorised, I maintain that they are key to understanding how hybridity and friction function in gendered ways in conflict-affected contexts such as Afghanistan.

As Róisín Read outlines:

> Humanitarians, especially in conflict-affected areas, increasingly serve as sources of information about the areas they work in and the people they work with; as such, it is important to critically interrogate their experiences and knowledge.[2]

The particularly gendered experience of these actors is key to recognising the gendered nature of peacebuilding and the intersections between feminist approaches and CPS concepts. In this article, like Read, I am interested in how female internationals are marked by and articulate for

---

[1] I use this term loosely to encompass a range of international civil society actors who participate in what are understood to be peacebuilding activities – for instance aid and development work, education and security sector reform, institutional capacity-building. These individuals mostly work for NGOs, international organisations or big donor entities. I refer to them in this paper as internationals for simplicity, though I am aware that this category of person is expansive and varied.
[2] Róisín Read, 'Embodying Difference : Reading Gender in Women's Memoirs of Humanitarianism,' *Journal of Intervention and Statebuilding* Online First (2018), 2.

themselves, specific kinds of difference, and how this 'difference is always embodied and is imbued with meanings, regardless of the degree to which there is conscious awareness of these meanings'.[3] Like McLeod, I am interested in the ways that feminist thinking intersects with and enhances the analytical scope of hybridity by centring on the significance of the 'personal' amongst international actors and paying attention to peace and post-conflict labour as lived experience.[4]

In the context of peacebuilding, hybridity is a 'meeting between international and local norms, actors and practices' creating 'new arrangements, which display hybrid features where for instance liberal and illiberal norms co-exist'.[5] Following this, I am exploring the 'third gender' as the term for female internationals who, in their own perception, combine female bodies and 'liberal' gender expectations with traits, access and behaviour associated strongly with masculinity in 'illiberal' Afghanistan. In the coming together of two apparently divergent sets of gender norms, a new gender arrangement forms as the 'third gender', socio-culturally rather than biologically. I argue that the 'third gender' acts as a hybrid identification framework in everyday praxis, symptomatic of the liberal peace paradigm in Afghanistan in which 'international' and 'local' norms interact.[6] This interaction creates friction – movement back and forth between paradigms, ideas and expectations[7] – demonstrating the coming together of the 'international' and the 'local', mixing different perceptions and performances of social orders and creating a kind of hybridity with aspects of both.

Afghanistan was the site of global 'war on terror' military intervention in 2001 and a subsequent liberal peacebuilding project running alongside ongoing military activity which incorporated a vast array of international and non-governmental organisations (IOs and NGOs), institutions and donors. Broadly speaking Afghanistan has been understood as a classically patriarchal country[8] meaning that women face unequal treatment in the legal system, education system, governance and security structures and within socio-cultural norms.[9] As such women's rights and freedoms were a key focus in the liberal peace project, and a key site of politicisation by multiple actors including Afghan political elites, donors and intervening states.[10] The idea of Afghanistan as a context in which a problematic gender order, particularly the patriarchal treatment of women, was pervasive, forms an important backdrop to my exploration of the 'third gender' in this article. Moreover, while 'gender' in peacebuilding, donor programming and international institutions, in Afghanistan and more

---

[3]Ibid., 2.
[4]Laura McLeod, 'A Feminist Approach to Hybridity: Understanding Local and International Interactions in Producing Post-Conflict Gender Security,' *Journal of Intervention and Statebuilding* 9, no. 1 (2015): 48–69.
[5]Annika Björkdahl and Kristine Höglund, 'Precarious Peacebuilding: Friction in Global – Local Encounters,' *Peacebuilding* 1, no. 3 (2013), 290.
[6]For a critique of the idea of the 'local' and this binary in CPS see Nick Lemay-Hebert and Stephanie Kappler's article in this issue.
[7]Ibid.,
[8]Jennifer Fluri, 'Armored Peacocks and Proxy Bodies: Gender Geopolitics in Aid/Development Spaces of Afghanistan,' *Gender, Place & Culture: A Journal of Feminist Geography* 18, no. 4 (2011), p. 525.
[9]Valentine M. Moghadam, 'Patriarchy in Transition: Women and the Changing Family in the Middle East,' *Journal of Comparative Family Studies* 35, no. 2 (2004): 137–62.
[10]See Lila Abu-Lughod, 'Do Muslim Women Really Need Saving? Anthropological Reflections on Cultural Relativism and Its Others,' *American Anthropologist* 104, no. 3 (2002): 783–90; Julie Billaud, 'The Making of Modern Afghanistan: Reconstruction, Transnational Governance and Gender Politics in the New Islamic Republic,' *Anthropology of the Middle East* 7, no. 1 (2012): 18–37; and Michaele L. Ferguson, '"W" Stands for Women: Feminism and Security Rhetoric in the Post-9/11 Bush Administration,' *Politics & Gender* 1, no. 1 (2005): 9–38.

generally, is a key consideration and site of study, few scholars have explored the gender dynamics of the actors that undertake peacebuilding labour and occupy humanitarian spaces. This means that the operation of gender *within* the everyday praxis and experience of peacebuilding is under-theorised and despite the compatibility of feminist thought with critical peace scholarship,[11] the latter does not sufficiently envisage the centrality of gender as an organising principle in post-conflict lifeworlds. Equally, a criticism levelled at CPS is that it tends to homogenise the actors it discusses – 'locals' or 'internationals' for example[12] – and paying attention to the complex gender dynamics within groupings mitigates against that critique. Illustrating this, Julian et al. in this special issue elucidate the possibilities for a feminist-inspired methodological engagement with the diversity of situated knowledges articulated in 'local' spaces,[13] while Kappler and Lemay-Hebert outline an approach based on the 'intersectionality of peace', in order to capture the complexity of power and privilege which are layered, cross-cutting and relational within particular contexts.[14]

This article makes a contribution to both CPS and feminist peace and conflict studies. It builds on the pioneering work of scholars such as Roger Mac Ginty and Oliver Richmond,[15] whose work on hybridity helped to reframe the debates around the liberal peace paradigm, by deploying these ideas in feminist terms and through the prism of certain gendered experiences of Afghanistan. It uses original interview data to unpack the unexplored concept of the 'third gender' as a site of embodied everyday experience in peacebuilding and thus contributes to a growing feminist literature on the complexities of (post-)conflict ecosystems and the ways that race, gender and power intersect to produce particular systems of privilege, distance and difference in the 'post-war moment'.[16]

I focus on Afghanistan because it was during my research into the gendered practices of intervention and peacebuilding there that I came across the notion of the 'third gender'. Moreover, because of the centring of gender in the rhetoric and representation of post-conflict Afghanistan, it is a very important context in which to explore how gender threads through the everyday praxis of peacebuilding. However, as I suggest in my conclusion, there is room for fruitful further research into other contexts.

The article progresses in three parts; I develop the framework of gendered hybridity further and outline the notion of the 'third gender' and its use in Afghanistan, I then use my interview data to explore how the 'third gender' concept functioned as one kind of embodied, performed hybridity; a manifestation of friction and hybridity in the lived

---

[11]McLeod, 'A Feminist Approach to Hybridity'.
[12]Jenny H Peterson, 'A Conceptual Unpacking Of Hybridity : Accounting For Notions Of Power, Politics And Progress In Analyses Of Aid-Driven Interfaces,' *Journal of Peacebuilding & Development* 7, no. 2 (2012), 15.
[13]Rachel Julian, Berit Bliesemann de Guevara and Robin Redhead 'From Expert to Experiential Knowledge: Exploring the Inclusion of Local Experiences in Understanding Violence in Conflict'.
[14]Lemay-Hebert and Kappler 'From Power-Blind Binaries to the Intersectionality of Peace: Connecting Feminism and Critical Peace and Conflict Studies'.
[15]See for example Roger Mac Ginty, 'Hybrid Peace: The Interaction Between Top-Down and Bottom-Up Peace,' *Security Dialogue* 41, no. 4 (2010): 391–412; and Oliver Richmond, 'Becoming Liberal, Unbecoming Liberalism: Liberal-Local Hybridity via the Everyday as a Response to the Paradoxes of Liberal Peacebuilding,' *Journal of Intervention and Statebuilding* 3, no. 3 (2009): 324–44.
[16]See for example Cynthia Cockburn and Dubravka Zarkov, eds., *The Post-War Moment: Militaries, Masculinities and International Peacekeeping* (London: Lawrence and Wishart, 2002); Claire Duncanson, *Gender and Peacebuilding* (Cambridge, Malden: Polity Press, 2016); Gina Heathcote and Dianne Otto, eds., *Rethinking Peacekeeping, Gender Equality and Collective Security* (Palgrave Macmillan, 2014); and Paul Higate and Marsha Henry, *Insecure Spaces: Peacekeeping, Power and Performance in Haiti, Kosovo and Liberia* (London, New York: Zed Books, 2009).

experiences of international peacebuilding actors. Embodiment here refers to the centrality of the body as a site of identification and experience,[17] while performance indicates those behaviours enacted to conform to societal expectations in particular ways. In the third and final section of the article, I unpack what the 'third gender' as an idea can tell us about the gendered and racialised ordering of the liberal peace paradigm in Afghanistan. Before I move to the body of the article, I will outline a few points on my methodology.

My methodological approach is based on original interview data from semi-structured interviews. While I focus on and cite from six interviewees in this article, these interviews are part of a wider research project on Afghanistan which included further semi- and un-structured conversations (I have interviewed 41 participants formally and others outside of those cited here also mentioned the 'third gender' term and similar ideas), as well as a visit to Afghanistan in 2014. During my research, I interviewed civil society and military actors who are working or had worked in Afghanistan, both Afghans and 'internationals'. Those mentioned in this article are German, American, Australian and Afghan-Canadian and are all female. One cited interview took place in person in Kabul in 2014, the rest were contacted via a closed online network for people living and working in, but largely not from Kabul, and took place via Skype in 2017. Those who easily identified with the 'third gender' or those who were referred to as doing so are described as 'international' in the sense that they did not identify as Afghan nationals and mostly worked for NGOs, IOs, donors, institutions such as the International Security Assistance Force (ISAF), etc. that involve actors, mandates and financing developed or originating outside of Afghanistan.

My focus on the 'third gender' comes from it being mentioned several times in interviews and while I make no claim to generalise for all female 'internationals' (especially given the number of participants cited), I infer from my interviewees' comments on its ubiquity that it was a common term and framework. My respondents referred to 'third sex' and 'third gender' interchangeably at points. I have settled on the consistent use of the term 'third gender' in this article because I am conducting a feminist analysis attuned to the operation of gender and because this categorisation was something social and performed, not implying a biological difference. There is much more to be said here on the distinction between sex and gender and the productivity of the space between them that I do not have the scope to say, and it needs to be acknowledged that I also discuss the concept of the 'third gender' in one particular way, referencing women whose sexuality I do not engage with. There is a wealth of queer theory that deals much more fully with the complexities of non-binary sexualities and gender performativities which I overlook in this article due to restrictions of space and focus.[18] However, my narrow and unusual engagement with the 'third gender' allows me to explore the nuances and ambiguities within certain lived experiences of hybridity and friction and thus contribute to scholarly work on peacebuilding and humanitarian spaces.

---

[17]See Catherine Baker and Tarja Väyrynen in this special issue for further theorisation and expansion of the role of embodiment in feminist peace studies.

[18]See, for example, William B. Turner, *A Genealogy of Queer Theory*, (Philadelphia: Temple University Press, 2000).

A feminist approach to hybridity

Drawing on feminist scholarship, in particular Laura McLeod's work, I engage a feminist approach to hybridity in this article. This approach provides space for a 'textured' understanding of power relations between different actors and centres experience as an entry point.[19] Doing this allows for two types of analytical shift; firstly, it allows for the muddying of our understanding of how power works in peacebuilding contexts and importantly, how it *travels*. Since it looks for nuance and change in power relations, a feminist approach to hybridity might pay close attention to the ways that non-local actors 'translocate their own positionalities (i.e. class, culture, gender and ethnicity/race)' to their peacebuilding context,[20] As such it has parallels with Kappler and Lemay-Hebert's intersectionality of peace approach (in this special issue) and can recognize how gendered power relations intersect with other kinds of difference and privilege differently at different sites, exploring the non-linear ways that power(/lessness) is carried from context to context while being shaped, perceived and felt on an everyday, situated level. For Kappler and Lemay-Hebert these nuances of power are better articulated outside of the concept of hybridity due to its dichotomizing tendencies. As per their critique, I am guilty of replicating the binary between 'international' and 'local' in this article for the purpose of analysis. However, I also illustrate that this binary is not clear-cut when we approach it from a feminist perspective and thus demonstrate that a feminist application of the concept of hybridity can contribute to an understanding of the relational and felt nature of power. Second, the centering of experience within the concept of hybridity requires us to engage with how it is lived out, embodied, remembered and represented. For instance, I am interested in how my respondents described their gendered feelings, experiences and perceptions. Even taking into consideration the so-called 'local' and 'everyday' turns in CPS, the concept of hybridity in peace research often still foregrounds collective, public or abstract phenomena such as cultures, institutions and norms (even if they are locally based, or everyday ones).[21] A feminist approach to hybridity, paying attention to the complexities of gender, directs us to different sites and ways of being such as the individual, the private, the lived and performed and the *ambiguity* of the everyday. A feminist approach to hybridity is interested in embodied experiences as forms of peace or conflict work in and off themselves which are taking place at the intersections of different kinds of privilege and marginalization, without losing track of the broader structural forces that shape conflict-affected lives and spaces. If as Peterson suggests:

> [a]nalytically, it is the notion of the 'contact zone' (i.e. between local and external) and the creation of 'new forms' (i.e. non-liberal or post-liberal) that resonate most clearly in current usages of hybridity within the fields of peace and development studies,[22]

then feminist explorations of hybridity in this vein might look to the 'new forms' of gender identity, perception, performance and difference that intersect with other

---

[19]McLeod, 'A Feminist Approach to Hybridity'.
[20]Roger Mac Ginty and Gurchathen Sanghera, 'Hybridity in Peacebuilding and Development: An Introduction,' *Journal of Peacebuilding & Development* 7, no. 2 (2012), 3.
[21]Jonathan Goodhand, 'Contested Boundaries: NGOs and Civil–military Relations in Afghanistan,' *Central Asian Survey* 32, no. 3 (2013): 287–305; and Mac Ginty, 'Hybrid Peace: The Interaction Between Top-Down and Bottom-Up Peace.'
[22]Peterson, 'A Conceptual Unpacking of Hybridity', 11.

dynamics (race, status, etc.) in the 'contact zone' of conflict-affected places. These new forms can be framed in terms of experience, imaginaries and the felt everyday, perhaps 'new' only in the sense of being perceived, constructed or experienced as such.

As I outline more fully in the following sections, I see the 'third gender' in the context of international usage in Afghanistan as a kind of embodied, performed hybridity. The Afghan context and perceived gendered expectations in Afghanistan are mixed with the bodies, behaviours and expectations of international women to form something that contains gendered elements of masculinity, femininity, the 'illiberal' and the liberal social orders.

Hybridity, understood through feminist lenses, and in line with the original postcolonial understanding of the term,[23] is potentially disruptive to the hegemonic project of the liberal peace because it destabilizes decontextualised projects and their universal templates.[24] I argue here that, with the addition of a feminist lens, it also disrupts the very framework of the 'liberal' as it takes account of the multiplicities of gendered hierarchies that cut through *both* liberal and non-liberal social orders.

Friction in peacebuilding literature is a term often applied to policy implementation, it points to the distinction between expectations and reality, between an idea and its actualization in praxis. Friction in peace literature focuses on 'conflictual encounters' between external ideas or norms and 'local' ones, it is similar to hybridity in that it is about the drawing together of different actors/norms but it focuses on the *process* of contestation.[25] Because friction is attuned to the operation of power, agency and struggle, it is again well aligned with feminist thinking. While I suggest that the 'third gender' is a hybridity-infused framework, I also argue that it allows us to see processes; sites of friction within gendered experiences of the peacebuilding paradigm. By this I mean moments where embodied identities are being pulled in different directions, and divergent expectational parameters are coming up against each other.

It is important to recognise that I am using the notion(s) of hybridity (and friction) analytically in a specific way here. I am suggesting that it is productive to view the notion of the 'third gender' as a hybridized identity framework, which draws a 'liberal' understanding of gender – women as professional and societal equals – into confluence with an 'illiberal' one – women who *behave as equals* are masculinised, and not real women but something else. In this way, it is possible to explore the nuance and complexity that emerges from the lived, gendered, racialised experience of a certain kind of hybridity. To be clear, I am not attempting to suggest that this is anything other than one way to frame and deploy the analytical concept of hybridity in feminist terms. I am also not reifying the idea that liberalism is *actually* conducive to gender-equality, that Afghan women are *actually* passive/always silenced or that Afghanistan is only ever patriarchal, but rather using this notion of the 'third gender' as a window through which to explore some elements of the operation of gender within the Afghan liberal peace project.

---

[23]Ibid.,.
[24]See also Kappler and Lemay-Hebert in this special issue.
[25]Björkdahl and Höglund, 'Precarious Peacebuilding', 292.

The 'third gender' in Afghanistan

The third sex or gender has mostly been a way to describe a person or people who transcend sex and/or gender-based dimorphism. This happens in lots of ways, through genitalia, hormonal make-up, sexuality and performativity that do not fit neatly into the sex or gender-based distinctions between male (/masculinity) and female (/femininity). There are historical associations between citizenship, colonialism, race and the queer and/or non-binary body. As Cynthia Weber points out, the depiction of a savage, racialised Other as sexualised, deviant and 'homosexual' actually 'played a role in licensing Victorian sovereign states to subject entire colonialized populations to imperial rule'.[26] Queerness is also a trope deployed in Orientalist framings of a racialised Other, including in western media depictions of Afghanistan.[27] Those such as intersex persons, queer individuals and others who have been associated with the term 'third gender' have often faced discrimination, as the limits of what constitute acceptable gender behaviours are policed within different social worlds.[28] As late as the latter part of the twentieth century, children who were born in the UK and elsewhere who fell outside of the gender binary for various reasons were medically reassigned without their consent.[29] Thus, internationals using this term in Afghanistan are drawing, probably unconsciously, on a trajectory of meaning which situates them in a wider history of both subversive sexuality and imperial as well as medical violence. They call to action a term which indicates non-binary liberation from gendered heteronormativity as well as suppression and discrimination, thus illustrating the way that fragments of meaning travel, carrying aspects of their original significance while gaining significance anew as they become remoulded through embodied and discursive use.

While a full discussion of the history and use of the 'third gender' concept falls outside of the scope of this article, it is important to note that both biological and social aspects of sex and gender exist on a spectrum whereby a simple dichotomy between male/masculine and female/feminine is clearly false, yet feminist scholarship consistently demonstrates that this dichotomy structures multiple facets of our world, from language to war.[30] Thus the idea of a 'third gender' potentially contests the power-laden gender dichotomy between male and female, but, as I demonstrate in this article, could equally be understood to reinforce that dichotomy as well as other kinds of difference. During my research, I discovered that the 'third gender' was being used in an unexpected way by international women and those who spoke about them. On respondent described it like this:

---

[26] Weber, 'Queer Intellectual Curiosity as International Relations Method: Developing Queer International Relations Theoretical and Methodological Frameworks,' *International Studies Quarterly* 60, no. 1 (2016), 12.
[27] See Nivi Manchanda, 'Queering the Pashtun: Afghan Sexuality in the Homo-nationalist Imaginary', *Third World Quarterly*, 36 no. 1 (2015): 130–146.
[28] See Jake Scobey-Thal 'Third Gender: A Short History', *Foreign Affairs*, 30 June 2014, https://foreignpolicy.com/2014/06/30/third-gender-a-short-history/, last accessed 17/09/18.
[29] See Colette Bernhardt, 'The Third Sex: The Truth about Gender Ambiguity' *The Independent* 20 March 2010, https://www.independent.co.uk/life-style/health-and-families/features/the-third-sex-the-truth-about-gender-ambiguity-1922816.html, last accessed 17/09/18.
[30] See for example Carol Cohn, 'Sex and Death in the Rational World of Defense Intellectuals,' *Signs: Journal of Women in Culture and Society* 12, no. 4 (1987): 687–718; Cynthia Cockburn, 'Gender Relations as Causal in Militarization and War: A Feminist Standpoint,' in *Making Gender, Making War: Violence, Military and Peacekeeping Practices*, ed. Annica Kronsell and Erica Svedberg, Kindle (London, New York: Routledge, 2012), 19–34; and Cynthia Enloe, *Bananas, Beaches, and Bases: Making Feminist Sense of International Politics* (Berkeley: University of California Press, 1989).

Women there, foreign women, are kind of this third gender for Afghans, especially Afghan men. From an Afghan male perspective, I'm generalising, but in general there are men and foreign men, and then there are Afghan women and then there are foreign women. For them foreign women are just sort of this like strange amalgamation of woman and man (Anna, American Education worker)

Within the notion of the 'third gender' in Afghanistan was the idea that foreign women were not entirely women but not men either. It contained a complex uncertainty that was both gendered and racialised.[31] The interaction between some concept of the 'foreign' and some concept of the 'female' played out as a site of friction in which 'porous boundaries'[32] between different notions of *woman* were marked by distinctions between foreign and local bodies in terms of differential freedom and access. Kate exemplified this well in the following comments: '[p]eople talk a lot about foreign women being like the third sex. I don't really like the analogy but there is certainly things that you can do, that Afghan women can't do …' (Kate, Australian research consultant).

Liberal citizenship (not specific to bodies of a particular race) is a citizenship association with countries – especially in the 'west' – that identify as liberal democracies with gender-equitable value systems (in theory). Liberal citizenship creates a sense of confusion and unease around the notion of 'woman' in contexts understood as illiberal. It bestows expectations around how women can behave, their capacity to enter the public sphere and at least a nominal sense of individual professional authority, equality and freedom. What comes up continually within the notion of the 'third gender', is the disruption but not dispersal of these expectations, the uneasy in-between-ness that comes with bringing ideas about liberal and illiberal womanhood into confluence.

Speaking about needing to get a tyre fixed on her motorbike, Eva said:

[A]n Afghan female could never do that, and you had a huge amount of freedoms and you became kind of more conscious about this freedom, because you had a direct comparison so to speak (Eva, German ISAF civilian personnel).

Foreign womanhood here is understood through a conceptualisation of agency and freedom that becomes *more significant* as against an apparently 'direct comparison' with non-agency and un-freedom. Respondents described their gendered identities as constituted by a process of negotiation due to their hybridity-infused experience as females who were not, in their understanding, fully *feminised* in the Afghan context. Luise illustrated that the very ownership of a gender identity became context-dependent:

[B]ecause my socialisation is German, or European, I would certainly identify, if I would identify, I would identify as a woman, like I would never say I identify as third gender. I identify as third gender in the *Afghan context* if that makes sense (Luise, German UN worker).

Luise's way of framing her gender identity as context-specific in Afghanistan speaks to the complex 'performative infrastructure'[33] involved in simply being a foreign female,

---

[31]Hannah Partis-Jennings, 'The (In)security of Gender in Afghanistan's Peacebuilding Project: Hybridity and Affect' *International Feminist Journal of Politics* 19, no. 4 (2017): 411–425.
[32]Niels Nagelhus Schia and John Karlsrud, '"Where the Rubber Meets the Road": Friction Sites and Local-Level Peacebuilding in Haiti, Liberia and South Sudan,' *International Peacekeeping* 20, no. 2 (2013), 246.
[33]Luiza Bialasiewicz et al., 'Performing Security: The Imaginative Geographies of Current US Strategy,' *Political Geography* 26, no. 4 (2007), 415.

the understanding that gender was fluid and contingent for internationals. Equally, there is again an implicit suggestion that by comparison, it was not so fluid and contingent for Afghans. Eva stated that: 'the Afghans see you...as a female of course but more like a third gender...not ... their Afghan females' (Eva, German ISAF civilian personnel) implying a knowable and static femininity against which the foreign woman was defined.

In terms of the ubiquity of the 'third gender' as a discursive currency, Luise recounted that she was told about the concept almost as soon as she arrived in Afghanistan (Luise, German UN worker), while Eva explained its frequent use in experiential terms – 'you take it up as a notion which makes sense to describe the *actual experience*' Eva, German ISAF civilian personnel, emphasis added). This experience was always a mixing together of the 'local' context/gender norms with the 'international' body/gendered expectations that was felt and performed though it did not necessarily imply a substantial change in actual behaviour:

> So that I guess what is behind this notion of the third gender that it is, it really provides you with a way to behave or feel very freely, you don't necessarily engage in seriously strange, different behaviour than normally, it is just this feeling that you are really not bound by the normal society rules in a way ...That really is kind of strange [sic] (Eva, German ISAF civilian worker).

Eva positions the 'third gender' and her life in Afghanistan as one that offered felt liberation from the constraints of gender norms and this offers up a view of the liberal peace paradigm as a space of exception, especially for bodies marked by liberal citizenship. The 'third gender' framework frees the international woman, allowing a sense of liberation from gendered expectations and adherence to gender binaries yet, equally, this is only made possible when the binary itself can be understood to originate with Afghan socio-cultural norms. The Afghan gender order can be transcended by the privilege of liberal citizenship, yet it also shapes the very idea of womanhood in the peacebuilding context, arguably crafting the idea of a 'new form' in the hybrid space of the 'contact zone',[34] one that is felt and lived.

Unpacking the 'third gender'

While hybridity and friction focus on the dynamics between the 'international' and the 'local', this section unpacks what the 'third gender' can tell us about peacebuilding and explores how a feminist engagement with hybridity can capture the shifting and situated intersectional interactions between elements of race, status, citizenship and gender. For instance, the experience of Afghan-Canadian respondents demonstrated the ways that 'womanhood' is policed and navigated *through, alongside and within* the boundaries of racial expectations in varied ways within the peacebuilding context.

Safia, an Afghan-Canadian IO worker, described the negotiated nature of her everyday life: 'I'm trying to fit in, I don't fit in, but then sometimes I don't really want to fit in.' She talked about the way some colleagues would assign her 'local' status. Yet she felt her identity was in fact a complicated and hybridised one: 'I think that the way they see

---

[34]Peterson, 'A Conceptual Unpacking Of Hybridity', 11.

it is I'm just a local I can go hang out with the locals, but I work here as an international'. There is a certain agency evidenced in her identity framework, sometimes she *has no desire to* 'fit in' with either 'local' or 'international' identity categories.

Yet Safia also spoke to the friction at work within her performance as an 'international' whose body (in the eyes of others) tied her to different expectations than those placed on foreign bodies. She gave the example of how foreign-educated Afghan men reacted to her dismissively, including making 'weird comments' about the legitimacy of her PhD (suggesting that it might be fake), insisting on 'putting an Afghan label' on her, resenting her salary and having difficulty accepting that a woman who appeared physically as Afghan was not easily categorised according to their gendered expectations: 'because they are men, and they are foreign-educated but they are still Afghan, I don't know, I feel I am sensing more of an issue with that, the way that I am not actually an Afghan woman, but I look like it' (Safia, Afghan-Canadian IO worker). Her Afghan-ness is bound to her in a bodily way, and she somehow ought to perform Afghan femininity in line with her bodily image, but she is equally tied to a sense of her own foreign-ness which also shapes her gendered identity and performative expectations of her work and lifestyle.

Safia talked about the 'third gender' as something she could see and hear about among foreigners, but also as a category that she did not neatly fit herself. Here, she is talking about noticing others (foreign women) fitting into the category of the 'third gender' in her workplace:

> I remember I read this article about this woman who said you know she was allowed to pass through the genders whether it was male or female, through the different spaces. And I notice it you know every day at work, I literally notice it every day (Safia, Afghan-Canadian IO worker).

When I asked her if she was ever understood through the prism of the 'third gender' she stated: 'it can be true for me – if I play that card. If I completely deny that Afghan connection, if I say that I don't speak the local languages'. Her words illustrate that this category of the 'third gender' for her required a performative rejection of the 'local' and locally situated knowledge.

Masha, another Afghan-Canadian respondent, also illustrated that the elements of gendered identity which shaped her experience were often defined externally and that she experienced a friction between expectations and realities which was deeply frustrating. She articulated this sense of frustration to me directly: 'so I kind of want to sometimes just scream and say: "well if I'm foreign then let me do whatever the hell I want, and if I'm not, stop calling me foreign"' (Masha, Afghan-Canadian NGO programme director). Thus, these participants who were both 'local' and 'international' (Canadian), by birth, did not associate themselves easily with the 'third gender' framework because their race and 'localness' tethered their gender differently, producing particular categories of difference and navigation within the peacebuilding paradigm.

Importantly, the categorisation of the 'third gender' seems to participate in the construction and reproduction of certain racialised ideas about Afghan men and Afghan women/femininity. It implies that Afghans (especially men) are so deeply wedded to their understanding of women as subordinate, that in order to cope with women who, by virtue of their relative wealth, status and international origins could not be subordinated, they must see them as *not women*. There is a racialised homogenisation of the Afghan male and social order implicit in this categorisation, perhaps indicative of what one respondent described as 'an international prejudice against the Afghan people and them not being able to actually listen to intelligent people [who were female]' [sic] (Luise, German UN worker). This traces the idea, as articulated by Nivi Manchanda, that the 'Afghan man' is framed as always already 'monstrously misogynistic'.[35]

Thus, in abstracted terms, this idea of the 'third gender' in Afghanistan speaks to the crashing together of a liberal order in which cultural (if not always actual) gender equality is a pillar of market democracy and individualism,[36] with that which is understood to be an illiberal order, marked by inequality and lacking in progressive norms.[37] As many feminist scholars have pointed out in relation to the intervention in Afghanistan, this crashing together is rendered intelligible by negating Afghan women's agential subjectivity, collapsing them into a monolithic victim, foil to the patriarchal, 'monstrously misogynistic' Afghan male as well as the liberated 'western' woman.[38] Thus the 'third gender' as a means of (self-)identifying the foreign female body is at once a judgement upon the capacity of Afghan men to fully accept a gender order beyond their own, and a positioning of Afghan women as the truly *feminised* in this context, where feminisation is equated to passivity and victimhood. Eva stated that as a member of the 'third gender':

> you are different to the Afghan man than an Afghan female would be who is of course very protected and very seen in that Afghan traditional kind of style in a way, because you are open, you are outspoken, I think they are respecting you [sic](Eva, German ISAF civilian personnel).

She indicates a distinction between 'traditional' and liberal values, where the latter allows for respect and the former is marked by voicelessness. Again, as so often, gender here does not manifest as a relation of power that exists in a vacuum, but rather functions as 'part of the processes that also constitute class and race as well as other lines of demarcation and domination'.[39] In Eva's words, Afghan women in Afghanistan are *truly female*, and the implication is that they are truly subordinated, so that subordination and true femininity are somehow linked, while having freedom, authority and access in Afghanistan mean a performative negation of subordination/femininity. Eva did not particularly want to generalize, and she was self-reflexively awkward about using terms such as 'their females' to describe Afghan women, and yet found this language her only mechanism to explain her experiences. Arguably, however, the 'third gender' as a framework of meaning is made possible in this context because of the circulation of the troubling idea that 'brown men' are

---

[35]Manchanda, 'Queering the Pashtun', 130.
[36]Nancy Fraser, 'Feminism, Capitalism and The Cunning of History,' *New Left Review* 56, no. March/April (2009): 97–117.
[37]Julie Billaud, 'The Making of Modern Afghanistan: Reconstruction, Transnational Governance and Gender Politics in the New Islamic Republic,' *Anthropology of the Middle East* 7, no. 1 (2012): 18–37.
[38]Ferguson, '"W" Stands for Women'; Keally McBride and Annick T. R. Wibben, 'The Gendering of Counterinsurgency in Afghanistan,' *Humanity: An International Journal of Human Rights, Humanitarianism, and Development* 3, no. 2 (2012): 199–215.
[39]Joan Acker, 'Gendering Organisational Theory,' in *Gendering Organisational Theory*, ed. A.J. Mills and P. Tancred (Thousand Oaks, CA: Sage Press, 1992.), 567.

somehow backward, traditional and oppressive, and 'brown women' are silenced and powerless.[40]

However, to suggest that the 'third gender' is *purely* based on a racialised assumption of Afghan patriarchal conditions would be to fail to capture the complex site of friction and hybridity that the term entails. The 'third gender' is also a contradictory space that demonstrates simultaneously a pulling away from the restraints placed upon the (liberal) female body *and equally* a reaffirmation of its subordination. To illustrate the first dimension, respondents would point to the fluidity and potential afforded by the 'third gender' categorisation. Luise stated that: 'because I feel like every human being should be able to do what they want to do, and by falling in-between being a man and being an Afghan woman you *can* actually'. She suggested increased possibilities in her work as a result: 'ultimately, when it comes to the work, I actually think as that third gender you actually have access… you are a lot better equipped to talk to both parts of society' (Luise, German UN worker).

The 'third gender' could function as a space of agency, where the restrictions of feminisation could be detached from the female body and discarded, a de-gendering performance which opens up possibilities for access and enjoyment without any loss or distancing from the sexed female body itself. There is a sense of sexual liberation associated with it, as well as an increased power, voice and authority. One respondent described how, despite never learning to drive in the UK or Germany, she had used a motorbike to see the city of Kabul when she was based there, allowing her to be independent and adventurous. She went on to say:

> when I think about the time in Afghanistan, a female in Afghanistan, working for the military, living in a military installation in a country which is patriarchal to the core, and I still *felt the most free in my life* (Eva, German ISAF civilian personnel, emphasis added).

Another international described how some women (like some men) would take off their wedding rings as soon as they entered Afghan airspace (Anna, American education worker) implying a space of social of exceptionalism. Most respondents described the respect they were shown by Afghans in the workplace particularly. This first dimension is thus indicative of a fascinating agency, freedom, exceptionalism and respect bestowed upon the female international body in this conflict-affected context. The 'third gender' thus indicates a performative space in which liberation could be enacted despite the huge variety of restrictions at work in Afghanistan in different ways; seen like this it marks a site of 'liberal' values in the embodied and ideational sense, where women could access a 'masculine' domain of power and authority but without being *masculinized* according to their own social standards (they are not seen *as men*). Moreover, for some, it could offer a sense of freedom *in relation to* home or a 'western' context: 'you felt very free from even values, stuff, behaviour you would usually, which is expected from you in a western society as normal kind of behaviour' (Eva, German ISAF civilian personnel). This demonstrates the way the lived experience of the liberal peace constructs a space and imaginary of exception; a shift in and release from certain normative parameters and behavioural expectations.

---

[40]Nicola Pratt and Sophie Richter-Devroe, 'Critically Examining UNSCR 1325 on Women, Peace and Security,' *International Feminist Journal of Politics* 13, no. 4 (December 2011): 489–503.

In this space of exception, international women could leverage their hybrid gender identity framework, seeking to transcend boundaries and facilitate work they recognised to be important in ways that promoted inclusivity. As Luise suggested:

> [I]t is possible to talk to men, but it is also possible to talk to women, and especially when you work on peace and if you talk about it in terms of inclusive peace, if you want to build an inclusive peace process actually as a woman you are a lot better equipped to talk to both parts of society, in most cases (Luise, German UN worker).

By carefully retaining both woman-hood and access/authority, my respondents could try to situate themselves as culturally dissonant but respectful guests helping to link together different strands of the Afghan social order and ensure that Afghan women's voices were heard.

The second dimension, however, is quite different. Respondents who identified with the categorisation of the 'third gender' in Afghanistan also pointed to their experiences of hyper-sexualisation or patriarchal expectations *within the international domains*. Eva talked about the way that international men could view their female counterparts as sexually available and subordinate: 'the perception changes to "oh these women in Afghanistan, who are working here and who are here just for the fun and the wild parties and we don't have to take them really equal"'. She suggested a distinct lack of equality in this space: 'as a female, all of the kind of bad stuff we had before emancipation kind of kicks in. You are kind of not so much an equal as you are in the UK or Germany or any kind of normal environment, it is really different' [sic] (Eva, German ISAF civilian personnel).

Moreover, the backdrop of a tense and threatening conflict-affected country, in which internationals and their organisations are frequent targets of attacks carried out by the Taliban or Islamic State affiliates, renders a masculinised security environment commonsensical.[41] In particular, private military security contractors are emblems of masculinised security practice which centres on weapons, stoicism and a constancy of risk.[42] Safia described how the attitude of the private security personnel (who hold significant authority as harbingers of security) in her various places of work 'was very much like "I've got a gun, I've got a machine-gun", a full display of masculinity or sort of the *militarised version* of it... it is all about violence, guns and you hear the stories about how tough they are... very macho, very macho' (Safia, Afghan-Canadian IO worker, emphasis added). Certain respondents reported a distinctly gendered experience of male security personnel, contrasting the freedom and sense of liberation discussed earlier.

Luise posited a kind of gendered governmentality in her everyday life. She described 'international men being really worried about my personal life, which I do think is related to my gender', particularly a situation where

> one of the security officers at a party and he is the guy that is responsible for tracking where we are most of the time. He said ..."I know you stayed over at the US embassy, do you have a boyfriend there?"

---

[41] Mark Duffield, 'Risk Management and the Bunkering of the Aid Industry,' *Development Dialogue* 58 (2012): 21–36; and Róisín Shannon, 'Playing with Principles in an Era of Securitized Aid: Negotiating Humanitarian Space in Post-9/11 Afghanistan,' *Progress in Development Studies* 9, no. 1 (2009): 15–36.
[42] Partis-Jennings *Hybridity and Affect* .

She told me that many women faced inappropriate, searching questions such as this, somehow framed as tied to their security (where men did not) and a lack of any faith in their ability to look after themselves, despite, as in Luise's case, greater knowledge of Kabul than the security personnel themselves. She commented that because of this gendered treatment: 'I feel like I am really in prison' as well as noting that 'in terms of discrimination, and structural discrimination, a lot of the discrimination against women actually comes from the international community'. (Luise, German UN worker)

Here then, once again, the trope of the 'third gender' manifests as a duality whereby these women are truly free of gendered constraints *only where there is an illiberal Other against which to be defined*. The abstention from the constraints of femininity and the association to *almost masculinity* that comes with the possession of a foreign body is temporally and spatially situated. It is only in a particular place at a particular time that womanhood can be abandoned and only if one's body conforms to liberal subjectivity. Without the foil of the vague and static subordinated Afghan woman, or the unshakably traditional Afghan male, the international female body slips into a site upon which to map sexualisation and over which to seek control.

Conclusions

Read, focusing on aid worker memoires articulates that:

> [t]he ways in which female aid workers narrate their experiences of the spaces of humanitarianism offer an important contribution to the construction and maintenance of a distinctly humanitarian social imaginary, which highlights the complex and intersecting hierarchies of gender, race, class, nationality, and age that are deeply embedded in humanitarian practices.[43]

With a similar understanding in mind, I have suggested in this article that within this one embodied, the experiential label of the 'third gender' are bound different uncertainties about what it means to be a foreign female in a peacebuilding context, as well as different kinds of pre-knowledge and perception about how Afghan men view women.[44] The category of the 'third gender' does not fundamentally change the sexual identity of women, but instead collapses their race and international status onto their gender in particular ways; ways that are rendered intelligible only in relation to specific understandings of the Afghan context – it can encompass the dualities of freedom and restraint, empowerment and disempowerment.

What is clear, and a contribution this article to the wider liberal peace scholarship, is that sites of hybridity, friction and the everyday mixing together of liberal/'international' ideas, expectations and bodies with 'local' ones are only fully elucidated by looking at gender identities. Gendered expectations weigh upon different bodies differently and shape different experiences of peacebuilding in particular ways, mapped and ossified through routine behaviours.[45] The 'third gender' as a category is unstable, it is both and neither, in-between and something else. Yet arguably it is dominant because it

---

[43]Read, 'Embodying Difference', 2.
[44]Partis-Jennings, 'Hybridity and Affect'.
[45]See Judith Butler, *Gender Trouble: Feminism and the Subversion of Identity*, Routledge, Anniversar (New York, Oxon, 1999).

is unstable, as it speaks to the constancy of hybridity and friction in the 'liberal' order and its inability to create identity or meaning without reference to the 'illiberal' Other. In being always already in-between a perception of Afghan 'tradition' and expectation of liberal 'modernity' the female body and its meaning is suspended, kept uncertain and unstable. Moreover, that uncertainty stuck to and shaped experiences, and was generated by the affective sensation of difference, of liberal rights and freedoms and of the racialised physical, psychological and everyday distinctions made within liberal peace-building between international and Afghan bodies.[46]

The 'third gender' and the friction between and within gender orders that it signals illustrates the work that individual women do to try to navigate their gender and the (dis)advantages it implies, in ways that are acceptable to their perceived context. They can *self*-negate as 'typical' 'females' by self-identifying with or accepting or embracing a (temporary and situated) distancing from woman-hood in service of non-disruption, to protect their work and illustrate respect. Therefore, while the category of the 'third gender' is problematic, it echoes elements of the relational approach to peace described by Tarja Väyrynen in this issue in which the Other (and their perspective) is acknowledged and accommodated.[47] It is also potentially indicative of what Laura Shepherd might call 'hopefulness' in conflict-affected spaces, a desire for compromise on multiple sides and a willingness or attempt to adapt to social structures without excessive imposition,[48] and this element of the 'third gender' merits further study.

While it falls outside of the scope of this article to generalise to other contexts, or to investigate the appearance of the term 'third gender' used in similar ways outside of Afghanistan, I suggest that the insights I gain from exploring the Afghan context are likely to also map onto other conflict-affected spaces. Róisín Read's work demonstrates that some of the core dynamics that I explore here – such as distinction from 'local' populations, in-betweenness and the performance of gender roles by female humanitarians in very specific and negotiated ways – manifest in other contexts as well.[49] Similarly, further research into the differently racialised experiences within 'international' domains, Afghan men and women's perspectives on (and experiences of) the concept and other facets of analysis are necessary to fully understand the 'third gender' in Afghanistan.

However, and crucially, this article has demonstrated the importance of paying attention to gendered dynamics as a form of hybridity within the 'international' space, it has illustrated that this can elucidate nuance within gendered orders, demonstrating that, for instance, international women may perceive themselves as a kind of 'new form' in relation to an Afghan gender order which they believe cannot recognise them fully as women, while at the same time finding the so-called 'liberal' international gender order in Afghanistan to be the restrictive one in typically patriarchal ways. The liberal peace paradigm as a whole is characterised by contradiction and disjuncture,

---

[46]See Jennifer Fluri, '"Foreign Passports Only": Geographies of (Post)Conflict Work in Kabul, Afghanistan,' *Annals of the Association of American Geographers* 99, no. 5 (2009): 986–94.
[47]Tarja Väyrynen 'Mundane Peace and the Politics of Vulnerability: A Nonsolid Feminist Research Agenda'.
[48]Laura J. Shepherd, 'The Road to (and from) "Recovery": A Multidisciplinary Feminist Approach to Peacekeeping and Peacebuilding,' in *Rethinking Peacekeeping, Gender Equality and Collective Security*, ed. Gina Heathcote and Dianne Otto (Basinstoke and New York: Palgrave Macmillan, 2014): 99–117.
[49]Read, 'Embodying Difference'.

sites of slippage and hybridity,[50] and a feminist, gender-focused lens brings to the fore the deeply political nature of everyday encounters.

A feminist lens gives us the tools to explore how – as with the category of the 'third gender' at the micro-level – the existence of the liberal paradigm at the macro-level is dependent upon an 'illiberal' Other, which anchors it, and which, once deflated in significance, elucidates the instability and negotiation inherent within liberal ideas of progress and equality. Without a feminist engagement, we cannot grasp the full ambiguity and uncertainty of the 'liberal' order itself, nor exactly how it fragments, pulls-apart and reforms when it encounters different contexts, and this, I suggest, is vital if we want to understand how peace work feels, is lived and what it might produce.

Acknowledgments

I would like to thank Maria O'Reilly and Laura McLeod for all their incredible work on this special issue as well as the editors of Peacebuilding and the anonymous reviewers for their help improving this article. I would also like to thank all of the contributors to this issue for their inspiring scholarship as well as Claudia Aradau for her advice on an early draft.

Disclosure statement

No potential conflict of interest was reported by the author.

ORCID

Hannah Partis-Jennings http://orcid.org/0000-0002-5882-6951

---

[50]Mac Ginty and Sanghera, 'Hybridity in Peacebuilding and Development'; O. P. Richmond, S. Kappler, and a. Bjorkdahl, 'The "Field" in the Age of Intervention: Power, Legitimacy, and Authority Versus the "Local,"' *Millennium – Journal of International Studies*, 2015, 1–22.

Care as everyday peacebuilding

Tiina Vaittinen, Amanda Donahoe, Rahel Kunz, Silja Bára Ómarsdóttir and Sanam Roohi

ABSTRACT
Analyses of everyday peace provide a critical response to existing peace practices. However, absent from these discussions is the feminist research that theorizes peace through everyday practices of care. We argue that contemporary debates on everyday peace should engage with this largely forgotten tradition. We explore the contributions of this research through case studies that span the north-south divide: from Northern Ireland to Aceh, and Kashmir to Reykjavik. Demonstrating how care is an essential ingredient of everyday peace, we suggest that a care lens allows us to reframe the understanding of everyday peace to provide a fuller picture that also addresses the complex and contradictory nature of social relations involved in everyday peacebuilding. By resolving conflicts over immediate care needs and building the capacity of communities in ways that subtly challenge the fixity of conflict, care cumulatively creates possibilities for peaceful transformation.

Introduction

A tradition focusing on everyday peace is emerging in contemporary Peace and Conflict Research.[1] Related to the 'local turn'[2] and contributing to 'post-liberal peacebuilding', this

---

[1] E.g. Roger Mac Ginty, 'Everyday Peace: Bottom-Up and Local Agency in Conflict-Affected Societies', *Security Dialogue* 45, no. 6 (2014): 548–64; Pamina Firchow and Roger Mac Ginty 'Measuring Peace: Comparability, Commensurability, and Complementarity Using Bottom-Up Indicators', *International Studies Review* 19 (2017): 6–27; Oliver Richmond, *A Post-Liberal Peace*(London: Routledge, 2011); Roger Mac Ginty and Oliver P. Richmond, 'The Local Turn in Peacebuilding: A Critical Agenda for Peace', *Third World Quarterly* 34, no. 5 (2013): 763–83; Helen Berents, 'An Embodied Everyday Peace in the Midst of Violence', *Peacebuilding* 3, no. 2 (2015): 1–14; Sukanya Podder, 'The Power In-Between: Youth's Subaltern Agency and the Post-Conflict Everyday', *Peacebuilding* 3, no. 1 (2014): 36–57; Laura McLeod, 'Feminist Approach to Hybridity: Understanding Local and International Interactions in Producing Post-Conflict Gender Security', *Journal of Intervention and Statebuilding* 9 (2015): 48–69; Gearoid Millar, 'For Whom Do Local Peace Processes Function? Maintaining Control through Conflict Management', *Cooperation and Conflict* 52, no. 3 (2017): 293–308; Elisa Randazzo, 'The Paradoxes of the "Everyday":

literature develops understandings of how 'simple everyday activities present the realm of the possible'[3] in situations where conflicts within or between social groups are ongoing, or are likely to erupt.[4] Examining people's lived experiences of conflicts, the everyday peace literature grows from a critique of liberal approaches to peacebuilding,[5] criticised for limiting their attention to institutions, while 'sacrificing concern for community, local needs, and everyday experience.'[6] The everyday peace literature emphasises social practices and 'bottom-up, localized and particularistic conflict-calming measures,' thus going beyond negative peace as an absence of war, and 'towards everyday diplomacy or people-to-people activities that can move a society towards conflict transformation.'[7]

Despite its important openings, the contemporary everyday peace literature ignores many feminist accounts of the everyday,[8] including a rich tradition that theorises peace and conflict through the ethics of care.[9] For instance, the Everyday Peace Indicators (EPI) project, by Pamina Firchow and Roger Mac Ginty, has mapped a wide range of indicators for measuring everyday peace, many of which point to dimensions of care and caring.[10] However, the EPI project is yet to engage with existing peace theories on everyday practices of care. In general, as shown by Vaittinen elsewhere, the contemporary critical peace studies tend to ignore this feminist tradition.[11] This is glaring, since different kinds of care needs are present in all contexts of human life, including situations of conflict and peacebuilding.

Scrutinising the Local Turn in Peace Building', *Third World Quarterly*, 1–20 (2016); Christelle Rigual, 'Rethinking the Ontology of Peacebuilding. Gender, Spaces and the Limits of the Local Turn', *Peacebuilding* 6, no. 2 (2018); and Tarja Väyrynen, 'Mundane Peace and the Politics of Vulnerability: A Nonsolid Research Agenda', in this issue.

[2] See for example Rachel Julian, Berit Bliesemann de Guevara and Robin Redhead, 'From Expert to Experiential Knowledge: Exploring the Inclusion of Local Experiences in Understanding Violence in Conflict', this issue.

[3] Podder, 'The Power In-Between', 56.

[4] Mac Ginty, 'Everyday Peace', 549.

[5] See Susanna Campbell, David Chandler, and Meera Sabaratnam. *A Liberal Peace?: The Problems and Practices of Peacebuilding* (Zed Books, 2011); and John Heathershaw, 'Unpacking the Liberal Peace: The Dividing and Merging of Peacebuilding Discourses', *Millennium* 36, no. 3 (2008): 597-621.

[6] Berents, 'An Embodied Everyday Peace', 191.

[7] Mac Ginty, 'Everyday Peace', 549. See also Stefanie Kappler and Nicolas Lemay-Hébert, 'From Power-Blind Binaries to the Intersectionality of Peace: Connecting Feminism and Critical Peace and Conflict Studies', in this issue.

[8] Juanita Elias and Adrienne Roberts, 'Feminist Global Political Economies of the Everyday: From Bananas to Bingo', *Globalizations* 13, no. 6 (2016): 787–800.

[9] E.g. Sara Ruddick, *Maternal Thinking: Towards a Politics of Peace*. (New York: Ballantine Books, 1990); Joan C. Tronto, *Moral Boundaries: A Political Argument for an Ethic of Care*. (New York and London: Routledge, 1993); Linda Rennie Forcey, 'Women as Peace Makers. Contested Terrain for Feminist Peace Studies', *Peace and Change* no. 4 (1991): 331–54; Alison Bailey, 'Mothering, Diversity and Peace Politics', *Hypatia* 9, no. 2 (1994): 188–98; Fiona Robinson, *Globalizing Care: Ethics, Feminist Theory, and International Relations*. (Westview Press: Boulder, 1999); Fiona Robinson, *The Ethics of Care: A Feminist Approach to Human Security*. (Temple University Press: Philadelphia, 2011); Sigal Ben-Porath, 'Care Ethics and Dependence: Rethinking Jus Post Bellum", *Hypatia* 23, no. 2 (2008): 61–71; Virginia Held, *The Ethics of Care: Personal, Political and The Global*, (Oxford University Press: Oxford and New York, 2006); Kimberly Hutchings, 'Towards Feminist International Ethics', *Review of International Studies* 26 (2000): 111–30; Carol Cohn '"Maternal Thinking" and the Concept of Vulnerability in Security Paradigms, Policies and Practices', *Journal of International Political Theory* 10, no. 1 (2014): 46–69; Fiona Robinson and Catia Confortini, 'Symposium: Maternal Thinking for International Relations? Papers in Honor of Sara Ruddick', *Journal of International Political Theory* 10, no. 1 (2014): 38–45; Hannah Partis-Jennings, 'The "Third Gender" in Afghanistan: A Feminist Account of Hybridity as a Gendered Experience', in this issue; Väyrynen, 'Mundane Peace and the Politics of Vulnerability'; and Kappler and Lemay-Hébert, 'From Power-Blind Binaries to the Intersectionality of Peace'.

[10] Among the indicators are codes such as social cohesion and interdependence, education, access to health care, routine for social practices, conflict resolution, and so on – many of which found in feminist peace literature on care. See Everyday Peace Indicators Project: 'Codebook – EPI Categories – May 2016', https://everydaypeaceindicators.org/research/ (accessed May 18, 2018).

[11] For a detailed discussion and examples, see Tiina Vaittinen, The Global Biopolitics of Needs: Transnational Entanglements Between Ageing Finland and the Global Nurse Reserve of the Philippines, Tapri Studies in Peace and Conflict Research 103 (Tampere: TAPRI, 2017), http://urn.fi/URN:ISBN:978-952-03-0505-5, 51–64, 158–61.

When care is not explicitly addressed in analyses of peace, it follows that various mundane practices of caring that are crucial in creating trust and peaceful conflict transformation are either taken for granted, or remain invisible. Consequently, the intricate processes of everyday peacebuilding are not fully understood. We address this gap by examining different conflicts through a *care lens*, which provides a critical understanding of conflict management and peacebuilding that goes beyond the dominant accounts of everyday peace. The care lens reframes our understanding of peace, by providing a fuller picture of the complex and contradictory nature of building and sustaining social relations involved in peacebuilding.

Our aim in the article is not to add a new code for caring to the indicators for everyday peace, however. Nor do we suggest that feminist theories of care should replace other approaches to everyday peace. Rather, we want to emphasise that care, and the gendered power relations that go with it, *cut through* social practices in all contexts of peace and conflict. For the understanding of everyday peace, engaging with feminist theories of care is therefore crucial.

As we show in this article, everyday practices of care not only sustain life through direct acts of care-giving, but in various gendered ways involving caring human beings they also sustain and help to build trust among and within communities. They open the potential for peaceful transformation in circumstances, where such transformation seems unlikely if not impossible. In conflict and post-conflict societies, possibilities for peace thus emerge from *non-linear cycles of care, trust, and transformation*.[12] Simultaneously, given the detailed insights of feminist care literature into the power dimensions of care, the care lens avoids romanticising everyday peace, allowing for an alternative gendered reading of peace and peaceful transformations.

In what follows, we briefly revisit the feminist peace research tradition that addresses care, after which we show through four case studies how different dimensions of care contribute to everyday peace, and what a reading of peacebuilding through a care lens reveals. Our case studies range from the Troubles in Northern Ireland to 'post-conflict' Aceh to conflict-ridden Kashmir to the financial crisis in Iceland. We have selected a disparate sample of case studies in order to demonstrate the ways in which care *in its multiple dimensions* emerges as a site, source, and catalyst of everyday peace in different conflict contexts.[13] We do not seek to provide a uniform or exhaustive account of care as a means for peaceful transformation, or a comparative analysis. Rather, we ask how and what kind of care is present, and what relations of care do for everyday peace and the potential for transformation in conflict or post-conflict societies. Such questions, we suggest, should become a standard practice in all analyses of everyday peacebuilding.

Care as peacebuilding

The contemporary everyday peace literature challenges theories and practices of liberal peacebuilding.[14] Since the 1980s, feminist care and peace theorists have done something

---

[12]This resonates with debates around the potential of non-linear understandings of peacebuilding (see D. Chandler, 'Peacebuilding and the politics of non-linearity: rethinking "hidden" agency and "resistance"', *Peacebuilding* 1, no. 1 (2013): 17–32.
[13]The article builds on our discussions in the first Feminist Peace Research Network (FPRN) Workshop in Tampere, June 2016, where care as everyday peacebuilding in different conflicts turned out to be a common theme from our disparate fieldwork experiences. For FPRN, see: http://www.uta.fi/yky/en/feministpeaceresearch/index.html.
[14]See note 1 and 4 above.

very similar, by drawing attention to the situated necessities of care and human relatedness that liberal abstractions of political subjectivity tend to ignore. This feminist literature maintains that practices of care give rise to distinct moral and political thinking, which derives from the existential fact of human vulnerability and relatedness, and the capacity to recognise and respond to the needs of others.[15] Such alternative moral thinking, care ethicists argue, is capable of challenging militarism and the customary thinking of global justice, while providing avenues for re-imagining just peace.[16]

In her pioneering book *Maternal Thinking*,[17] Sara Ruddick for instance argued that the thinking that arises from mothering may be used as a 'standpoint from which to criticize the destructiveness of war and begin to reinvent peace'.[18] Despite some interpretations to the contrary,[19] mothers and maternal thinking in this account do not refer to 'women' but to any 'responsible adult', who 'takes on responsibility for children's lives and for whom providing child care is a significant part of *her or his* working life'.[20] As Ruddick's maternal thinking, feminist care ethics also more generally goes beyond the understanding of care as 'women's' reproductive labour.[21] Whereas the term 'care' in popular parlance carries connotations of feminised kindness that comes out 'naturally', especially from 'women', care ethicists recognise care as a field of complex political struggle. They acknowledge that care relations are power relations, imbued with the potential of dominance, exploitation, and even direct violence – and difficult choices as to whose care needs matter.[22]

For care ethicists then, care practices give rise to situated, embodied ethics, and mundane practices of conflict management. This understanding unsettles the more abstract frameworks of liberal peacebuilding that emphasise institutions and universalist solutions. In this regard, feminist ethics of care presented a theory of 'post-liberal' peace well before the contemporary accounts of the same.[23] Simultaneously, the care lens provides a more nuanced picture of social relations that goes beyond a romanticised understanding of care and empathy. It challenges dichotomous representation of liberal versus non-liberal and rationality versus empathy, questioning some of the tendencies in the post-liberal peace literature.[24]

The largely forgotten tradition of feminist peace research that focuses on care asks us to scrutinise the situated and often difficult *peacebuilding work that gendered relations of care and caring do* in conflict-prone situations, beyond inter-personal practices of caregiving. Here, care is understood as a form of social and corporeal relatedness,

---

[15]See note 8 above.
[16]Catia C. Confortini and Abigail Ruane, 'Sara Ruddick's Maternal Thinking as Weaving Epistemology for Justpeace', *Journal of International Political Theory* 10, no. 1 (2014): 70–93.
[17]Ruddick, *Maternal Thinking*. For discussion, Robinson and Confortini, 'Symposium'; Vaittinen, 'The Global Biopolitics of Needs', 51–5; and Väyrynen, 'Mundane Peace and the Politics of Vulnerability'.
[18]Ruddick, *Maternal Thinking*, 12.
[19]E.g.: Laura Duhan Kaplan, 'Woman as Caretaker: An Archetype that Supports Patriarchal Militarism', *Hypatia* 9, no. 2 (1994): 123–33; Tarja Väyrynen, 'Gender and peacebuilding', in *Palgrave Advances in Peacebuilding: Critical Developments and Approaches*, ed. Oliver P. Richmond (Basingstoke: Palgrave Macmillan, 2010), 137–53.
[20]Ruddick, *Maternal Thinking*, 40, 41.
[21]E.g., Tronto, *Moral Boundaries*; and Tiina Vaittinen, 'The Power of The Vulnerable Body: A New Political Understanding of Care', *International Feminist Journal of Politics* 17, no. 1 (2015): 100–18.
[22]E.g. Robinson, *Globalizing Care*, 128; Robinson, *The Ethics of Care*, 5.
[23]E.g. Richmond, *A Post-Liberal Peace*.
[24]Oliver P. Richmond, 'Becoming Liberal, Unbecoming Liberalism: Liberal-Local Hybridity via the Everyday as a Response to the Paradoxes of Liberal Peacebuilding', *Journal of Intervention and Statebuilding* 3, no. 3 (2009): 324–44.

enacted by the moral and political demands of care by human beings who are, by default, vulnerable and dependent on multiple others within the society.[25] Consequently, relations and practices of care cut through, and are conditioned by, the entire social strata, tying together social structures beyond the inter-personal and intimate practices of caregiving, as our case studies below demonstrate.[26]

Northern Ireland: care as community-building and peacebuilding[27]

From the late 1960s until the Good Friday Agreement in 1998, Northern Ireland experienced political violence known as the 'Troubles,' between 'Catholics' and 'Protestants'.[28] What began as a non-violent civil rights movement, transformed into a violent contest over the 'constitutional question': should Northern Ireland remain part of the United Kingdom or instead unite with Ireland? In 1972, following increasing levels of violence, the local Stormont Government was disbanded in favour of direct rule. The ensuing political vacuum was filled by the violence of the Troubles on the one hand, and the necessary caring efforts of community-building on the other. The 'community and voluntary sector' that thereby emerged contributed to everyday peace in the midst of violence, and remains critical for peacebuilding in Northern Ireland.[29] With seventy-five percent of paid positions in the community and voluntary sector being held by women in Northern Ireland,[30] our first case study draws attention to women's role in community-building.

Building on Ruddick's work, Catia Confortini and Abigail Ruane argue that '[f]or mothers, the relationship with the other is a condition for knowing the world'.[31] For women in Northern Ireland, caring relationships within the community and across communal divides became a condition for knowing the Troubles in ways that allowed spaces of everyday peace to emerge. On both sides of the divide, women formed groups to meet the needs of their families and neighbours, confronting overlapping forms of deprivation created by the conflict and a failing economy. Knowing the conflict was thus mediated through the care needs of others that ensued from the violence. On both sides of the conflict, women saw children being caught up in paramilitaries and sought to occupy them in play schemes and after school programs. They saw their families and neighbours' families suffering from hunger, and developed urban gardening, nutrition, and catering projects. They saw violence in their own homes and sought to protect each other by locating safe spaces, legal support, and health and counselling services. To achieve their goals, they sought various forms of training and education, from primary education and childcare to grant writing and project development. They professionalized and challenged gender dynamics in their communities.

---

[25] See also Väyrynen, 'Mundane Peace and the Politics of Vulnerability'.
[26] Cf. Berenice Fisher and Joan C. Tronto, 'Toward a Feminist Theory of Caring', in *Circles of Care: Work and Identity in Women's Lives*, ed. Emily K. Abel and Margaret K. Nelson (Albany: State University of New York Press, 1990), 35–61; Tronto, *Moral Boundaries*; and Vaittinen, 'The Power of The Vulnerable Body'.
[27] This section draws on fieldwork carried out by Amanda E. Donahoe in Northern Ireland from July-December 2012. Semi-structured interviews, focus groups and ethnographies were conducted along both sides of the social divide.
[28] Use of the terms 'Protestant' and 'Catholic' in Northern Ireland are placeholders for more complex clusters of political identities including British, Unionist, or Loyalist in the case of 'Protestant'; and Irish, Nationalist, or Republican in the case of 'Catholic.' However, as these terms are commonly used in Northern Ireland, they will suffice here.
[29] Amanda E. Donahoe, *Peacebuilding through Women's Community Development: Wee Women's Work in Northern Ireland* (New York: Palgrave Macmillan, 2017).
[30] NICVA, 'Working Patterns by Gender', in *State of the Sector: Workforce Chapter* (DetailData: Northern Ireland Community and Voluntary Association, 2014).
[31] Confortini and Ruane, 'Sara Ruddick's Maternal Thinking', 73.

The operation of women's community groups on both sides of the divide is an example of care as societal healing, a crucial dimension of peacebuilding. An important aspect in their work is networking across the communal divide, extending care to the side of the other. The Catholic Falls Women's Centre, for instance, one of the first in Belfast, helped the Protestant Shankill Women's Centre get organized to care for the women of its community, despite the fact that these two centres are located on either side of one of the most well-known interfaces in Belfast. Thus, women who could have identified as enemies engendered trust. Years later, when funding was denied to the Falls Women's Centre amid accusations that they were politically associated with the violence, the Shankill Women fortified this trust by standing with the Falls Women and calling on the city to grant the funding.

The collaboration of these two centres is unexceptional. Managers and organizers of women's centres across Northern Ireland regularly share best practices and collaborate on projects and funding applications. They belong to and utilise resources of umbrella groups like the Women's Support Network, or the Women's Resource and Development Agency. This network contributes to the standardization of women's centres such that similar classes, trainings, and services are available across Northern Ireland. These collaborations not only help build resources to care for the members of individual communities, but the shared practices and knowledges continue to foster peaceful relations across the communal divides.

Thus, the ethics of care that was born from recognising the everyday care needs within one's own community has, over time, fostered collaboration, trust, and care across communities. For instance, women attend events or weekend 'residentials,' in which they engage with the 'other', share stories and work on joint projects. Though women who participate in residentials rarely directly challenge power relations that reinforce the communal divide in their own communities, these experiences foster relational awareness and compassion, which keeps such prospects open for the future. Relating concretely with the other transforms women's community politics, as women identify needs in common rather than in competition with their acquaintances from the other community. This compassion is extended, for example, when they moderate children's slurs against the other. Thereby, the relational logic of knowing the Troubles through the everyday needs of the 'other' – and not only through the 'other's' violence – continues to foster a peaceful transformation.

The case of community development in Northern Ireland demonstrates how a care lens allows us to account for activities and social relations that are essential to everyday peacebuilding across communities. However, care is not necessarily 'women's work'; the maternal practices of knowing conflicts through the needs of the 'other' takes many forms. In the following section, we illustrate this through the care practices of mostly male leaders in Aceh.

Aceh: village leader's caring and everyday acts of kindness as peacebuilding[32]

Since shortly after Indonesian independence in 1945, Aceh's politics have been dominated by calls for independence from Indonesia, leading to repeated armed

---

[32]This case study draws on research carried out by Rahel Kunz in the context of a collective project *Gender Dimensions of Social Conflicts, Armed Violence and* Peacebuilding, supported by the Swiss Programme for Research on Global Issues for Development co-funded by the Swiss Agency for Development and Cooperation and the Swiss National Science Foundation (400240). Inspiring collaboration with Mimidoo Achakpa, Henri Myrttinen, Joy Onyesoh, Elisabeth Prugl, Arifah Rahmawati, Christelle Rigual and Wening Udasmoro is gratefully acknowledged. The case study draws on interview and focus group discussion material collected in 2015–2016. Special thanks go to the data collectors Arifah Rahmawati, Raihal Fajri, Wening Udasmoro and Tabrani Yunis and the respondents. Pseudonyms are used to guarantee anonymity.

insurrections.[33] From 1976 to 2005, the independence movement in the form of the Free Aceh Movement (Gerakan Aceh Merdeka, GAM) waged an armed struggle against the central government, which ended with the signing of a peace agreement that granted Aceh wide-ranging political autonomy.[34] The desire for independence is a complex matter, motivated among other things by issues of economic disparity, political subordination, and differing understandings of Islam.[35]

During the thirty years of conflict, Acehnese people found themselves in various positions, in between the Indonesian military and GAM, drawn into supporting GAM, or trying to remain neutral, or doing both. In the conflict literature, civilian populations are often perceived as passive victims of armed violence. In Aceh, many civilians took active roles in conflict, defying notions of victimhood. Various forms of mediation, reconciliation and healing played a key role in negotiating conflict situations and building peace. Communities and individuals mobilised their resources and social positions for conflict de-escalation and peacebuilding, during and after the conflict.[36] These, we argue, should be understood as *practices of care* that happened mostly from the bottom up as a micro-politics, involving thousands of leaders of villages, clans, churches, mosques, and community members.[37]

In Acehnese communities, important roles are performed by a few key figures, mostly men. These include the village chiefs (*Keuchik*), *adat* cultural figures (*Tuhapeut*), religious figures (*Tengku*), and sometimes also (male) youth leaders. During the conflict these figures played an important role in protecting villagers, preventing the escalation of violence or reducing its effects, meditating between the community, the Indonesian military and GAM, and building peace. A community in East Aceh, in one of the most conflict-affected regions with a strong GAM presence, remained comparatively peaceful during the conflict and became a place of refuge for surrounding villages.[38] In this community, the *keuchik* and a *tengku* carried out numerous practices of care, managing to build trust. For instance, both reportedly used their personal material and social capital to negotiate with the GAM and the Indonesian military to free suspected GAM members detained by the Indonesian military.[39] As one community member reports, the *keuchik* sold one of his houses to use the money to protect the community: he would check on the village even during the night and if a community member was taken away by the GAM or the military, he would use his resources to free them, without taking sides in the conflict.[40]

The *tengku* turned the space of his house and the mosque in front of it into a safe space, where men could come and pray or even mediate conflict.[41] When social gatherings were strictly forbidden, and men's mobility was sometimes even more restricted than women's, due

---

[33] Edward Aspinall, *Islam and Nation: Separatist Rebellion in Aceh, Indonesia* (Stanford: Stanford University Press, 2009), http://www.eastwestcenter.org/publications/islam-and-nation-separatist-rebellion-aceh-indonesia.
[34] M. Amin Zuhri, 'Membayangkan Aceh Sebagai Negara Bangsa: Sejarah Gerakan Nasionalisme Lokal' (PhD diss., Yogjakarta: Universitas Gadjah Mada, 2015).
[35] Rizal Rizal Sukma, *Security Operations in Aceh: Goals, Consequences, and Lessons* (Washington, DC: Easte-West Center, 2004).
[36] Rahel Kunz, Henri Myrttinen, Wening Udasmoro, 'Preachers, pirates and peace-building: Examining non-violent hegemonic masculinities in Aceh', in *Asian Journal of Women's Studies* 24, no. 3 (2018).
[37] John Braithwaite, 'Traditional Justice', in *Restorative Justice, Reconciliation, and Peacebuilding*, ed. Jennifer J. Llewellyn and Daniel Philpott (Oxford: Oxford University Press, 2014), 225; and Jacqueline Aquino Siapno, 'Living through Terror: Everyday Resilience in East Timor and Aceh', *Social Identities* 15, no. 1 (2009): 58.
[38] Focus Group Discussion, March 2016.
[39] Ibid.
[40] Ibid.
[41] Interview with Mana, March 2016. It has to be noted, however, that the gatherings in his house were sometimes also used by the Indonesian military to verify who was present and thus presumed as not associated with GAM.

to the military's suspicions that they might be GAM members, these religious gatherings allowed men to meet up with friends, fostering the maintenance of everyday social relations within the community. These acts of care fostered relations of trust among inhabitants of the community, and between the community, the GAM, and the military. Through a cycle of trust and transformation then, caring practices contributed to a transformation of the relationships between the community and the armed actors, which de-escalated the situation in the everyday.

The caring practices of these male leaders could be read as a story of patriarchal practices of leadership, reproducing gendered power relations. Yet, reading them through a lens of care – and not only as patriarchy – can help us better comprehend the work that *different kinds of* gendered care relations do for everyday peace, and how caring, while gendered, contributes to everyday peace in all its forms. Indeed, the acts of care that helped to transform relationships in peaceful ways in Aceh were never limited to community leaders. The everyday care work of women continued to sustain lives and communities during the conflict. In addition, different kinds of everyday acts of kindness occurred. For instance, offering a ride to a community member of another religion, or 'the loan of a Muslim-owned lawn mower to cut the grass of the Christian church'[42] helped to bring people closer, transforming assumptions about the 'other' and building trust.

Similarly, community rituals contributed to bringing people closer and transforming assumptions about and reconciling with the 'other'.[43] *Peusijuek* ceremonies, for instance, were used to prepare conflicting parties for negotiations, to bless conflict victims, or to reintegrate returned GAM members.[44] These caring rituals facilitated dialogue between conflicting parties and the transition of combatants and victims to citizens and community members, helping to dissolve conflict and build reconciliation and peace. As in Northern Ireland, such caring relations across community divides were crucial not only for everyday peace and conflict management, but also for keeping open the hope and the potential for large-scale, long-term peace and reconciliation. As elaborated below, similar inter-community relations are visible in Kashmir, albeit there, the everyday peace across communities is partly enabled by the lack of state care, and the communities' shared experiences of mistrust of the state.

Kashmir: inter-and intra-communal care as fostering everyday peace[45]

Kashmiris live in one of the world's most heavily militarised zones.[46] The Indian state utilises the discourse of security to legitimise this status quo by constructing Kashmiris

---

[42] Braithwaite, 'Traditional Justice', 227.
[43] Braithwaite, 'Traditional Justice'; Siapno, 'Living through Terror'; and World Bank, 'GAM Reintegration Needs Assessment: Enhancing Peace through Community-Level Development Programming', http://documents.worldbank.org/curated/en/554011468259735196/GAM-reintegration-needs-assessment-enhancing-peace-through-community-level-development-programming.
[44] In a survey, 76.7% of GAM indicated that such ceremonies had been held in their village. World Bank, op.cit, 25.
[45] This section draws on fieldwork carried out by Sanam Roohi in Srinagar during October 2016, with a brief follow up interviews in November 2017 in Bangalore. Interviews and group discussions were conducted with Muslims of different denominations, and Sikhs, when the town was undergoing intense and at times violent stand-off between the Indian State and the separatists, after a militant called Burhan Wani was killed by the armed forces in July 2016.
[46] According to verbal estimates, the Kashmiri conflict since 1948 has led to some 100,000 Kashmiris being killed, yet a more accurate figure is around 47,000 deaths since 1989 (see https://edition.cnn.com/2013/11/08/world/kashmir-fast-facts/index.html) often at the hands of the Indian security forces who are protected from prosecution under the Armed Forces Special Powers Act.

as a threat to the establishment of an increasingly Hinduising state.[47] The present conflict with the Indian state dates back to late 1980s, three decades after Kashmir was annexed to India in 1948.[48] Since then, the region has seen a spate of militant activities, demanding freedom from India. India has consistently responded with military force,[49] often delegitimising these struggles as interference from Pakistan.

Unlike the other cases analysed in this article, the conflict in Kashmir is ongoing, and potentially expanding, to an extent that violence has become normalised. Yet, despite frequent eruptions of conflict and regular incidences of violence, mundane life goes on, as do everyday practices of relational care that maintain the possibilities of peace. Kashmiri Muslims of different denominations make up roughly 96% of the population in the valley. While other communities like Hindus, Sikhs, and Buddhists form the remaining 4% of the population,[50] these minorities are considered very important to the fabric of Kashmir as encapsulated through the term 'Kashmiriyat': a centuries old tradition of living together amidst religious diversity and peaceful coexistence among different religious groups.[51] Looking at inter- and intra-community engagements in Kashmir among Kashmiri Muslims of different denominations and between Sikhs and Muslims, we show how relations of care provide momentary relief from conflict, making everyday life possible, and at times, even peaceful.

The state repression and violence against Muslims not only politicises the Muslim community, it simultaneously fosters intra-communal relations of care. Within this backdrop of historically problematic state-community relations, forging a solidary Muslim identity has brought the community together, often united against the 'occupation' of Indian state. Muslims may assert, for instance, that any person killed in a crossfire, or stone-pelting, whatever their religion, are their own sons and daughters. Hundreds and even thousands of Muslims attend the burial of these victims of state violence to mark their solidarity and protest. These instances show how the realm of care is by no means apolitical, but entangled with the socio-political circumstances where relations of care emerge – in this case as a community response and even as a form of resistance.

While Muslims in Kashmir are divided in their political and sub-religious affiliations, the shared Islamic and place-based affinity allows for the creation of strong affective ties within the Muslim community across these and other divisions including gender.[52] For instance, in 2016, during a shutdown and violence when the data for this case study was collected, a supporter of the People's Democratic Party[53] was visibly distressed to narrate how children were getting injured by the pellet guns used by security forces. He asserted that those getting

---

[47] For a detailed history of the Kashmiri struggle, see Mridu Rai, *Hindu Rulers, Muslim Subjects: Islam, Rights, and the History of Kashmir* (Princeton University Press, 2004).
[48] A. G. Noorani, *The Kashmir Dispute, 1947–2012* (Tulika Books, 2013) offers insight into the conflict as it stands today.
[49] The Armed Forces Special Powers Act introduced in Kashmir in 1990 gives Indian army special powers to maintain law and order, often giving them indemnity from legal proceedings in case of excesses.
[50] During the height of Islamic militancy, some 100,000 Hindu Kashmiri Pundits left the valley in fear in 1990 and were settled in different parts of India, including Jammu region of the state of Jammu and Kashmir. Hindus were relocated in different parts of India and provided with affirmative actions and were often provided with government jobs. Yet a few thousand Hindus still remain in Kashmir today.
[51] B. Puri, 'Kashmiriyat: the vitality of Kashmiri identity', *Contemporary South Asia* 4, no. 1 (1995): 55–63.
[52] Inshah Malik, 'Imaginations of self and struggle: women in the Kashmiri armed resistance', *Economic and Political Weekly* 50, no. 49 (2015): 60–6.
[53] The People's Democratic Party is the local ruling party in the state of Jammu and Kashmir, which has forged alliance with the Bharatiya Janata Party, the ruling Hindu right-wing party in India.

injured are '*hamare bacchhe*' or our children, and prayed for the use of pellet guns to stop. This example speaks to Ruddick's emphasis that 'mothering' can be done by anyone taking responsibility for children's lives. For the Muslim community, being exposed to state violence *as a community*, fostered intra-communal care relations, which are not limited to victims of violence. For instance, during the 2016 shut downs, villagers sent truckload of vegetables to the city to feed the inhabitants who were facing food shortages. Such relational ties, formed under the asymmetric threat from a common oppressor, holds social life in Kashmir together – helping to maintain everyday cordiality amongst Muslims, regardless of the social, political and other differences within the community. While such communal affinities may protract the conflict between the state and the community, in towns like Srinagar, these affinities create 'fictive' kinship ties that help make everyday life possible and, at times, peaceful.

Similar transformational potential is visible in inter-community relations of care. Research among Muslims and Sikhs in Kashmir shows that both communities' relations with the state are undergirded with memories of violence and feelings of neglect.[54] Therefore, pragmatism reigns, with an instrumentalist understanding of the Indian state. Sikhs have been making demands on the state for affirmative actions in the region given their minority status, without necessarily seeing the state as an ally. This neglect also unites the Muslims and Sikhs in their distrust of the state, which in turn fosters inter-communal relations of care, trust, and everyday peace.

Between the Muslim and Sikh communities, differences of opinion and suspicion based on political and other affiliations create mistrust. Yet, such mistrust can be offset by a strong sense of shared Kashmiri identity, irrespective of the religious or political affiliation. In the name of *Kashmiriyat*, or co-existence, people extend care to one another, and stories of everyday acts of care and concern between the communities abound. In the interviews, many Sikhs cited this reason behind their desire to continue living in the Muslim majority Kashmir, despite ongoing unrest and violence. While Muslims see Sikhs as an important part of their multi-ethnic social fabric, Sikhs are aware that the patronage of Muslims is vital for their survival as a minority community. Sikhs realise that Muslim violence is directed toward the state, and not aimed at them. Amongst the Sikhs interviewed for this research, stories of how Muslims and Sikhs have not had any instance of communal riots in the region was a common refrain. Sikhs also consider Kashmir a safe place, with less inter-personal violence, rape, thefts, and other crimes that plague the rest of India, and see it as an important reason for staying in Kashmir.

Sikhs and Muslims attend each other's weddings and funerals, provide social and psychological support as neighbours and respect each other's customs and taboos. Stories of Sikh families regretting their decision to relocate after 2008 or 2010 violence (between Indian security forces and Muslims) were also common. Additionally, stories about how Muslims have provided care to Sikhs in a 'big brotherly' manner thrive. For instance, one young Sikh man explained how Muslims always respected their religious sentiments.[55] Another, much older man explained that when stone-pelting is on, no stone is pelted at Sikhs, and when they celebrate their festivals during times of violence, the stone-pelters give them way and allow

---

[54]The desecration of golden temple and the anti-Sikh riots of 1984 following the then Prime Minister Indira Gandhi's assassination where officially 3,000 Sikhs were killed by Hindus, provoked by the Congress Party is a traumatic memory for the Sikhs.

[55]Interview conducted on 12 November 2017 in Bangalore, India.

their processions to pass peacefully. In addition, a 25-year old Sikh woman, a schoolteacher, spoke very warmly about the parents of her Muslim students. Another Sikh woman narrated that when a relative had unexpectedly required hospitalization in Srinagar, a Muslim family, whose ward was in the adjoining bed, came to their rescue, providing food and cash. The Sikh woman's slipper had broken in the rush to the hospital, and the Muslim lady gave the Sikh woman her slippers to go back home.[56] These instances exemplify Kashmiriyat or Kashmiri ethics of care, which continues to build a sense of place, uniting the communities in Srinagar irrespective of their diverse religious identities, especially during the time of conflict.

In a place like Srinagar amidst an undeclared war between the Indian state and the people, conflict is externalized with the Indian state, and peace in the form of co-existence and provision of care is internalized, paving the way for life to 'go on.' Practices of caregiving both sustain life in a conflict situation and prevent communal enmity from becoming the defining feature of Muslim-Sikh relations, which protects Kashmiriyat. As such, care practices are transformational. For the majority in Kashmir, internalized building of relations of care allow for not only relations and bonds of trust to deepen, but also for the potential for future peaceful coexistence, if *Azaadi* (freedom) is to be eventually realised in Kashmir.

From Kashmir, we now turn to the post-financial crash Iceland – a case, which would traditionally not be understood as a conflict in peacebuilding literature. Yet, shattering the economy, the crash (re)produced gendered structural violence, uncertainty, and precariousness, in similar ways as situations of direct violence do. Here, too, caring enabled life to go on.

Iceland: the women's collective as care-givers in post-crash Reykjavík[57]

The Icelandic economy was one of the earliest and most prominent victims of the financial crisis of 2008, also known as 'the great recession.' The country's three largest banks, privatized only a few years earlier, had been aggressively internationalized. When combined, the three bankruptcies, which took place over the course of only ten days, rank as the third largest corporate bankruptcy in the world.[58] As Iceland is one of the world's smallest sovereign countries, its residents felt the impact intensely.

A crisis of this magnitude could easily lead to civil unrest, and even violent conflict. Icelanders, however, do not have access to weapons; there is no military in the country and the police is mostly unarmed. Thus, when Icelanders gathered in October 2008 to protest their government's lack of response to these unprecedented events, the demonstrations were largely peaceful. A spontaneous organization, *Raddir fólksins* (i.e. The People's Voices) emerged to organize speakers around three main demands: the resignation of the government, the resignation of the boards of the Central Bank and the Financial Supervisory Authority (FME).[59] These meetings were held from 11 October 2008 until 24 January 2009,[60] when the government finally resigned on Monday, 26 January 2009.[61]

---

[56]These interviews were conducted during October 2016.
[57]This chapter is based on Silja Bára Ómarsdóttir participation in and notes from the Women's Collective.
[58]Jenny Anderson, 'How Iceland Emerged from its Deep Freeze', *New York Times*, July 3, 2015, https://www.nytimes.com/2015/07/05/business/international/how-iceland-emerged-from-its-deep-freeze.html.
[59]Baldur Arnarson, 'Reiðin ráði ekki för', *Morgunblaðið*, September 30, 2010, http://www.mbl.is/frettir/innlent/2010/09/30/reidin_radi_ekki_for/.
[60]Raddir fólksins: '#16 – Laugardagur 24. Janúar' http://raddirfolksins.info/?cat=6&paged=2.
[61]Only in the week before, upon the first meeting of parliament after the Christmas break, did violence erupt, although some acts of sabotage had been registered before.

Concurrently with the People's Voices, a series of open meetings was held,[62] where the organizers attempted to engage authorities with the public. Women's movements criticized both series of meetings for promoting a masculine perspective on the crisis and responses to it. Iceland consistently ranks as one of the best places in the world to be a woman,[63] but men were at the helm of all the banks, with a rare woman running the domestic side of the business. When the economy faltered, it was men who were profiled in the media, e.g. the rugged fishermen who left their homes and families behind and looked to the sea for survival.[64] The international press focused on a different narrative, paying more attention to milestones of the reconstruction, such as a woman becoming prime minister, women elected to parliament in record numbers, and women taking over the hollowed-out banks[65] – of which nothing remained but the domestic operations.

As the economy faltered, Icelanders were faced with significant uncertainty. The economy is heavily reliant on imports and with a suddenly worthless currency, supply lines closed on many companies and no one knew for how long. In economic downturns, women are usually the first to lose their jobs but in Iceland, it was the men, who were working in the high-risk side of the banking sector. Women had worked in the front-end positions that remained necessary for daily operations, very much fitting the narrative Prügl describes of the 'reckless man and responsible woman [that] offers insight into the unfamiliar of the crisis.'[66] This left women in Iceland, particularly in the urban area around Reykjavík, facing an even heavier second shift than before. Many women needed to find ways to meet the daily needs of their families on a single income, they could not be certain that they would have the same access to imported goods they used to have, and it was clear that the austerity policies would result in cutbacks of the welfare state. As Kantola and Lombardo note, the 'neoliberal policy solutions to the crisis ... require cutting down the public sector [and] tend to rely on and reproduce the gender roles that delegate major responsibility for care to women.'[67] It is in this context that a women's collective emerged, creating a feminist ethic of care in a precarious situation.

While many men lost their jobs, their voices were certainly not silenced. Noting that women were rarely heard in the post-crash environment, Reykjavík city councillor Sóley Tómasdóttir created a Facebook group, called 'the women's emergency government' (Neyðarstjórn kvenna), and issued a manifesto for a women's collective that would promote the reconstruction of a community based on humane values, emphasizing respect for the individual, community, life, nature and the environment. The collective declared that since men had so clearly been unable to develop a society that served the needs of the many, it was time for women to step forward.[68] Within a few days, the group had grown to 1,600

---

[62]Wikipedia.is, 'Opinn borgarafundur', https://is.wikipedia.org/wiki/Opinn_borgarafundur (accessed May 15, 2018).
[63]Sigmarsdóttir, Sif, 'Once more, Iceland has shown it is the best place in the world to be female', *The Guardian*, January 5, 2018, https://www.theguardian.com/commentisfree/2018/jan/05/iceland-female-women-equal-pay-gender-equality.
[64]Charles Forelle, 'As banking "Fairy-Tale" Ends, Iceland Looks Back to the Sea', *Wall Street Journal*, October 10, 2008, https://www.wsj.com/articles/SB122359763876821355.
[65]Ruth Sunderland, 'After the crash, Iceland's women lead the rescue', *The Guardian*, February 22, 2009, https://www.theguardian.com/world/2009/feb/22/iceland-women.
[66]Prügl, Elisabeth, '"If Lehman Brothers Had Been Lehman Sisters...": Gender and Myth in the Aftermath of the Financial Crisis', *International Political Sociology* 6:1 (2012), 21–35.
[67]Johanna Kantola and Emanuela Lombardo, 'Feminist Political Analysis: Exploring Strengths, Hegemonies and Limitations', *Feminist Theory* 18:3 (2017), 323–341.
[68]Wikipedia.is: 'Neyðarstjórn kvenna' https://is.wikipedia.org/wiki/Ney%C3%B0arstj%C3%B3rn_kvenna. (accessed May 15, 2018).

members and expanded to 3,000 within a few weeks. Real-life meetings were planned and dozens of women attended the first brainstorming session on what could be done to ensure that women's voices would be heard and that women were not excluded from the reconstruction of Iceland's economy.

The women's collective developed organically. It tried to engage the political elite, get women active in politics and considered running a women's list for parliament, if and when elections would be called. In addition to political mobilization, an interesting response appeared in everyday acts of caring for each other. Women shared their willingness to teach each other skills that could be useful in a barter economy; they organized workshops on cutting hair, making new clothes from old ones, and so on. As many companies were going bankrupt, office buildings were left unoccupied and the group was given control over a bright and spacious office where women could spend their days working on creative projects and hold workshops. The space was operational for about a year, and contributed to the work of graphic designers, seamstresses, artists, web developers and more.

The women's collective promoted a variety of causes over the 3–4 months it was most active, publishing three volumes of a newsletter that served as an outlet for women's views on the crisis. A simple four-page leaflet, each volume featured an interview with a woman, intellectuals and workers alike, commented on the gender bias of the media and the protests, and had a dedicated slot for a 'woman's soap box.'[69]

Inside and outside of the women's collective, people realized they needed to run their households differently, and started returning to more traditional foods. Lamb sales grew rapidly,[70] and families started spending time together in preparing 'slátur', a traditional liver sausage and blood pudding reminiscent of the Scottish haggis. Municipalities advertised community garden plots, available to anyone who was interested and many people started growing potatoes and root vegetables to supplement their families' diet and lowering the amount of money they spent on food.[71] Knitting became popular again, as a way of earning money and calming the mind during this time of uncertainty.[72] The traditional Icelandic woollen sweater 'lopapeysa' became a fashion statement and showed that the consumerism of the past years was disappearing.[73] In this way, women took on the role of constructing a new national identity through protecting and transmitting culture and values, but also by contesting what had been the dominant national project.[74]

The women's collective faded quickly. In January of 2009, the government resigned and elections were scheduled for the spring. With elections set so soon, many women returned to the political parties they had been active in – in particular the two left-wing

---

[69] *Kvennastjórnartíðindi*, 1:1 2008 https://rafhladan.is/bitstream/handle/10802/11466/1.%20tbl.%20-%20prent%C3%BAtg..pdf?sequence=2, *Kvennastjórnartíðindi* 1:2 2008 https://rafhladan.is/bitstream/handle/10802/11466/2.%20tbl.%20-%20prent%C3%BAtg..pdf?sequence=3, *Kvennastjórnartíðindi* 1:3 2008 https://rafhladan.is/bitstream/handle/10802/11466/3.%20tbl.%20-%20prent%C3%BAtg..pdf?sequence=4. (accessed May 15, 2018).
[70] *visir.is* 'Stóraukin sala á lambakjöti', July 14, 2010, http://www.visir.is/g/2010131785766. (accessed May 15, 2018).
[71] *visir.is* 'Fleiri matjurtagarðar í sumar', January 29, 2009, http://www.visir.is/g/2009178508607. (accessed May 15, 2018).
[72] Rannveig Karlsdóttir, 'Að prjóna saman samfélag: Hlutverk og gildi handverks eftir bankahrunið árið 2008' (MA Thesis in Ethnology, University of Iceland, 2014), https://skemman.is/bitstream/1946/17879/1/A%C3%B0%20prj%C3%B3na%20saman%20samf%C3%A9lag.pdf .
[73] Karlsdóttir, 'Að prjóna saman samfélag'.
[74] Umut Erel, 'Saving and reproducing the nation: Struggles around right-wing politics of social reproduction, gender and race in Austerity Europe', *Women's Studies International Forum* (in press). https://doi.org/10.1016/j.wsif.2017.11.003; and Nira Yuval-Davis, 'Women, Citizenship and Difference', *Feminist Review* 57 (1997): 4–27.

parties, both of which identified as feminist. Some women remained true to the collective and attempted to organize a run for parliament, with the caveat that they would first pressure the established parties to ensure equal representation of women and men.[75] The attempt fizzled and did not result in a women's list in the April 2009 elections.

It is true that the women's collective did not bring about a revolutionary change in the political system. However, offering a 'strategy for organizing,'[76] the collective's impetus on caring was transformational in the time of the crisis. It awakened a sense of care with the women who participated in it, and in the wider society. Political ambitions for the women's collective faltered, the focus on caring for each other and the community, which members perceived as needing support rather than a struggle, resulted in confidence building and trust towards one another. Through their organising and caring practices, women were able to rely on one another for support. The trust they built through care enabled many women to get by, emotionally and financially. By focusing their energy on constructive projects in the midst of a crisis, the women engaged their neighbours, colleagues and peers in a network to build a stronger and more cohesive community.

Concluding remarks

Our different case studies contribute to the discussions on everyday peace that argue against universally applicable schemas of peacebuilding, calling attention to the geopolitical, historical, and socio-cultural specificities of conflicts. We build upon a long tradition of feminist peace research that since the 1980s has examined how everyday practices of care give rise to alternative moral and political thinking, while feeding into alternative practices of conflict resolution. We argue that the care lens promoted by this tradition is pivotal for a fuller picture of the conditions and practices of peacebuilding within and across communal divides.

We show how different gendered forms of caring shape the political space in the midst of conflicts. In all the cases, relations of care emerge as a dynamic for processes of trust-building, community-building, and peaceful transformation. We began with an analysis of women's community groups' work in Northern Ireland. This case draws attention to the relational logic that led women from both sides of the conflict to take over several organisational tasks of care, when the state structures failed, and how these shared activities helped to breach inter-communal divides, creating spaces for everyday peace. Drawing attention to the care activities in Aceh carried out by men in patriarchal environments, we argue that regardless of the temptation to read such acts as instances of patriarchal governance, reading them as gendered care helps to understand how *different kinds of* caring relations work for everyday peace.

The case of Kashmir, in turn, illuminates the ways in which conflicts may foster inter- and intra-communal care relations amongst and within ethnic groups differentially affected by state-led violence. A shared place-based affiliation to *Kashmiriyat* encourages relations of care, which in turn create possibilities for peace and co-existence in an intensely strife

---

[75]*Morgunblaðið*, 'Verði þrýstiafl á stjórnvöld', March 14, 2014. https://www.mbl.is/frettir/innlent/2009/03/14/verdi_thrystiafl_a_stjornvold/. (accessed May 15, 2018).
[76]Tronto, *Moral Boundaries*, 175.

ridden zone. Post-financial crash Iceland would traditionally not be understood as a conflict. Yet, the shattered economy (re)produced gendered structural violence, overshadowed by the voices of (elite) men. To this, women responded by organising joint caring activities that contribute to a more stable and cohesive community.

These four cases exemplify, how feminist care ethics *as a theory of human relationality* adds to our understanding of everyday peace. This does not mean that care should be romanticised as eternally peaceful human activity, or that carers should be automatically read as peacemakers. Rather, caring, while embedded in gendered relations of power, continues to manifest itself beyond the intimate practices of caregiving. For better 'post-liberal' practices of peacebuilding, we argue that it is crucially important to read human relatedness and subjective action as practices of caring. Furthermore, understanding particular relations and practices of care as everyday peacebuilding helps us to better comprehend the localised and particular needs of people – that is, the everyday sources of suffering and deprivation – that must be responded with care, in order for trust and peaceful transformation to emerge.

Our suggestion to pay attention to care in peacebuilding, and account for the feminist peace research tradition, is fully compatible with most critical accounts of everyday peace. Indeed, we argue that the care lens complements critical peace studies in important ways. By resolving conflicts over immediate care needs and building the capacity of communities in ways that subtly challenge the fixity of conflict, care cumulatively creates possibilities for peaceful transformation. Therefore, it is crucially important to ask, not only in feminist accounts but in *all* contexts of peacebuilding: how care is present, what kind of care is present, and what particular relations of care do for everyday peace and the potential for transformation in conflict and post-conflict societies. If we do not address these questions, we cannot claim to understand, what it takes to sustain life during conflicts, and in their aftermath. For life does not go on without the varied gendered dimensions of care and caring.

Disclosure statement

No potential conflict of interest was reported by the authors.

Funding

The coauthoring of the article was made possible by NOS-HS Workshop Grant number [2015-00127]; for the establishment of Feminist Peace Research Network. In addition, Vaittinen's research was made possible by the Academy of Finland [grant number 297053]; and Kunz' research was supported by the Swiss Agency for Development and Cooperation and the Swiss National Science Foundation [grant number 400240].

ORCID

Tiina Vaittinen ⓘ http://orcid.org/0000-0002-8349-1487
Rahel Kunz ⓘ http://orcid.org/0000-0001-9275-9900
Silja Bára Ómarsdóttir ⓘ http://orcid.org/0000-0003-4478-4890
Sanam Roohi ⓘ http://orcid.org/0000-0002-2483-841X

From expert to experiential knowledge: exploring the inclusion of local experiences in understanding violence in conflict

Rachel Julian, Berit Bliesemann de Guevara and Robin Redhead

ABSTRACT
Critical peace and conflict scholars argue that to understand fully conflict dynamics and possibilities for peace research should incorporate 'the local'. Yet this important conceptual shift is bound by western concepts, while empirical explorations of 'the local' privilege outside experts over mechanisms for inclusion. This article explores how an epistemology drawing on feminist approaches to conflict analysis can help to redirect the focus from expert to experiential knowledge, thereby also demonstrating the limits of expert knowledge production on 'the local'. In order to illustrate our arguments and suggest concrete methods of putting them into research practice, we draw on experiences of the 'Raising Silent Voices' project in Myanmar, which relied on feminist and arts-based methods to explore the experiential knowledge of ordinary people living amidst violent conflict in Rakhine and Kachin states.

Introduction

Knowledge production about conflict, violence and peace matters. Accepted or shared knowledge creates reality by shaping the norms that define what we think of as conflict and by framing what we look for or expect to see in conflict analyses. Critical peace and conflict studies have drawn attention to this construction of 'truths' and have shown how different frames and interpretations may lead to competing problematisations of violent conflict, which differ with regard to questions about its origins, its root causes, who the perpetrators and victims of violence are, and what potential conflict solutions arise from these problematisations.[1] In the last two decades, different strands of research have highlighted the importance of 'the local'[2] in knowledge production

---

[1] Oliver Ramsbotham, Tom Woodhouse and Hugh Miall, *Contemporary Conflict Resolution*, 4th ed. (Cambridge: Polity Press, 2016); Peter Wallensteen, *Understanding Conflict Resolution*, 2nd ed. (London: Sage, 2007); Berit Bliesemann de Guevara and Roland Kostić, eds., *Knowledge and Expertise in International Interventions: The Politics of Facts, Truth and Authenticity* (London: Routledge, 2018).

[2] Thania Paffenholz, 'Unpacking the local turn in peacebuilding: a critical assessment towards an agenda for future research', *Third World Quarterly* 36, no. 5 (2015): 857–874; Thania Paffenholz, 'International peacebuilding goes local: analysing Lederach's conflict transformation theory and its ambivalent encounter with 20 years of practice', *Peacebuilding* 2, no. 1 (2014): 11–27; Timothy Donais, 'Empowerment or Imposition? Dilemmas of Local Ownership in Post-conflict Peacebuilding Processes, *Peace and Change* 34, no. 1 (2009): 3–26; Severine Autesserre, 'International Peacebuilding and the local success: assumptions and effectiveness', *International Studies Review* 19, no. 1 (2017): 1–19.

This is an Open Access article distributed under the terms of the Creative Commons Attribution-NonCommercial-NoDerivatives License (http://creativecommons.org/licenses/by-nc-nd/4.0/), which permits non-commercial re-use, distribution, and reproduction in any medium, provided the original work is properly cited, and is not altered, transformed, or built upon in any way.

about conflict. In the midst of all violent conflicts there are people who carry experiential conflict knowledge as a result of their lived experience of violence. Yet while many organisations, which intervene with projects designed to address the needs of people experiencing direct and indirect violence, acknowledge the centrality of 'the local' for protection and conflict transformation work,[3] the everyday experiences of those living amidst violent conflict are not always part of the conflict analysis processes that guide these projects. Often the scale and urgency to end violence and resolve conflict favour more traditional outsider-expert analyses that quickly identify overarching patterns over more time-consuming and messy analyses which include everyday experiences of those living amidst conflict.

In this article we argue that local people's experiences of conflict must be included in conflict analysis because, even in the context of time and resource constraints, these experiences enrich our understanding of conflict and improve peacebuilding and aid work. In this context, we use the notion of everyday (or everyday life) to describe the people's routine activities – assuring their livelihood, raising a family, being member of a community etc. – which in this case happen in and are shaped by sites and times of violent conflict. By experiential knowledge we mean ways of knowing, and stocks of knowledge, that are based on practice or being in a situation. It relies on listening to how those experiencing conflicts describe these knowledges. Finally, we use the adjective 'local' to include the people who are directly affected by a localised violent conflict, as combatants or civilians, but without disputing that localised violent conflicts usually have national and international causes and/or dimensions, which may not be explored fully through local experience.

We begin with an analysis of critical scholarly literature in peace and feminist studies to illuminate how the use of the category 'the local' has not led to an inclusion (beyond mere recognition) of experiential knowledge in conflict analyses. This enables us to critique the work of organisations who recognise the importance of 'the local', but whose epistemic practices lead to exclusions of local people's experiences from organisational knowledge production.

We then explore how a feminist epistemology helps to cherish the value of experiential knowledges in understanding violent conflict. A key finding here is that the everyday activities of those living with violent conflict give us different, more nuanced insights into the nature and complexity of a conflict, which complement in rich ways the interpretations by outsiders.

Finally, we draw on the example of the 'Raising Silent Voices' research project conducted between 2016 and 2018 in Myanmar to illustrate what an inclusive methodology for conflict analysis can look like in practice.

'The local' in conflict analysis and the privileging of expert knowledge

By directing the research focus away from global and national elites and processes in peacemaking, peacekeeping and peacebuilding, critical peace and conflict studies have over the

---

[3]Dylan Mathews, *War Prevention Works: 50 Stories of People Resolving Conflict* (Oxford: Oxford Research Group, 2001); European Centre for Conflict Prevention, *People Building Peace: 35 Inspiring Stories from Around the World* (Utrecht: European Centre for Conflict Prevention, 1999); John Paul Lederach, *Memoirs of Nepal: Reflections Across a Decade* (London: Blurb Books UK, 2015).

last two decades contributed greatly to a now almost common-sensical recognition of 'the local' into our thinking about conflict transformation. Different strands such as scholarly critiques of the liberal peace,[4] the rise of participatory analyses in development studies,[5] studies of civil society's role in peace and conflict,[6] and approaches that seek to rebalance power in terms of bottom-up peacebuilding,[7] or stress the importance of listening,[8] have all contributed to a general acceptance that scholars and practitioners working on peace and conflict must recognise 'local people'. Often, the latter are conceptualised as 'insiders'[9] and thus bearers of 'local knowledge', which is seen as crucial to understanding causes at different scales of a violent conflict and thus finding better tailored solutions.[10]

Yet, although 'the local' is now accepted as a crucial arena for scholarly scrutiny and governance action in the field of peace and conflict, the meaning and use of the term is contested and its usefulness for bringing 'local voices' into conflict analysis has been argued to be limited. For one, local actors and processes, and their relevance to the dynamics of violent conflict, are identified, classified and understood differently by different actors in both academia and practice, hinting at less clarity about the role of 'the local' in the transformation from war to peace than the rise of the concept might suggest.[11] More importantly for the argument of this article, scholars have also drawn on feminist and other traditions of critique to explore 'the local' within a context of multiple levels of engagement, hybridity and relationships to international policy.[12] What many of these observations and critiques of the use of the notion of 'the local' and related concepts amount to, is that 'the local' is an inherently western concept, which by its very virtue of claiming to recognise and include 'the other' pretends to be inclusive and non-hierarchical, while in reality reinforcing

---

[4]Roger Mac Ginty, *International Peacebuilding and Local Resistance: Hybrid Forms of Peace* (New York: Palgrave Macmillan, 2011); Oliver Richmond, 'Becoming Liberal, Unbecoming Liberalism: Liberal-Local Hybridity via the Everyday as a Response to the Paradoxes of Liberal Peacebuilding', *Journal of Intervention and Statebuilding* 3, no. 3 (2009): 324–44.

[5]David K. Leonard, 'Social Contracts, Networks and Security in Tropical African Conflict States: An Overview', *IDS Bulletin* 44, no. 1 (2013): 1–14.

[6]Thania Paffenholz, ed., *Civil Society and Peacebuilding: A Critical Assessment* (Boulder: Lynne Rienner, 2010), 65–78.

[7]John Paul Lederach, *Building Peace* (Washington: USIP, 1997).

[8]Tom Woodhouse and John Paul Lederach, *Adam Curle: Radical Peacemaker* (Stroud: Hawthorn Press, 2016).

[9]Reina C. Neufeldt, '"Frameworkers" and "Circlers" – Exploring Assumptions in Impact Assessment', in *Advancing Conflict Transformation: The Berghof Handbook II*, eds. B. Austin, M. Fischer and H.-J. Giessmann (Opladen and Farmington Hills, MI: Barbara Budrich, 2011).

[10]Severine Autesserre, *Peaceland: Conflict Resolution and the Everyday Politics of International Intervention* (New York: Cambridge University Press, 2014); Severine Autesserre, 'Going Micro: Emerging and Future Peacekeeping Research', *International Peacekeeping* 21, no. 4 (2014): 492–500.

[11]Conflict Sensitivity Consortium, *How to Guide to Conflict Sensitivity* (Conflict Sensitivity Consortium, February 2012); Hannah Reich, *Local Ownership in Conflict Transformation Projects* (Berlin: Berghof Centre, 2006); Carolyn Hayman, 'Local First in Peacebuilding', *Peace Review* 25, no. 1 (2013): 17–23. For different understandings of 'the local' in academia, compare e.g.: Autesserre, *Peaceland*; Autesserre, 'Going Micro'; Roger Mac Ginty, 'Indigenous Peace-Making versus the Liberal Peace', *Cooperation and Conflict* 43, no. 2 (2008): 139–63; Mac Ginty, *International Peacebuilding*; Oliver Richmond and Audra Mitchell, eds., *Hybrid Forms of Peace: From Everyday Agency to Post-Liberalism* (Basingstoke: Palgrave Macmillan, 2012).

[12]Laura McLeod, 'A Feminist Approach to Hybridity: Understanding Local and International Interactions in Producing Post-Conflict Gender Security', *Journal of Intervention and Statebuilding* 9, no. 1 (2015): 48–69; Nicole George, 'Institutionalising Women, Peace and Security in the Pacific Islands: Gendering the "architecture of entitlements"?' *International Political Science Review* 37, no. 3 (2016): 375–89; Hannah Partis-Jennings, 'The (In)Security of Gender in Afghanistan's Peacebuilding Project: Hybridity and Affect', *International Feminist Journal of Politics* 19, no. 4 (2017): 411–25; Laura Shepherd and Caitlin Hamilton, *Understanding Popular Culture and World Politics in the Digital Age* (London: Routledge, 2016); Hannah Partis-Jennings 'The "Third Gender" in Afghanistan: A feminist account of hybridity as a gendered experience' *Peacebuilding* 2019; Nicholas Lemay-Hebert and Stephanie Kappler, 'From power-blind binaries to the intersectionality of peace: connecting feminism and critical peace and conflict studies' *Peacebuilding* 2019.

entrenched power hierarchies and forms of exclusion.[13] This observation is of crucial importance when it comes to the inclusion of so-called 'local knowledge' or 'local voices' into conflict analyses with the aim to make these more relevant to the contexts in which peace research and peace work take place.

In particular, 'the local' is positioned and defined in relation to 'the international', thus reflecting (neo-)colonial attitudes and reproducing hierarchical ways of imagining international politics that are embedded in the type of conflict analysis that the critical peace and conflict studies literature seeks to critique.[14] Equally important, who or what constitutes 'the local' is defined, grouped and categorised externally and a priori. Such 'local' categories include, most prominently, women (of a specific locale or ethnic, religious, etc. group), youth (often understood as urban, violent, or unemployed), victims (e.g. of war atrocities, wartime sexual violence), ex-combatants, rural communities, or urban populations, which are all externally defined with no or little involvement of the thus-grouped (and often essentialised) individuals in the construction of these categories. Rather, the source of the categories are more often than not the international policy agendas they relate to and which drive not only peacebuilding planning – such as programmes for youth in peacebuilding, women-related programmes, or disarmament, demobilisation and reintegration programmes – but also much of our scholarly production of knowledge.[15]

Hence, although recognising 'the local' has undoubtedly led to a broader range of perspectives on the dynamics of violent conflict and opportunities for peace than the sole focus on the role of states and elites, which had dominated peace and conflict studies before, the problem with the 'local turn' is that the *recognition* of local actors is different from their *inclusion*. In terms of the quality of conflict analyses, this is a crucial point since it means that the privilege of outsider expertise has remained largely unchallenged despite the heightened attention to 'the local'. On the one hand, this relates to the politics of categorising discussed above. The inclusion (as opposed to mere recognition) of local experiences and knowledge requires a challenging of the power structures which construct the relationship 'international–local' and the categories within which the local is conceived and constructed, because it is this construction which gives power to outsiders and experts from the so-called 'international community'.[16]

On the other hand, a change from recognition to inclusion of the local must challenge experts' ideas of what constitutes knowledge and valid ways of knowing.

---

[13] Shahar Hameiri and Lee Jones, 'Beyond Hybridity to the Politics of Scale: International Intervention and "Local" Politics', *Development and Change* 48, no. 1 (2017): 54–77.

[14] Phillip Darby, 'Recasting Western Knowledges about (Postcolonial) Security', in *Rethinking Insecurity, War and Violence: Beyond Savage Globalisation*, eds. D. Grenfell and P. James (London: Routledge, 2009): 98–109; Philip Cunliffe, 'Still the Spectre at the Feast: Comparisons between Peacekeeping and Imperialism in Peacekeeping Studies Today', *International Peacekeeping* 19, no. 4 (2012): 426–42; Chandra Talpade Mohanty 'Under Western Eyes: Feminist Scholarship and Colonial Discourses' *Boundary 2* 12, no. 3 (1984), 333–58.

[15] See, for instance, United Nations Security Council Resolution 2250 (2015) on youth, peace and security; UN Women, *Preventing Conflict, Transforming Justice, Securing the Peace: A Global Study in the Implementation of the Global Study on the Implementation of the United Nations Security Council resolution 1325* (New York: UN Women, 2015); United Nations Disarmament, Demobilization and Reintegration Resource Centre, www.unddr.org (accessed June 9, 2018).

[16] Andreas T. Hirblinger and Claudia Simons, 'The Good, the Bad, and the Powerful: Representations of the "Local" in Peacebuilding', *Security Dialogue* 46, no. 5 (2015): 422–39; Heather L. Johnson, 'Narrating Entanglements: Rethinking the Local/Global Divide in Ethnographic Migration Research'. *International Political Sociology* 10, no. 4 (2016): 383–97.

Driven not least by donors' demands to evaluate projects and evidence impact,[17] outsider expertise that feeds into international and national aid organisations' conflict analyses and peacebuilding strategies builds on an (implicitly or explicitly) positivist understanding of knowledge and recognised knowledge production methods. These tend to privilege quantifiable data (e.g. household surveys) or written/spoken text (e.g. interviews, focus groups) over other forms. To ensure generalisability of findings, research often involves either large numbers of participants/data, or concentrates on individuals and organisations such as village leaders or community-based organisations, whose views are taken as representative of the larger category of 'local people' they are seen to represent. In short, expert knowledge about the local, albeit focusing more at a micro level, still looks for the universal rather than the particular and context specific knowledge about conflict and peace. Stemming from the organisational necessity to come to systematised findings[18] that can guide action that benefits the majority of people and does no harm, situated and embodied forms of knowledge usually do not figure in these reports, or are only incorporated in the form of illustrative single-case stories aimed to bring a broader (generalizable) point to life and/or to arouse empathy in the target audience.

Our findings, from reviewing Myanmar-related conflict analysis documents available publicly or from the project partner, confirm scholarly critiques that preconceived framings of 'the local' by 'outsiders' (researchers, consultants, experts) constrain their level of engagement. Even when they recognise the importance of 'the local' for comprehensive and meaningful knowledge production, outsiders approach conflict analyses with ways of categorising research participants and methods that seek to find the general in the particular, which limits the inclusion of the 'the local' because they are not always represented by the general.[19] This is not to say that international organisations do not aim to employ methodologies that capture local conflict dynamics as accurately as possible, while ensuring that their programmes address people's needs and do no harm to beneficiaries. Nonetheless, in the reports that were available to us, experiential knowledge was only considered in very few cases and only to inform broader patterns and conclusions, rather than speaking to the diversity and intersectionality in conflict experience, which may provide new, additional insights.

There is thus a gap in the way conflict analysis models and methods are constructed. There is no position, language or expectation on how the direct experience of people living in the midst of violent conflict can, or should, be included (rather than merely recognised) in the knowledge produced. This raises the question of what methodologies are available to capture the knowledge arising from the experience of living amidst violent conflict and feasible within the institutional context and constraints of conflict knowledge production by international peacebuilding and aid organisations.

---

[17]Rachel Julian, 'Is it for donors or locals? The relationship between stakeholder interests and demonstrating results in international development', *International Journal of Managing Projects in Business* 9, no. 3 (2016): 505–27.
[18]See for instance ActionAid, *Resource Pack on Systematization of Experiences* (The Hague: ActionAid, 2006).
[19]See Appendix A.

The importance of the everyday and personal experience in understanding peace and war is well established in feminist literature,[20] where peace is seen as an everyday mundane process.[21] Feminist scholars argue for the inclusion of 'voices' and life stories of people who experience war and violence in international politics, whereby they also highlight the importance of women and family in understanding peace and conflict. Our methodology of inclusion, inspired by feminist epistemologies,[22] ensures direct involvement of local people in the collection and dissemination of experiential knowledge. This provides a basis for extending the inclusion of local 'voices', experiences and life stories to conflict analysis.

Feminist epistemology and the analysis of violent conflict: experiential knowledge

A feminist epistemology asks why socially marginalised groups are absent from the design and conduct of research about them and seeks to transform those political practices that legitimate this exclusion.[23] This involves the inclusion of the researched in the research, revealing the power dynamics between researcher and researched and stressing the value of local knowledges or experiences.[24] It demands scrutiny of our own practices as scholars as well as a commitment to transformative politics.[25] Knowledge is understood as an intersubjective process, it is produced through encounters with others.[26] This means that knowledge is 'not just "out there", but the result of a particular engagement in a particular context as a continuous way of "becoming"',[27] highlighting the crucial role the researcher-researched relationship plays in (conflict) knowledge production – a role that is usually written out of conflict analyses.

---

[20]Sara Ruddick, *Maternal thinking: Toward a politics of peace* (The Women's Press, 1990); Elise Boulding, *Cultures of Peace: The Hidden Side of History* (New York: Syracuse University Press, 2000); Vivienne Jabri and Eleanor O'Gorman, *Women, Culture and International Relations* (Boulder: Lynne Rienner, 1999); Jo Woodiwiss, Kate Smith, and Kelly Lockwood, *Feminist Narrative Research: Opportunities and Challenges* (Palgrave Macmillan 2017); Catherine Baker, 'Veteran masculinities and audiovisual popular music in post-conflict Croatia: a feminist aesthetic approach to the contested everyday peace', *Peacebuilding* (2019).

[21]Tara Vayrynen, 'Mundane Peace and the politics of Vulnerability: A nonsolid feminist research agenda', *Peacebuilding* (2019); Tina Vaittinen, Amanda Donahuoe, Rachel Kunz, Silja Bara Omarsdottir and Sanam Roohi, 'Care as Everyday Peacebuilding', *Peacebuilding* (2019).

[22]Brooke Ackerly, Maria Stern and Jacqui True, *Feminist Methodologies for International Relations* (Cambridge: Cambridge University Press, 2006); Maria Eriksson Baaz and Maria Stern, 'Making sense of violence: voices of soldiers in the Congo (DRC)', *The Journal of Modern African Studies* 46, no. 1 (2008): 57–86; Maria Eriksson Baaz and Maria Stern, 'Fearless Fighters and Submissive Wives: Negotiating Identity among Women Soldiers in the Congo (DRC)', *Armed Forces and Society* 39, no. 4 (2012): 711–39; Carolyn Nordstrom, 'Global Fractures', *Social Analysis* 52, no. 2 (2008): 71–86; Carolyn Nordstrom, 'Women, Economy and War', *International Review of the Red Cross* 92, no. 877 (2010): 161–76.

[23]Marianne Janack, 'Standpoint epistemology without the "standpoint"? An examination of epistemic privilege and epistemic authority', *Hypatia* 12, no. 2 (1997): 125–39.

[24]Bat Ami Bar On, 'Marginality and Epistemic Privilege' in *Feminist Epistemologies*, eds. L. Alcoff and E. Potter (New York: Routledge, 1993), 83–100.

[25]Daphne Patai, 'U.S. Academics and Third World Women: Is Ethical Research Possible?', in *Women's Words: The Feminist Practice of Oral History*, eds. S.B. Gluck and D. Patai (New York: Routledge, 1991), 137–53.

[26]Liz Stanley and Sue Wise, 'But the empress has no clothes! Some awkward questions about the "missing revolution" in feminist theory', *Feminist Theory* 1, no. 3 (2000): 261–88.

[27]Tine Davids and Karin Willemse, 'Embodied engagements: Feminist ethnography at the crossing of knowledge production and representation – An introduction', *Women's Studies International Forum* 43 (2014): 2.

The feminist approaches we draw on highlight everyday experience as crucial to knowledge. Feminist ethnographies, for instance, consider the 'everyday' activities of people to show the complexities of local-global relations.[28] They 'listen to the unsaid'[29] in the everyday and produce 'sincere and reliable knowledge'.[30] The feminist approach accounts for embodied knowledge: how we make sense of the world based on our own experiences in it.[31] While experience is universal in the sense that we all experience everyday social reality, it is also personal in that it cannot be generalised or categorised by an external actor. It incorporates what is of central importance to the person having the experience, including the perceptions, narratives, myths and relationships that surround it. In much the same way that the study of practice challenges the norms of institutionalised politics, an understanding of the importance of everyday experience challenges the dominance of the outside expert in creating knowledge about conflict, violence and peace in several ways. Inspired by these insights of feminist methodologies,[32] underpinning the research agenda of 'Raising Silent Voices' was a strong commitment to developing and valuing experiential knowledge, which re-defined what counted as 'knowledge' in understanding conflicts.

Feminist approaches provide us with at least two reasons why including everyday experiences into our analyses of violent conflict enhances understanding. Firstly, experiences cannot be categorised by group (e.g. the experience of all women), but rather need to be treated as a set of narratives from which we can learn more and which may challenge the assumptions or systematising analyses of outsiders. Thus, understanding that there are different knowledges that emerge from lived experiences, and that all these experiences have value, is essential. This also means that not all specific or personal experiences can be represented solely by community leaders or civil society representatives. Civil society and community leaders are not interest-free conduits of knowledge, but their position is already a manifestation and a potential source of the power struggles in the conflict area. This is an important insight when considering that community and civil society leaders feature prominently in conflict analysis approaches, where these actors are often taken to be able to speak on behalf of those they represent. Feminist approaches remind us that we need many experiential knowledges in order to achieve a fuller picture, not all of which can be represented by 'local elites'.

Studying 'ordinary people' rather than starting with 'local elites' promises to unearth insights, knowledges and strategies that currently tend to remain hidden in conflict analysis which starts with outsider views. Indeed, what emerges from our research is that those who live amidst violence, seek to protect people, or create peace, are far from 'ordinary', but are courageous, creative and extraordinary people who have interwoven relationships and protection into their everyday lives in order to deal with the fears, insecurities and threats they face. Using a feminist conception of knowledge production opens up spaces to allow for different actors and actions to form part of the knowledge

---

[28] Isabel Dyck, 'Feminist geography, the "everyday", and local–global relations: hidden spaces of place-making', *The Canadian Geographer* 49, no. 3 (2005): 233–43.
[29] Paul Dresch and Wendy James, 'Fieldwork and the passage of time', in *Anthropologists in a Wider World: Essays on Field Research*, eds. P. Dresch, W. James and D. Parkin (New York: Berghahn Books, 2000), 122–25.
[30] Samar Kanafani and Zina Sawaf, 'Being, doing and knowing in the field: reflections on ethnographic practice in the Arab region', *Contemporary Levant* 2, no. 1 (2017): 4.
[31] Robin Redhead, *Exercising Human Rights: Gender, Agency, and Practice* (New York: Routledge, 2015).
[32] Woodiwiss, Smith and Lockwood, *Feminist Narrative Research*.

that is seen as valid in these circumstances. This may ultimately have a positive impact on everyday peace strategies, for when someone is recognised as an actor, they are empowered with the capability to act and with that comes recognition of the validity of their actions. In this idea of inclusion of local agency and people's everyday actions, we are not following the much debated 'participatory' models, which can reproduce hierarchies of power and expertise in their own right, but rather the idea of 'capacity recognition',[33] which begins with the understanding that people already have agency, that their actions have value and importance in the local context, and that people's everyday experiences based on these actions make them valuable holders of experiential knowledge that gives them the capacity to act knowingly (i.e. with an awareness of what they are doing). This form of empowerment-through-inclusion raises the significance of everyday activities to more than a local matter,[34] and writes them into the dominant narratives and practices of peacebuilding.

Secondly, experiences are important for conflict analyses because they are likely to defy any uncritical form of universal or generalizable narrative coherence. By their virtue, experiences are diverse, producing many knowledges. Including the diversity of experiences – including past, present and future thinking – into conflict analyses, reveals how people's varied interpretations and perceptions create a set of different knowledges, which all contribute to understanding the web of conflict and potentials for peace. People living amidst violent conflict know the significance of details – that it matters what they wear, which symbols are of importance in identifying allegiances, which routes, roads and paths are safe and at which times, who is aligned with whom, and how to find safe escape routes when necessary. They see conflict and violence in their many forms, and they also know what peace looks like. Especially for work in the areas of protection and conflict transformation, such experiential micro-insights are invaluable.

This leads us to the question of how to access experiential knowledge methodologically, without reproducing the power hierarchies inherent in outsider-expert knowledge production discussed above. While ethnographic approaches seem promising as a way of knowing experiences and are now used more frequently in peacebuilding studies,[35] Macaspac has shown that most of this ethnographic research still revolves around the experience of researchers from the Global North, thus perpetuating the outsider-expert view on conflict at the cost of a more meaningful inclusion of local experiential knowledge.[36] Furthermore, ethnography usually presupposes a longer-term engagement with 'the field' in which the ethnography takes place, thus making this methodology difficult to realise within the time and financial constraints of international organisations' project work. Critical peace and conflict studies scholars have provided some ideas on how to foreground the centrality of local people's knowledge and experiences (rather than that of the Northern researcher) in violent conflict and conflict

---

[33]'Capacity recognition' is one of the good practices of unarmed civilian protection (UCP) work that emerged from workshops organised by Nonviolent Peaceforce to capture UCP practitioners' experiences in different world regions when trying to protect other civilians from political violence.
[34]Dyck, 'Feminist geography, the "everyday", and local–global relations'.
[35]Gearoid Millar, *An Ethnographic Approach to Peacebuilding: Understanding Local Experiences in Transitional States* (London: Routledge, 2014); Adam Moore, *Peacebuilding in Practice: Local Experience in Two Bosnian Towns* (Ithaca: Cornell University Press, 2013); Autesserre, *Peaceland*; Autesserre, 'Going Micro'.
[36]Nerve Valerio Macaspac, 'Suspicion and Ethnographic Peace Research (Notes from a Local Researcher)', *International Peacekeeping* 25, no. 5 (2018): 677–94.

transformation. These include approaches based on reflective practice,[37] empowerment and emancipation through listening,[38] and patience and humility.[39] Lederach has used some of these approaches in his argument that some people in the midst of conflicts can become key catalysts and produce dramatic results, describing them as 'critical yeast', that is, people who are engaged in constant and growing 'web-weaving' (or building of relationships between people) to make them connected and stronger.[40] Ideas of reflexivity, listening, critical yeast and web-weaving all provide clues for how we can re-think peace and conflict studies in ways that give primacy to local experiences and overlap with feminist epistemology.

A shared insight is that revealing experiential knowledge requires research methods which involve trust and a recognition of the power or agency of the local everyday experience. Standard social science methods often find their limits when applied to topics that involve complex or strong experiences, emotions and/or cultural taboos and shame, which may resist objectification in language. For one, human knowledge constitutes more than just that which can be put into words, or as Polanyi writes about tacit knowledge: 'The fact that we can possess knowledge that is unspoken is of course a common-place and so is the fact that we must know something yet unspoken before we can express it in words.'[41] Furthermore, health and psychology research suggests that people may find it hard to voice traumatic or tabooed experiences, especially in front of others, or that they simply lack the words to describe how an experience makes them feel, to make the unheard and invisible heard.[42] Sexual violence, torture and other common conflict-related experiences are prone to fall into this category, but also situations that do not constitute an unspeakable issue in one culture (e.g. that of the aid worker) may resist direct reporting in the context of different cultural conventions and norms.[43] Methods to reveal experiential knowledge thus ideally need to create safe space for sharing and provide tools that empower people to do so.[44]

Exploring experiential knowledge also involves revealing and working to mitigate power relations between researcher and researched, since the use of methods that do not challenge power would risk perpetuating the norms created by 'external experts' and encourage local people to 'just tell you want they think you want to know'. Therefore, overcoming the shortfalls of outsider/expert methods is the task of studies that try to include experiential knowledges of ordinary people living amidst violent

---

[37]John Paul Lederach, Reina Neufeldt and Hal Culbertson, *Reflective Peacebuilding: A Planning, Monitoring, and Learning Toolkit* (London: International Alert, 2007).
[38]Woodhouse and Lederach, *Adam Curle*.
[39]John Paul Lederach, 'Keynote address at Adam Curle' (Adam Curle Symposium, Bradford University, Bradford, 5-6 September 2016).
[40]John Paul Lederach, *The Moral Imagination: The Art and Soul of Building Peace* (Oxford: Oxford University Press, 2005); Lederach, *Memoirs of Nepal*.
[41]Michael Polanyi, 'Sense-giving and Sense-reading', *Philosophy* 42, no. 162 (1967): 306; cf. also Michael Polanyi, *The Tacit Dimension* (Chicago: The University of Chicago Press, 1966).
[42]Marilys Guillemin, 'Understanding Illness: Using Drawings as a Research Method', *Qualitative Health Research* 14, no. 2 (2004): 272–89; Louis Tinnin, 'Biological Processes in Nonverbal Communication and Their Role in the Making and Interpretation of Art', *American Journal of Art Therapy* 29 (1990): 9–13.
[43]An example discussed in the aforementioned UCP workshops organised by NP is the under-reporting of violent incidences in refugee and IDP camps in the Middle East due to the shame male heads of family feel vis-à-vis their inability to protect their families.
[44]This includes recognising the risk of re-traumatisation by re-living experiences. In the next section we explain the steps taken during our 'Raising Silent Voices' project to give control to the people sharing their experiences in order to reduce the risk.

conflict. In 'Raising Silent Voices' we have developed a methodology that achieves inclusion. It is to this we will now turn.

Applying an experiential knowledge methodology to violent conflict in Myanmar

'Raising Silent Voices' is an Arts and Humanities Research Council UK (AHRC) project, funded under the AHRC's Partnership for Conflict, Crime and Security Research (PaCCS) programme. Its project partner is the Myanmar office of Nonviolent Peaceforce (NP), an international non-profit organisation working 'to promote and implement unarmed civilian protection as a tool for reducing violence and protecting civilians in situations of violent conflict'.[45] One of the project's main objectives is to explore how local experiential knowledge can be accessed and incorporated into the conflict analysis and protection work of its partner organisation. Our interest as researchers is in understanding the way in which the roles and tasks of civilians who protect other civilians are influenced by their everyday life and experiences, and how they use their experiential knowledge in their community and protection work. Building on Rachel Julian's previous work with Nonviolent Peaceforce, we know that civilian peacekeepers hold knowledge which is not captured in 'normal reporting mechanisms'.

Our methodology investigating this experiencing knowledge challenges the conventional researcher-researched relationship because it moves the 'expert' role to include those who live in, and experience, conflict and violence. Our approach to inclusion is understanding that it is the local people's choice to share their experiences, and it is the local people's direct involvement, rather than being represented, which defines it as inclusive. We begin with listening to local people and reflecting back to them their stories so they can analyse their own practice. This form of experiential knowledge production can then feed into expert knowledges increasing the rigour and efficacy of conflict analysis.

In the remainder of this article we show how we explored three different ways through which to turn the general principles of this research into research practice. Firstly, the involvement of Burmese research associates throughout the design and activity of the fieldwork; secondly, conversations with Yangon-based artists and peace activists as a 'different' initial entry point to conflict knowledges; and thirdly, the use of arts-based workshops as a sensitive and non-intrusive method to access experiential knowledge of ordinary people living in two violent conflict areas of Myanmar.

Working with Burmese research associates

Our first research strategy was to work with Burmese research associates. Beyond practical necessity, there was a strong epistemological reason for our choice to work closely with Burmese research associates, since we hoped that their involvement would help challenge the power relationships that exist in the collection of information that creates knowledges. The practical reasons were the need for translation and (cultural) interpretation given our lack of Burmese language knowledge; time and budget constraints both of our own research project and of our partner organisation Nonviolent Peaceforce; and most importantly

---

[45]Nonviolent Peaceforce website: http//www.nonviolentpeaceforce.org/ (accessed June 9, 2018).

Myanmar authorities' access restrictions for foreigners to the conflict zones we were interested in. The three persons (S, B and R) we worked with in this project were initially contacted through personal networks of our core research team in an organic and iterative manner. All three live in Yangon but come from different parts of Myanmar: S is a female Arakanese Buddhist entrepreneur from Rakhine state in western Myanmar, B a female artist from Myanmar's southeast region bordering Thailand, and R identifies as a male Christian of Kachin ethnicity from Northern Shan state on the border with China. All three areas of origin are conflict zones, and Kachin and Rakhine state also constituted the two areas in addition to Yangon where our research took place.

S, B and R's initial role was to facilitate our research conversations with artists and peace activists in Yangon. But through discussion and identification of shared values in the objectives of the research our initial facilitators soon became partners in the research and we built more long-standing friendships with them. The involvement of local people as part of the researcher team in collecting data is not unproblematic. As Macaspac has shown, despite their cultural understanding and language familiarity, local researchers may not be seen as 'neutral', and their interrogations may create risks for them and turn them into objects of suspicion.[46] Aware of these risks, we worked together to ensure their safety, and the safety of research participants. The three Burmese research associates brought an insider understanding of the places, cultures and histories our research addressed, a deep care about people which was visible in their respective own charitable and activist work, and an existing commitment to understanding more about conflict, violence and peace that arose out of their own interest in, and family experiences with, violent conflict. By working with S, B and R, we co-created the drawing workshop method in a culturally acceptable (if in part a little unusual) way enabling them to express and share their experiences. The implementation of our drawing workshops by the Myanmar researchers (the international researchers chose not to attend the workshops) helped challenge the power hierarchies between researchers and researched, and showed that it is possible to produce 'sincere and reliable knowledge' in 'local-local' conversations.

To achieve this co-design of the drawing workshops, we deliberately tried not to control the process. The Myanmar researchers had the decision-making roles in the arts workshops. They chose the venue and appropriate levels of staffing for logistics and cooking, contacted potential participants and arranged travel, and had all communication with the participants. The researchers from the UK and USA each made a video about themselves and their life stories, which were translated and shown at each workshop. We had an 'always available' communication approach using email, WhatsApp and social media to provide support and advice where needed and wanted, but without aiming to control or steer the research process from afar. We also tried to give the Myanmar researchers the budget responsibility for the workshops but they declined, so we managed the overall accounts based on their good bookkeeping. In addition to the actual workshops, we developed friendships which includes sharing aspects of our daily lives, offering support to challenges beyond the project and continuing to meet when travel plans meant we could overlap.[47]

---

[46]Macaspac, 'Suspicion and Ethnographic Peace Research'.
[47]While overall the collaboration between our western team and the Burmese research associates worked well, the process was not without frictions and occasional misunderstandings. See Katarina Kušić, 'Interpretation by Proxy? Interpretive Fieldwork with Local Associates in Areas of Restricted Research Access', in *Doing Fieldwork in Areas of*

Choosing a non-standard entry point to the field

Our second research strategy was to choose an entry point for our exploratory conversations that would not fall into the trap of outsider experts' preconceived (social-scientific or other) categories. To this effect, rather than visit international NGOs, government officials or academics, we started our research in Myanmar by visiting art galleries, monks, former political prisoners, small businesses, film makers and musicians in Yangon. We had conversations with them about their lives and how they understood the conflicts and peace process in their country. Our conversation partners talked about the transition from military rule (and in the case of an older man even British colonial rule) to the current democracy, and both the opportunities and problems that emerged from it, what they had learned, and how their experiential knowledge informed their actions now. Although these persons were in some ways the city elite in cosmopolitan Yangon, their insights into how their own knowledge about conflicts and peace in Myanmar had been formed demonstrated the diversity of understandings and knowledges about the conflicts.

From these open-ended conversations we realised that some ideas re-occurred, for example, challenges of the changing identity of the majority Burman population group as an 'ethnic' group, and the lack of self-identification as Burman, which contrasted with conflict analyses that conceptualise the Burmans as the largest among over 120 ethnic groups in the country. Another reoccurring insight was the complexity of identity in Rakhine state which stands in contrast to some outsider analyses which tend to concentrate on a simplified antagonism between Buddhist Arakanese and Muslim Rohingya as the major conflict line. These initial conversations showed that the experiences of people living in and coming from different parts of Myanmar would reveal important nuances and insights about conflicts and peace. Examples of other topics that were brought up as part of understanding the conflicts were i) the persecution of IDPs including being isolated and cut off, moved between camps, lacking education, and high levels of fear, ii) the constitution, iii) the limited education system including how it is uncritical and not available equally to everyone, iv) the treatment of political prisoners, and v) the lack of clear and open communications, and the extent to which many are still not aware of the conflicts and violence in other parts of the country.[48]

The stories from the personal experiences provide insights into the complexity of the relationship between identity, politics, social structures and violent conflicts in Myanmar and conflicts driven by narratives that are familial, generational, political, social and personal. The personal transformations that people experienced as they challenged the antagonising narratives that they had previously internalised were highly significant in forming their political and social views, which in turn informed their actions for positive change.

International Intervention: A Guide to Research in Violent and Closed Contexts, ed. B. Bliesemann de Guevara and M. Bøås (Bristol: Bristol University Press, forthcoming); Berit Bliesemann de Guevara, Ellen Furnari, and Rachel Julian, 'Researching with Local Associates: Power, Trust and Data in a Project on Communities' Conflict Knowledge in Myanmar' (forthcoming).

[48]These topics are explored more fully in our presentations and papers about the findings, and are included here as examples of how the local knowledges produced a range of influences on the conflicts.

Using an arts-based method to explore peoples' experiences

Our third research strategy consisted of two drawing workshops in Myitkyina (Kachin) and Mrauk U (Rakhine), with participants from a variety of ethnic groups in Kachin and Rakhine states. The co-designed arts workshops were for those experiencing violent conflict where they would have the time, space and support to communicate, through metaphor-centred drawing, their experiences and life stories, how they saw the conflicts, and their ideas of what peace would be like for them, their families and communities.

The arts workshops were residential, and inspired by DrawingOut, a method developed in health-related research of minority groups.[49] DrawingOut uses metaphor-centred drawing as a way to prompt and elicit participants' ideas and stories and is able to mitigate the limits and disadvantages of standard data collection methods. The method works without preconceived frames and categories, and allows people to express experiences that might reject objectification in language. Metaphors are central to this method as they allow for the use of tangible imagery (e.g. things, animals, persons, or situations) to express something intangible such as feelings or thoughts. The three-day workshops in Kachin and Rakhine states allowed time to create safe space and trust for discussion and using arts enabled participants to control the speed, timescale, and boundary of their stories, thereby reducing as much as possible pressures to re-visit traumatic experiences. The workshops included spaces where participants could step outside the drawing activities and sit quietly or talk with others.

Our drawing method helped shift the starting-point of analysis from concepts and categories to the meanderings of lived experience. The feedback suggests, for instance, that the workshops enabled an equality of participants and their stories during the workshop. For example, about the Rakhine workshop, one of the facilitators said:

> In Rakhine, the majority tribe [Arakanese Buddhists] could listen to the minority tribe's [Mro] story, and also the educated man (a lawyer) had time to listen to very poor villagers of the Chin-Rakhine sub-tribe from the mountain – they had a chance to listen to each other, it was great and very interesting for the participants.[50]

B also reported the following workshop conversation, which hints at the workshop as a positive experience for participants beyond the immediate research aims, so research through arts is a potentially more respectful way of engaging with 'the local':

> I want to talk about something that really pleased me. There was a participant, a Christian from a very small minority group who is a Christian priest who works at a church. Recently there was a cyclone [in Rakhine], it caused flood and that destroyed his crop of betel, all the trees were gone, he had no money. He had some children schooling in the city who called him for some money, and his wife was complaining to him as well about the lack of money. He was very unhappy [...] at home. During the workshop in Rakhine, there was background music, and the man commented: "The first day I was boiling, they second day I became stable, now I am calm. I really liked the music while I was drawing".[51]

---

[49] Sofia Gameiro, Berit Bliesemann de Guevara, Alida Payson and Elisabeth El Refaie, 'DrawingOut – An innovative drawing workshop method to support the generation and dissemination of research findings', *PLoS ONE* 13, no. 9 (2018): e0203197.
[50] Skype conversation with B, research associate and workshop facilitator for Raising Silent Voices, 15 July 2017.
[51] Ibid.

Although the workshops had not been intended to provide a therapeutic space for participants – after all none of the team members were qualified to do any form of counselling – this story indicates how research methodologies can play a role in providing a space for people to actually 'raise their voice'. A Kachin workshop participant confirmed this when saying in a group discussion of the artwork:

> Let me speak in Jin Phaw Language. I had many things that I was afraid of, because of family, because of environment, because of war. So many things that I am afraid of. I fully participated in yesterday's discussion and what I reflected myself was that I had never had a chance to express things inside my mind. Now I have got the chance to express and it makes me feel something, I feel I have got something [positive].[52]

In this sense, the arts-based workshops and opportunities to realise tacit knowledge and bring it into a tangible form through drawing did seem to be of benefit to at least some participants. Not least, these experiences also had a profound effect on our local research associates, with B voicing a strong desire to become a healer, using art to help communities in her country.[53]

Conclusion

In this article we have argued that it is both desirable and possible to include the experiential knowledge of people living their daily lives amidst violence into understandings of conflicts. We first discussed that, despite the recognition of the importance of 'the local' and 'the everyday' in critical peace and conflict studies, the experiential knowledge of those people who live in the midst of violent conflict has been largely excluded. Far from this being a conscious disregard for local experiential knowledge, the demands of western academia and dominant ideas about objective and scientific truths predicated by the demands of 'white researchers', whose experiences remain a benchmark, have contributed to this.[54]

In the second part of this article, we have drawn on feminist approaches and epistemologies to argue that the inclusion of local experiential knowledge is desirable. There are three main points. The first is that an inclusion of lived experiences helps us avoid essentialising categorisations of 'local people' into specific groups or types of 'locals'. Secondly, a concentration on 'local elites', such as community or civil society leaders, bears the danger of privileging their representations at the potential cost of the experiences and aspirations of those whose voices are silenced by the violence. And thirdly, we have highlighted that a focus on the everyday experiences of local people helps reveal the 'small things' that may be crucial in navigating violence and building peace, and which are best accessed through explorations of lived experiences. We acknowledge that critical peace and conflict scholars have developed ideas of how to incorporate feminist approaches to power, experience and knowledge creation, for instance, by using 'collaborative and

---

[52] Male participant, drawing workshop in Kachin state, 25–27 May 2017.
[53] Skype conversation with B, research associate and workshop facilitator for Raising Silent Voices, 15 July 2017.
[54] Macaspac, 'Suspicion and Ethnographic Peace Research'.

practice-based inquiry' to produce knowledge 'in dialogue with' beneficiaries.[55] The more far-reaching approach we are suggesting here is that, rather than being beneficiaries of a project, ordinary people living amidst violent conflict may be key actors whose manifold, sometimes contradictory experiential knowledges need to be accessed in order to inform meaningful bottom-up strategies for protection from violence.

In the last section of the article we have then tried to demonstrate that accessing local experiential knowledge is possible even where time and resources are limited. Drawing on feminist epistemology and principles of trustfulness and empowerment in research relationships for the design of our research we have given three examples of what such methods could look like and which kinds of insights can be gained from them – not to substitute, but to complement more structural analyses. The feminist and critical peace studies literatures cited throughout this article provide many more ideas of how experiential knowledge could be brought into conflict analyses and to what benefit. For all these methods, the link between trust and what can be known is crucial. Our own research experience is that conversational and arts-based approaches such as (but by no means limited to) our drawing workshops, in conjunction with local research collaborations in which outsider researchers are prepared and willing to let go of the control over the data collection process, seem particularly well suited to create the trustful space needed to explore the experiential side of our knowing even in rather short-term encounters between researchers and researched. We hope that our insights and experiences encourage others to keep exploring the range of possibilities for how to shift from expert to experiential knowledge in understanding violence in conflict.

Acknowledgments

This work was supported by the Arts and Humanities Research Council (AHRC) under Grant AH/N008464/1. We are grateful to the guest editors of this special issue, Dr. Laura McLeod and Dr. Maria O'Reilly, to 'Raising Silent Voices' project researcher Dr. Ellen Furnari, and to two thorough and constructive peer-reviewers for their very helpful comments on earlier versions of this article.

Disclosure statement

No potential conflict of interest was reported by the authors.

Funding

This work was supported by the Arts and Humanities Research Council (GB) [AH/N008464/1].

---

[55]Philipp Lottholz, 'Critiquing Anthropological Imagination in Peace and Conflict Studies: From Empiricist Positivism to a Dialogical Approach in Ethnographic Peace Research', *International Peacekeeping*, online first (July 2017), doi:10.1080/13533312.2017.1350576.

ORCID

Rachel Julian http://orcid.org/0000-0003-4766-777X

Appendix A

We reviewed the following reports: Advisory Commission on Rakhine State, *Towards a peaceful, fair and prosperous future for the people of Rakhine: Final Report of the Advisory Commission on Rakhine State* (Advisory Commission on Rakhine State, August 2017); Burma News International (BNI), *Deciphering Myanmar's Peace Process: A Reference Guide*, several annual editions (Chiang Mai, Thailand: BNI, 2013–2017); Centre for Peace and Conflict Studies (CPCS), *Building Relationships across Divides: Peace and Conflict Analysis of Kachin State, 2016* (Siem Reap, Cambodia: CPCS, 2016); Centre for Peace and Conflict Studies (CPCS), *Listening to Communities – Karen (Kayin) State, Myanmar* (Siem Reap, Cambodia: CPCS, 2014); Centre for Peace and Conflict Studies (CPCS), *We want genuine peace: Voices of communities from Myanmar's ceasefire areas* (Siem Reap, Cambodia: CPCS 2016); Durable Peace Programme Consortium, *Durable Peace Programme Baseline Report* (Yangon: Oxfam, June 2016); Stephen Gray and Josefine Roos, *Intercommunal Violence in Myanmar: Risks and Opportunities for International Assistance* (Adapt Research and Consulting, April 2014); International Crisis Group (ICG), *Myanmar: A New Muslim Insurgency in Rakhine State*, Report 283 (Yangon/Brussels: International Crisis Group: 2016); International Crisis Group (ICG), *Buddhism and State Power in Myanmar*, Report 290 (Yangon/Brussels: International Crisis Group: 2017); Nonviolent Peaceforce, *Conflict Analysis Kayin State* (non-public document, Yangon: Nonviolent Peaceforce, 2014); Relief Action Network for IDP and Refugee (RANIR), *Community-led Peacebuilding in Kachin State: Findings and Recommendations* (Laiza, Kachin State: RANIR, 2016); Josefine Roos, *Conflict Assessment in Rakhine State* (consultancy report for anonymous organisations, February/March 2013); Saferworld, *A Community-led Approach to Conflict Sensitivity in Myanmar* (London: Saferworld, 2016); The Border Consortium, *Protection and Security Concerns in South East Burma/Myanmar* (Bangkok: The Border Consortium, 2014).

Veteran masculinities and audiovisual popular music in post-conflict Croatia: a feminist aesthetic approach to the contested everyday peace

Catherine Baker

ABSTRACT
In Croatia, campaigners for a more critical public reckoning with the memory of Croatia's 'Homeland War' (1991–5) and the national past confront embeddings of hegemonic myths of the war into everyday life. Among these are the stardom of a musician whose 'patriotic' music claims the same moral authority as the Croatian veterans' movement and whose public persona has embodied militarised masculinity since he became a wartime star. Popular music and youth engagement with it is thus among the sites where everyday understandings of peace are being contested. By exploring the audiovisual aesthetics of the song/video through which this musician re-engaged with veterans' activism in 1998, and showing that popular music spectatorship seeps into the everyday micropolitics of young people building and contesting peace, the paper argues that for critical peace and conflict studies to understand the affective politics of post-conflict masculinities, they must combine a feminist and aesthetic consciousness.

In summer 2018, not for the first time, Croatia's most contentious public figure was a musician. The controversy over Marko Perković Thompson's appearance at an open-air reception welcoming the Croatian men's football team home from the World Cup was intense enough to be reported internationally, but similar incidents have surrounded his high-profile public performances since the early 2000s, when left-wing journalists started problematising his appeal to youth.[1] Both critical and feminist peace and conflict studies (PCS), which now readily acknowledge the 'everyday' dimensions of peace,[2] should be equipped to understand moments like these as public contestations of peace from which they can learn – but even though they have drawn on 'visual' and 'aesthetic' turns in international theory to show how creative expression and participation might contribute to peacebuilding, they have largely been slower to understand the pleasures and meanings of popular culture and entertainment as part of the everyday peace. Nevertheless, popular culture is a significant site for youth engagement with gendered understandings of peace, conflict and the wartime past, including the phenomenon this paper explores in popular music: invitations to identify with veteran

---

[1] Ana Brakus, 'Neka prati koga smeta', *Novosti*, 27 July 2018, https://www.portalnovosti.com/neka-prati-koga-smeta (accessed October 5, 2018).
[2] See Vaittinen, Donahoe, Keane, Kunz, Ómarsdóttir and Roohi, this issue.

masculinities. The process of producing hegemonic veteran masculinities in Croatia began in the 1990s but continues into the present, where youth encounter them today. Through one case study of the construction of veteran masculinity in popular music, this paper asks what the affective politics of such identifications might be and why this matters in the everyday peace. The answer, it argues, requires an aesthetic consciousness that appreciates how sound, language, audiovisual images and embodied personas work together in popular music to produce meaning, and also how spectatorship of audiovisual material and live performance seeps into young people's everyday.

Today, as a post-conflict society, Croatia exemplifies a nation where young people grow up surrounded by the mythology of a war they did not witness. The incidents and audiovisual texts in this paper all exist within the context of a hegemonic 'mythic interpretation' of the 1991–5 Croatian war of independence (known in Croatia as the 'Homeland War'), embedded into everyday life through political discourse, media and education.[3] Croatian anthropologists have already called attention to contemporary Croatian nationalism's distinctive visual culture, and to how hegemonic narratives of national identity and history have permeated everyday media (including popular music). Their work illustrates how the processes Cynthia Enloe terms 'militarization' operated during and after wartime.[4] Amid political consensus that the war represented the fulfilment of the nation's sovereignty and the righteousness of its fight for freedom against an anti-democratic enemy aggressor, right-wing intellectuals and bishops defend their own ethnonationalist and religious discursive complex. This defence combines integralist nationalism, disavowal of the idea Croats could have committed war crimes in a defensive war, and readiness to rehabilitate the history and insignia of the collaborationist Independent State of Croatia (NDH) of 1941–5 as a patriotic ideology under attack from the Left. Popular culture, particularly popular music (and its interdependent relationship with national sporting institutions),[5] makes this position available to Croatian youth today. These young people have grown up in an education system which, human rights activists argue, does not equip them to think critically about the past or resist ethnonationalist politics of victimhood.[6]

From a feminist perspective, the central place of soldiers and veterans in Croatia's post-conflict historical mythology, and this mythology's conflation of veterans with masculinity (erasing 23,080 women veterans), makes struggles about the Homeland War in public culture inherently struggles over post-conflict masculinities as well.[7] In the study of disarmament, demobilization and reintegration programmes, conflict transformation, sexualised violence, and even implementations of the 'liberal peace', PCS recognises contestations of post-conflict masculinities as an important theme.[8] In Croatia, such struggles

---

[3] Dejan Jović, *Rat i mit: politika identiteta u suvremenoj Hrvatskoj* (Zagreb: Fraktura, 2017), 19, 32.
[4] Lada Čale Feldman, Ines Prica and Reana Senjković, eds., *Fear, Death and Resistance: an Ethnography of War: Croatia, 1991–1992* (Zagreb: IEF, 1993); Reana Senjković, *Lica društva, likovi države* (Zagreb: IEF, 2002). See Cynthia Enloe, *Globalization and Militarism: Feminists Make the Link* (Lanham, MD: Rowman and Littlefield, 2007).
[5] See Dario Brentin, 'Ready for the Homeland?: Ritual, Remembrance and Political Extremism in Croatian Football', *Nationalities Papers* 44, no. 6 (2016): 860–76, 873.
[6] Snježana Koren and Branislava Baranović, 'What Kind of History Education Do We Have after Eighteen Years of Democracy in Croatia?: Transition, Intervention, and History Education Politics (1990–2008)', in *'Transition' and the Politics of History Education in Southeast Europe*, ed. Augusta Dimou (Göttingen: V&R Unipress, 2009), 91–140.
[7] See Oliwia Berdak, 'Reintegrating Veterans in Bosnia and Herzegovina and Croatia: Citizenship and Gender Effects', *Women's Studies International Forum* 49 (2015): 48–56, 55.
[8] See Naomi Cahn and Fionnuala Ní Aoláin, 'Gender, Masculinities and Transition in Conflicted Societies', *New England Law Review* 44, no. 1 (2009): 1–24.

extend into popular music and its everyday reception. Thompson, the patriotic musician whom Croatian media has done most to produce as a celebrity, owes his stage-name to the rifle he carried as a wartime volunteer, thus his star persona makes the identities of musician and soldier/veteran inextricable. His debut hit in spring 1992, 'Bojna Čavoglave' ('The Čavoglave platoon', named after his home village in the Dalmatian hinterland),[9] was famously written at the front, and his veteran identity remains the foundation of his authority for moral claims about Homeland War memory, veterans' treatment, and present-day Croatia's social order.[10] Alongside public commemoration and veterans' sociopolitical activism, patriotic popular music is thus one more vector of militarisation in post-conflict Croatian society.

The institutionalised privileging of veterans' social identities and historical narratives in post-conflict societies, and the implications for peace when politicised veteran masculinities are made into common-sense national cultural archetypes, already concern critical and feminist peace and conflict researchers[11] – even though PCS has rarely appreciated that popular culture, including popular music, is a site of everyday contestation over veteran masculinities too.[12] Feminist security studies, meanwhile, offers important methodological tools for interpreting gendered narratives of politics, security and violence within popular culture, including Laura Shepherd's methodology for recognising such narratives in serial television through discourse analysis of spoken language, body language and non-linguistic signifiers.[13] This paper's methodology for audiovisual analysis builds on Shepherd but follows the music video scholar Andrew Goodwin in emphasising the juxtaposition of sound, language, embodied performance and moving images, plus the meta-text of stars' personas, as distinctive sources of audiovisual musical meaning.[14] Both these forms of meaning in general, and the affective politics of veteran masculinities in popular culture specifically, have so far been underappreciated even as PCS has taken its aesthetic turn.

Aesthetic approaches to the everyday in peace and conflict studies

PCS has already begun displaying an aesthetic consciousness as part of theorising peace and peacebuilding in the everyday. International theory's 'aesthetic turn', and resultant engagements with visual politics and embodied experience, gained pace in the late 2000s alongside critical peacebuilding research theorising the 'post-liberal' peace: in 2010, Oliver Richmond was already suggesting '[Roland] Bleiker's work on emotion and aesthetics' among the analytical tools that could help reveal 'the everyday' in the local contexts that critical peacebuilding scholars were arguing liberal theorists had failed to

---

[9]For background on veteran masculinities and religious nationalism in the Dalmatian hinterland, see: Michaela Schäuble, *Narrating Victimhood: Gender, Religion and the Making of Place in Post-War Croatia* (New York: Berghahn, 2014). Perković is his family name; 'Thompson' does not imply Anglophone descent.
[10]Marko Stojanovska Rupčić, 'Songs That Sound "Right"', in *Gender and Far Right Politics in Europe*, ed. Michaela Köttig, Renate Bitzan and Andrea Pető (London: Palgrave Macmillan, 2017), 289–303.
[11]E.g., Janine Natalya Clark, 'Giving Peace a Chance: Croatia's *Branitelji* and the Imperative of Reintegration', *Europe–Asia Studies* 65, no. 10 (2013): 1931–53; and Berdak, 'Reintegrating Veterans'.
[12]Though see Lesley Pruitt, 'Real Men Kill and a Lady Never Talks Back: Gender Goes to War in Country Music', *International Journal of World Peace* 24, no. 4 (2007): 85–106.
[13]Laura J. Shepherd, *Gender, Violence and Popular Culture: Telling Stories* (London: Routledge, 2013), 8–9.
[14]Andrew Goodwin, *Dancing in the Distraction Factory: Music, Television and Popular Culture* (Minneapolis, MN: University of Minnesota Press, 1992).

appreciate.[15] The aesthetics of sympathy produced through visual representations of suffering are a major theme in critical studies of humanitarianism and development, with which international peacebuilding interventions are often entangled.[16] The connections between emotion and visuality drawn by scholars like Emma Hutchison likewise help demonstrate how aesthetic techniques mobilise affects of empathy, compassion and solidarity[17] – important for motivating humanitarian donors through spectatorship, and also for engaging participants in everyday forms of arts-based peacebuilding.[18]

Arts-based peacebuilding is, indeed, where PCS engages aesthetics most directly. One relatively early study of arts-based peacebuilding suggested arts were marginalised in peacebuilding 'because they are seen as "soft" approaches (within an already "soft" field) to the "hard" issues of conflict and violence.'[19] Such marginalisation of aesthetic ways of knowing and feeling across a 'soft'/'hard' boundary is, of course, an implicitly gendered way of bounding a discipline, feminising and devaluing the 'soft'.[20] A growing number of studies of arts-based peacebuilding suggest that participatory artistic and cultural initiatives in post-conflict societies are spaces which can foster everyday empathy for those who were on other sides of the conflict, or where alternative narratives to hegemonic post-conflict nationalism, militarism and sectarianism can exist. These can include theatre and music projects staged in conflict zones or remediating survivors' experiences,[21] performance art,[22] murals,[23] community quilts,[24] and arts scenes where creators and audiences renegotiate the meanings of peace and legitimacy in ways the formal, ethnonationalistically-structured political sphere does not permit.[25] Even some mass-mediated popular culture, Siobhan McEvoy-Levy argues for contemporary English-language Young Adult fiction, potentially engages audiences in a 'politics of peace'.[26] Indeed, she and Helen Berents have suggested that aesthetic understandings of the everyday have particular insights to offer into the experiences and agency of young people, whose 'practices of resistance, rebellion and socio-political invention' in post-conflict societies are their own kind of responses to the liberal peace: '[h]ow', they ask, 'is peace conceptualised and/or hidden in the narratives [...] that young people both create [...] and embrace[?]'[27]

---

[15]Oliver P. Richmond, 'Resistance and the Post-Liberal Peace', *Millennium* 38, no. 3 (2010): 675. See Roland Bleiker, *Aesthetics and World Politics* (Basingstoke: Palgrave Macmillan, 2009).
[16]Tanja R. Müller, 'Celebrity', in *Visual Global Politics*, ed. Roland Bleiker (London: Routledge, 2018).
[17]Emma Hutchison, 'A Global Politics of Pity?: Disaster Imagery and the Emotional Construction of Solidarity after the 2004 Asian Tsunami', *International Political Sociology* 8, no. 1 (2014): 1–19.
[18]See Julian, Bliesemann de Guevara and Redhead, this issue.
[19]Michael Shank and Lisa Schirch, 'Strategic Arts-Based Peacebuilding', *Peace and Change* 33, no. 2 (2008): 217–18.
[20]Charlotte Hooper, *Manly States: Masculinities, International Relations, and Gender Politics* (New York: Columbia University Press, 2001), 165.
[21]Lesley Pruitt, *Youth Peacebuilding: Music, Gender, and Change* (Albany, NY: SUNY Press, 2013).
[22]Dena L. Hawes, 'Crucial Narratives: Performance Art and Peace Building', *International Journal of Peace Studies* 12, no. 2 (2007): 17–29.
[23]Tom Anderson and Bernard Conlon, 'In the Shadow of the Peace Walls: Art, Education, and Social Reconstruction in Northern Ireland', *Art Education* 66, no. 4 (2013): 36–42.
[24]Karen Nickell, '"Troubles Textiles": Textile Responses to the Conflict in Northern Ireland', *Textile* 13, no. 3 (2015): 234–51; Julian, Bliesemann de Guevara and Redhead, this issue.
[25]Stefanie Kappler, 'Everyday Legitimacy in Post-Conflict Spaces: the Creation of Social Legitimacy in Bosnia-Herzegovina's Cultural Arenas', *Journal of Intervention and Statebuilding* 7, no. 1 (2013): 23.
[26]Siobhan McEvoy-Levy, *Peace and Resistance in Youth Cultures: Reading the Politics of Peacebuilding from Harry Potter to The Hunger Games* (London: Palgrave Macmillan, 2018), 55.
[27]Helen Berents and Siobhan McEvoy-Levy, 'Theorising Youth and Everyday Peace(Building)', *Peacebuilding* 3, no. 2 (2015): 119.

This convergence of the aesthetic and the everyday also manifests when young people engage with popular culture that remediates hegemonic war memory and militarised masculinities, such as Thompson's music in Croatia.

'Youth' and 'young people' are, this paper acknowledges, culturally specific terms, especially when conflict has delayed or upended life courses.[28] The United Nations Development Programme concentrates principally on youth aged 15–24 but regards those aged up to 35 as youth where context requires.[29] Croatia's Ministry for Demography, Family, Youth and Social Policy defines youth as 15–30.[30] Where everyday peace and war memory are concerned, however, the most significant generational divide is between those who do or do not have lived experience of the war. While older Croatians have experiential knowledge of the war, youth in today's Croatia know about the war through 'postmemory', experienced vicariously.[31] Family, education and media shape their knowledge.[32] In a Croatian context, these are the youth with whom critical scholars of masculinities in peace and conflict, interested in 'how boys are encouraged to internalise their role as potential combatants from a very early age', would be concerned.[33] Whereas McEvoy-Levy argues that engagements with politics of peace through popular culture are part of young people's everyday, so too, this paper shows, are engagements with popular culture that contests peace. The prominence of veteran masculinities in this popular culture is additional reason for a gender lens.

While critical PCS has embraced the everyday in order to see peace-making and resistance at work beyond elite-driven and liberal forms of peacebuilding, the everyday has long been a feminist concern. Enloe's 'feminist intellectual curiosity' towards International Relations (IR) traces world politics into everyday, domestic and intimate spaces, and into the visible and less visible ways in which states, militaries and powerful financial institutions rely on women's labour and assent.[34] Everyday peace and conflict research, it might seem, is always already feminist peace and conflict research. Or it should be – but major interventions in critical peacebuilding studies have been perfectly able to theorise the everyday via authors like de Certeau and Lefebvre without building on feminist thought or giving gender dynamics any sustained attention.[35] Feminist peace and conflict scholars, in contrast, use gender lenses

---

[28] See Julian, Bliesemann de Guevara and Redhead, this issue.
[29] United Nations Development Programme, *UNDP Youth Strategy 2014–2017* (New York: UNDP, 2014), 9, http://www.undp.org/content/dam/undp/library/Democratic%20Governance/Youth/UNDP_Youth-Strategy-2014-17_Web.pdf (accessed October 5, 2018).
[30] 'Odjel za mlade', Ministarstvo za demografiju, obitelj, mlade i socijalnu politiku, https://mdomsp.gov.hr/istaknute-teme/mladi-i-volonterstvo/mladi-9015/odjel-za-mlade-9018/9018 (accessed October 5, 2018).
[31] See Dijana Jelača, 'Youth After Yugoslavia: Subcultures and Phantom Pain', *Studies in East European Cinema* 5, no. 2 (2014): 140.
[32] Tanja Vuckovic Juros, '"Things Were Good During Tito's Times, My Parents Say": How Young Croatian Generations Negotiated the Socially Mediated Frames of the Recent Yugoslav Past', *Memory Studies*, in press, http://journals.sagepub.com/doi/pdf/10.1177/1750698018790122 (accessed October 5, 2018).
[33] David Duriesmith, *Masculinity and New War: the Gendered Dynamics of Contemporary Armed Conflict* (London: Routledge, 2017), 32.
[34] Cynthia Enloe, 'Afterword', *International Peacekeeping* 17, no. 2 (2010): 308.
[35] See, e.g., Oliver P. Richmond, 'Becoming Liberal, Unbecoming Liberalism: Liberal–Local Hybridity Via the Everyday as a Response to the Paradoxes of Liberal Peacebuilding', *Journal of Intervention and Statebuilding* 3, no. 3 (2009): 324–44 (which twice credits feminism for theorising 'empathy', Richmond's bridge between liberal and local layers of peacebuilding, but does not address the gender politics of the everyday itself); Séverine Autesserre, 'Going Micro: Emerging and Future Peacekeeping Research', *International Peacekeeping* 21, no. 4 (2014): 492–500; and examples in Christine Rigual, 'Rethinking the Ontology of Peacebuilding: Gender, Spaces and the Limits of the Local Turn', *Peacebuilding* 6, no. 2 (2018): 148.

(on masculinities and femininities) to reveal the gender politics of international peacekeeping,[36] women's exclusion from negotiations such as those that ended the war in Bosnia-Herzegovina (BiH),[37] international peacebuilders' (dis)engagement with 'gender mainstreaming' strategies,[38] struggles for gender justice in domains from social welfare to the aftermath of wartime sexual violence (indeed sometimes both),[39] and spaces of women's agency and resistance.[40] All these are embodied, and part of the everyday.[41]

Yet the post-conflict everyday is also where peace-making efforts are contested and rejected, and where polarisation as well as reconciliation across the conflict's identitarian boundaries occurs. The aesthetics of the everyday, therefore, must also include the representations, messages and emotions that complicate and frustrate peace. Here, the insights of feminists using IR's experiential and embodied turn to explore the joys, pleasures and desires of war are just as important for PCS as the aesthetics and affects of peace itself.[42] For spectators and listeners of Thompson's music (both youth and older listeners, including veterans), the pleasures of spectatorship and listening are bound together with the emotions of identifying with the national myth of the Homeland War. Understanding that myth is essential to appreciating veteran masculinities' potential resonances for youth today.

Croatia and its public myths in peace and conflict studies

Croatia exemplifies a post-conflict society where myths of national heroism and sacrifice were hegemonic public narratives during the conflict and have continued to be reproduced as hegemonic into the present day. These narratives began to structure the public sphere during the war, through a discursive alliance between President Franjo Tuđman (founder of the ruling Croatian Democratic Union (HDZ) party) and institutions including state media, most private media, and the Church.[43] An oppositional right-wing variant of this historical narrative views the war's outcome as a betrayal of Croatian patriotism even though it ended in military victory, with the 'Oluja' ('Storm') offensive of August 1995 and a victorious entry into the town of Knin (which the separatist 'Republic of Serb Krajina' had made its capital).

Main points of the 'betrayal' narrative include the several years of international oversight Croatia had to undergo regarding Serb minority rights before the United Nations (UN) ended its transitional administration of eastern Slavonia; the socio-economic

---

[36]Cynthia Cockburn and Dubravka Žarkov, *The Postwar Moment: Militaries, Masculinities, and International Peacekeeping* (London: Lawrence and Wishart, 2002).
[37]Annika Björkdahl, 'A Gender-Just Peace?: Exploring the Post-Dayton Peace Process in Bosnia', *Peace and Change* 37, no. 2 (2012): 286–317.
[38]Laura J. Shepherd, 'Victims of Violence or Agents of Change?: Representations of Women in UN Peacebuilding Discourse', *Peacebuilding* 4, no. 2 (2016): 121–35.
[39]Maria O'Reilly, *Gendered Agency in War and Peace: Gender Justice and Women's Activism in Post-Conflict Bosnia-Herzegovina* (London: Palgrave Macmillan, 2018).
[40]See Claire Duncanson, *Gender and Peacebuilding* (Cambridge: Polity, 2016); and Laura J. Shepherd, *Gender, UN Peacebuilding, and the Politics of Space: Locating Legitimacy* (Oxford: Oxford University Press, 2017).
[41]Helen Berents, 'An Embodied Everyday Peace in the Midst of Violence', *Peacebuilding* 3, no. 2 (2015): 1–14; Väyrynen, this issue.
[42]See Julia Welland, 'Joy and War: Reading Pleasure in Wartime Experiences', *Review of International Studies* 44, no. 3 (2018): 438–55.
[43]See Gordana Uzelak [Uzelac], 'Franjo Tudjman's Nationalist Ideology', *East European Quarterly* 31, no. 4 (1997): 449–72; Senjković, *Lica društva*; and Jović, *Rat i mit*.

disenfranchisement of veterans, especially men in economically-depressed ex-front-line regions like the Dalmatian hinterland, compounded by the state's inability to meet disabled veterans' physical and psychosocial therapeutic needs;[44] and the fact that the UN and the European Union (EU) still required a victorious Croatia to co-operate with the International Criminal Tribunal for the Former Yugoslavia (ICTY) prosecutors who were investigating Croats for war crimes against Serbs or complicity in ethnic cleansing in BiH. To reverse this 'betrayal', the populist and clerical right looks towards a national regeneration around the values that male soldiers (or 'branitelji' ('defenders')) embodied during the Homeland War. Even though Croatia won the war, therefore, its post-conflict gender politics have much in common with 'defeated' nations, such as the attempted 'remasculinization of America' after the Vietnam War.[45] These contentions underlie the most commonly-researched Croatian cases for PCS, where hegemonic memory politics clash with efforts to improve inter-ethnic reconciliation.

The typical Croatian sites discussed in PCS are those where (some) refugees from the conflict have returned, and where struggles over minority rights are everyday political issues, especially if (as in Vukovar or Knin) the site also has symbolic significance in public narratives about the Homeland War. Particularly contentious struggles surround property restitution,[46] and Serbs' cultural autonomy and language rights.[47] Other struggles concern the 'competitive reconstruction' of Catholic and Orthodox religious sites,[48] the social reintegration of Croatian war veterans,[49] the building of war memorials,[50] and local perceptions of the ICTY.[51] The micropolitics of these struggles, in Vukovar and elsewhere, show that national contentions over Homeland War memory are linked to the everyday (in)security of Serbs in Croatia, LGBTQ minorities, left-wing, and feminist activists who are also targets of street violence from the nationalist right.

PCS also deals with Croatian nationalism when addressing the politics of Croat separatism in BiH. Bosnian Croat separatists seeking to create an ethnically homogenous Croat entity of 'Herceg-Bosna' during the war in BiH killed and persecuted Bosniaks and Serbs across the territory they aspired to unify with Croatia, and between January 1993 and January 1994 were openly in conflict with the Army of the Republic of Bosnia-Herzegovina (ARBiH): publicly avowing the wartime Croatian state's support for 'Herceg-Bosna' would undermine Croatian public myths of 1991–5 as a good, just, defensive war.[52] Within an ethnic cleansing strategy

---

[44]See Schäuble, *Narrating Victimhood*.
[45]Senjković, *Lica društva*, 189. See Susan Jeffords, *The Remasculinization of America: Gender and the Vietnam War* (Bloomington, IN: Indiana University Press, 1989).
[46]Carolyn Leutloff-Grandits, 'Post-Dayton Ethnic Engineering in Croatia Through the Lenses of Property Issues and Social Transformations', *Journal of Genocide Research* 18, no. 4 (2016): 485–502.
[47]Ivor Sokolić, 'My Neighbour, the Criminal: how Memories of the 1991–1995 Conflict in Croatia Affect Attitudes Towards the Serb Minority', *Nations and Nationalism* 23, no. 4 (2017): 790–814.
[48]Britt Baillie, 'Capturing Facades in "Conflict-Time": Structural Violence and the (Re)Construction [of] Vukovar's Churches', *Space and Polity* 17, no. 3 (2013): 309.
[49]Clark, 'Giving Peace a Chance'.
[50]Janine Natalya Clark, 'Reconciliation Through Remembrance?: War Memorials and the Victims of Vukovar', *International Journal of Transitional Justice* 7, no. 1 (2013): 116–35.
[51]See Tamara Banjeglav, 'The Micro Legacy of the ICTY in Croatia: a Case Study of Vukovar', in *Transitional Justice and Reconciliation: Lessons from the Balkans*, ed. Martina Fischer and Olivera Simić (London: Routledge, 2016).
[52]Ivor Sokolić, 'Denying the Unknown: Everyday Narratives about Croatian Involvement in the 1992–1995 Bosnian Conflict', *Südosteuropa* 65, no. 4 (2017): 639.

involving atrocities such as the massacre of Bosniak civilians at Ahmići in April 1993, the Croat Defence Council (HVO) besieged Mostar, separated it into 'Croat' and 'Bosniak' halves (including destroying the city's historic bridge in November 1993), and divided it along ethnicised lines that intangibly persist, with deliberate reinforcement, today.[53] At national level, meanwhile, Bosnian Croat demands for a 'third' (Croat) constitutional entity, which could potentially secede to join Croatia, have been regarded by opponents as a destabilising force in Bosnian politics.[54]

Ethnopolitical violence, as a form of war, manifests a characteristic everyday politics of peace and conflict. The processes through which ethnopolitical conflicts begin and alternatives to violence are closed down involve a reshaping of public consciousness from friendliness or at least coexistence with neighbours regarded as 'other', towards readiness to use violence or accept its legitimacy. The Yugoslav wars were just one conflict preceded by a tightening of symbolic boundaries between ethnic 'selves' and 'others', when ethnicity became a much more important primary dividing factor of social identities than in pre-war everyday life.[55] After conflict, markers of ethnopolitical identity – including political posters and newly-built religious symbols but also the sounds and symbols of patriotic popular music – demarcate social spaces as owned by one ethno-ideological group and off-limits to others, producing invisible but tacitly-understood ethnicised boundaries.[56] All these constructions of ethnicity and nationhood depend on constructions of gender, producing idealised ethnonational masculinities and femininities for differentiating self and other.[57] Individuals' everyday identifications with nationalist projects that were implicated in the last war, which could become reserves of sentiment for future conflicts, are thus an important part of the affective politics that complicate sustainable peace. Audiovisual popular culture's capacity to invite identifications with veteran masculinities can be observed through the music of Thompson, who reattached himself to veterans' activism in the late 1990s.

Thompson and the veterans' movement in the late 1990s

Scholars have already noted the production of nationalist narratives of identity in Croatia through patriotic popular music during and after the war, and the contested memory politics surrounding Thompson, as part of explaining how war and nationalism permeated everyday life after the break-up of Yugoslavia.[58] Thompson's primary theme since the turn of the millennium has been veterans' politicised disappointment

---

[53]Annika Björkdahl and Ivan Gusic, 'Sites of Friction: Governance, Identity and Space in Mostar', in *Peacebuilding and Friction: Global and Local Encounters in Post-Conflict Societies*, ed. Annika Björkdahl, Kristine Höglund, Gearoid Millar, Jair van den Lijn and Willemijn Verkoren (London: Routledge, 2016), 84–102.
[54]Vesna Bojicic-Dzelilovic, 'The Politics, Practice and Paradox of "Ethnic Security" in Bosnia-Herzegovina', *Stability* 4, no. 1 (2015), http://doi.org/10.5334/sta.ez (accessed May 23, 2018).
[55]See V. P. Gagnon, Jr., *The Myth of Ethnic War: Serbia and Croatia in the 1990s* (Ithaca, NY: Cornell University Press, 2004).
[56]Björkdahl and Gusic, 'Sites of Friction', 87.
[57]Dubravka Žarkov, *The Body of War: Media, Ethnicity and Gender in the Break-Up of Yugoslavia* (Durham, NC: Duke University Press, 2007).
[58]Svanibor Pettan, ed., *Music, Politics and War: Views from Croatia* (Zagreb: IEF, 1998); Senjković, *Lica društva*; Catherine Baker, *Sounds of the Borderland: Popular Music, War and Nationalism in Croatia since 1991* (Farnham: Ashgate, 2010); Brentin, 'Ready for the Homeland?'; Tomislav Pletenac, 'Accidental Celebrity?: Constructing Fame in Post-War Croatia', *Traditiones* 45, no. 1 (2016): 31–46; and Stojanovska Rupčić, 'Songs'.

with the nation's post-war condition and the attitude of its ruling elites, mixed with depictions of Croats' glorious, sacrificial traditions of fighting to defend their homeland which imply a state of grace Croatia might return to if present-day Croats overcome political differences and act on what he frames as the teachings of the Catholic Church. This populist message of national regeneration is simultaneously a call for the restoration of veterans' (masculine) dignity, a syncretic blending of present-day war with mythologised wars of the past (a common representational strategy throughout the Yugoslav wars)[59] and, critics contend, a rehabilitation of fascism through sympathy for the NDH. In fact, this role as Croatian popular music's main mediator of Homeland War memory and veterans' politics did not flow as naturally from the wartime fame he enjoyed in 1992–4 as his public image would now suggest. Most songs on his 1995 and 1996 albums resembled other rock-influenced newly-composed folk music from his home region. He started committing himself more to patriotic music – now as a veteran – in 1998, when he dedicated his song 'Prijatelji' ('Friends') to veterans suffering everyday social exclusion and depression, and (through its video) to the HVO colonel Tihomir Blaškić, then facing trial at the ICTY.

'Prijatelji', like 'Bojna Čavoglave' and the rest of Thompson's patriotic music, harnessed established codes of authenticity and sentiment in (post-)Yugoslav popular music to make truth claims and add emotional weight.[60] It appeared just as the veterans' movement was organising to make political claims on the Croatian state (still then governed by Tuđman and HDZ) from a position of oppositional, populist patriotism it maintains despite strong ties to the Croatian Party of Right (HSP), smaller far-right parties and the HDZ right wing. The unchallengeable moral authority that politicised veterans' associations claim on the grounds of their wartime sacrifice extends well beyond socio-economic welfare and bodily wellbeing, into the ethnopolitical issues that PCS observes more readily. Groups such as the Association of Croatian War Invalids from the Homeland War (HVIDRA) thus claimed – and the Croatian state and media have ascribed them – a wide-ranging social and political role as guardians of memory.[61] It is through Thompson's music that Croatian veterans' moral claims most permeate into popular culture, but examining his songs' lyrics alone would not fully explain how.

'Prijatelji', in its lyrics, was nevertheless framed already as a clear veterans' narrative. It contrasted a dangerous but proud and empowered past when the friends were at the front 'singing against death' with a present which is not good for the singer and his friends, when girls are no longer what they were and have run off into town, and when the narrator (and singer Thompson) can no longer 'see you all healthy' as he would have wished[62] – a line that some late-1990s Croatian listeners might have connected to

---

[59]See Ivan Čolović, *The Politics of Symbol in Serbia*, trans. Celia Hawkesworth (London: Hurst, 2002); and Ivo Žanić, *Flag on the Mountain: a Political Anthropology of War in Croatia and Bosnia*, trans. Graham McMaster and Celia Hawkesworth (London: Saqi, 2007).
[60]See Catherine Baker, 'Spaces of the Past: Emotional Discourses of "Zavičaj" (Birthplace) and Nation in Yugoslav and Post-Yugoslav Popular Music', *Southeastern Europe* 39, no. 2 (2015): 165–91.
[61]For BiH, meanwhile, Vesna Bojičić-Dželilović has described HVIDRA's Bosnian branch as among the main 'spoilers of peace' aligned with Bosnian Croat separatism: Vesna Bojicic-Dzelilovic, 'Peace on Whose Terms?: War Veterans' Associations in Bosnia and Herzegovina', in *Challenges to Peacebuilding: Managing Spoilers During Conflict Resolution*, ed. Edward Newman and Oliver Richmond (Tokyo: United Nations University Press, 2006), 200–18, 208.
[62]This summary is translated and closely paraphrased from Croatian lyrics available at https://web.archive.org/web/20170926202407/https://thompson.hr/albumi/39-vjetar-s-dinare (accessed May 7, 2018). For copyright reasons, lyrics are not quoted.

increasing suicides by male veterans.[63] The song's present is a time of disempowerment that has left veterans unable to fulfil the requirements of successful post-war masculinity (economic wellbeing, health, founding a family, and agency) and has left the nation divided, in contrast to wartime when the nation had been united and when the song's 'we' had been allowed to, and could, do everything, 'and were what we wanted to be'. Indeed, it has much in common with the disappointments expressed by many European veterans of World War I who became authors and/or paramilitaries.[64] Structurally, the stagnated aspirations of many Croatian veterans, and the ruptures this caused their sense of self, could be interpreted as another aspect of the general 'waiting-room' condition in which privatisation and neoliberal Europeanisation have left the Yugoslav region.[65] The organised veterans' movement, however, attributes their marginalisation to civilian society's disrespect for their sacrifice and, especially, to what their spokespeople often regard as a left-wing, neo-Communist political agenda that has sold the nation out to Euro-Atlantic institutions (the ICTY and EU).[66]

Interpreting the song's video (Table 1) requires thinking about how language, music, moving images and bodies (including stars' own biographical personas) work *together* to produce meaning in music video, that is, 'audiovisuality'.[67] Studies of popular culture and international politics privileging written, linear text thus miss much of what characterises audiovisual aesthetics. Importantly, music video editing conventions (which this video follows) present several different sequences of action or representation in one video and invite spectators to imagine the connections between them[68] – in other words, to perform the narrative work. Besides interpreting elements of meaning independently, analysing music video thus also requires interpreting how those elements are juxtaposed. Following this methodology shows how the video of 'Prijatelji' used Thompson's veteran identity to give authenticity to a narrative of disenfranchised masculinity and political betrayal after the Homeland War.[69]

Like many patriotic and regionally-themed videos from Croatia and the wider post-Yugoslav region, this video is offered to viewers in Croatia and the diaspora not just as a promotion of a song but also as an invitation to remember.[70] In some ways, its stimulus for a veteran viewer to remember their own experiences of conflict and readjustment is a more open text than Thompson's more recent videos (where the lyrics cast soldiers/veterans as more unambiguously heroic but Thompson tends to be the only veteran shown): the scenes where the depressed veteran watches or hallucinates

---

[63] See Dragica Kozarić-Kovačić, Mirjana Grubišić-Ilić, Frane Grubišić and Zrnka Kovačić, 'Epidemiological indicators of suicides in the Republic of Croatia', *Društvena istraživanja* 11. No. 1 (2002): 165.
[64] Senjković, *Lica društva*, 187–8. See George L. Mosse, *Fallen Soldiers: Reshaping the Memory of the World Wars* (Oxford: Oxford University Press, 1994).
[65] Stef Jansen, Čarna Brković and Vanja Čelebičić, 'Introduction: New Ethnographic Perspectives on Mature Dayton Bosnia and Herzegovina', in *Negotiating Social Relations in Bosnia and Herzegovina: Semiperipheral Entanglements*, ed. Stef Jansen, Čarna Brković and Vanja Čelebičić (London: Routledge, 2017), 17.
[66] See Tihomir Cipek, 'The Spectre of Communism is Haunting Croatia: the Croatian Right's Image of the Enemy', *Politička misao* 54, no. 1–2 (2017): 150–69.
[67] Carol Vernallis, *Unruly Media: YouTube, Music Video, and the New Digital Cinema* (Oxford: Oxford University Press, 2013), 6.
[68] Vernallis, *Unruly Media*, 160; and Goodwin, *Dancing*.
[69] 'Marko Perković Thompson "Prijatelji"', February 5, 2008, https://www.youtube.com/watch?v=O9e-yvaVeHA (accessed May 7, 2018).
[70] See Baker, 'Spaces of the Past'. As a spectator, I am outside the community it constructs: I speak Croatian but have no Croatian ethnic heritage (I am a white British woman).

Table 1. sections of Thompson's 'Prijatelji' video.

Section	Action	Key images in lyrics and music
Introduction (to 0.03)	Wartime footage of exploding house	Muffled explosion sound
Introduction (0.04–0.14)	Camera pans over rooftops of town in Dalmatian hinterland	Synthesised approximation of Dinaric bagpipes – ties the narrative to same region
Introduction (0.15–0.28)	Thompson ostensibly at home, reaching into wardrobe for leather jacket past his old army jacket Black-and-white photo of two soldiers in snowy woodland during war Camera picks out Thompson's army jacket again after he has left	Pipe phrase continues
Introduction (0.28–0.31)	Black-and-white photo of Thompson and his wartime platoon celebrating, holding rifles	Drums and guitars join the pipes
Verse 1 (0.31–0.50)	Thompson walking along road, singing; decoration of his brown leather jacket hints at military uniform (shoulder tabs, large globe-and-wings patch on sleeve) Cut to: dejected middle-aged man in suit passes two young, fashionable women beside car	
Verse 2 (0.50–1.10)	Thompson singing Intercut with montage of armed soldiers celebrating, training	Remembering proud days
Chorus 1 (1.10–1.52)	The older man walks across the playground Thompson has been passing Three boys are playing with toy guns Man's face falls as the boys mime pulling the trigger around him Thompson shakes hands with a third veteran Black-and-white photo shows third veteran's younger wartime self, uniformed and wearing Croatian volunteers' iconic black headband Thompson throws a basketball back to the boys	
Break (1.52–2.18)	Second veteran alone in bar, watching Blaškić's extradition and trial Briefer shots of: the boys' basketball game; veterans exchanging photos in the bar; another wartime photograph of Thompson's platoon; close-ups of several veterans juxtaposed with their photos from the war	Bagpipe phrase returns
Verse 3 (2.19–2.38)	Thompson greeting and reuniting veterans in the bar	Wishing to see 'you all' healthy again
Chorus (2.38–2.47)	Thompson puts coat back on, finds the second veteran outdoors walking towards a waterfall	
Chorus continues (2.48)	Brief clip from Blaškić extradition	Asking if 'you' are tired and if they have tricked you
Chorus continues (2.49–3.49)	Thompson adjusts the veteran's suit and tie, sartorially restoring his dignity, as they walk back Thompson puts his arm around the man's shoulder and takes him into the bar The reincorporated veterans toast each other with rakija (brandy)	
End (3.39–3.51)	Golden bird on war memorial	Music ends

boys playing with toy guns invite the viewer to draw *some* link between the imaginaries of war, play, soldiers and heroes offered to young boys and what soldiers actually experienced, but does not impose a single reading. It might connote the idea of the nation and its military tradition being reproduced through history as young boys grow up and are socialised into national culture; it might, on its own, permit a reading that (as in the strand of World War I literature epitomised by writers such as Robert Graves) these boyhood games were a lie; it might, as per anti-militarist veterans' activism and critical scholarship on masculinities and conflict, imply the public should be more critical of how children are socialised to be ready for war,[71] or that boys' identification with narratives of adventure and military heroism through play is itself, as Graham Dawson argues, a means of reproducing ideologies of nationalism and masculinity over time.[72] Its expressions of emotional support, intimacy and affection between male veterans, as an implicit precondition for psychological wellbeing, are unusual in a setting where men are expected to have managed war's emotional strain using their 'natural' masculine resilience, and where the state had not provided (and would not provide) veterans with sufficient psychosocial support.[73] And yet the video and its narrative is also linked to a heavily politicised issue in Croatia's post-war international relations, Blaškić's extradition and the populist 'betrayal' narrative about Croatian co-operation with the ICTY.[74]

Blaškić, the HVO colonel in whose area of responsibility the Ahmići massacre had taken place, had held a general's rank in the *Croatian* Army since November 1995, the same month the ICTY indicted him for war crimes on command responsibility grounds.[75] He had voluntarily surrendered to the ICTY in April 1996, and 'Prijatelji' appeared while his trial (June 1997–March 2000) was ongoing. This video, produced for a singer on Croatia's largest record label (Croatia Records), showed that popular music was a site where post-conflict contestations over transitional justice were taking place, and where they could reach young viewers watching music on television. It continued to be so after Tuđman, when the Croatian generals Mirko Norac and Ante Gotovina (who both fled from justice in 2001 after the ICTY indicted them) became even more symbolic than Blaškić of what the Croatian right portrayed as an unjust assault on the memory of Croatian wartime heroism. Thompson and the promotional infrastructure around him, plus certain other musicians, brought the Norac/Gotovina support campaign on stage and on to the airwaves, performing solidarity with HVIDRA and other veterans' organisations, commemorating the generals as heroes (Thompson's concert at Hajduk Split's stadium in 2002 famously left them two empty seats) and contributing to their mythologisation as contemporary expressions of 'hajduk' (highland outlaw) masculinity.[76] Their songs drew Homeland War veterans, medieval Croatian kings and knights, and folkloric hajduks into a single imaginative continuum. In 2005, Thompson began holding an annual open-air concert in Čavoglave to mark the Oluja anniversary, further establishing himself as a commemorative entrepreneur embodying veteran 'hypermasculinity'[77] and contesting the post-conflict peace.

Thompson's public meanings as a star are, however, not wholly under his control. Controversies over the attitude of Thompson and his fans towards the memory of the

---

[71]See Matthew Rech, 'Recruitment, Counter-Recruitment and Critical Military Studies', *Global Discourse* 4, no. 2–3 (2014): 244–62; and Duriesmith, *Masculinities*, 32.
[72]Graham Dawson, *Soldier Heroes: British Adventure, Empire and the Imagining of Masculinities* (London: Routledge, 1994).
[73]See Schäuble, *Narrating Victimhood*.
[74]See Christopher K. Lamont, 'Defiance or Strategic Compliance?: the Post-Tuđman Croatian Democratic Union and the International Criminal Tribunal for the Former Yugoslavia', *Europe–Asia Studies* 62, no. 10 (2010): 1683–705.
[75]Daresh Sarooshi and Malcolm D. Evans, 'Command Responsibility and the Blaškić Case', *International and Comparative Law Quarterly* 50, no. 2 (2001): 452.
[76]Vjeran Pavlaković, 'Croatia, the International Criminal Tribunal for the Former Yugoslavia, and General Gotovina as a Political Symbol', *Europe–Asia Studies* 62, no. 10 (2010): 1707–40: 1717.
[77]See Cahn and Ní Aoláin, 'Gender, Masculinities and Transition', 5.

NDH and the call-and-response slogan 'Za dom spremni' ('Ready for the Home') used by its Ustaša militia – which Thompson shouts and a group of male voices completes at the start of 'Bojna Čavoglave' – have been consistently part of his public image since 2003–4, when the web portal *Index* published a recording of Thompson and another man (Joško Tomičić) at a private concert in Osijek singing an offensive song that celebrated the NDH's Jasenovac and Stara Gradiška concentration camps.[78] Since 2004, venue owners and municipal authorities in several countries where Thompson has performed for diaspora audience have cancelled or banned his concerts, apparently understanding him as part of the international neo-Nazi music scene. Authorities more familiar with the context of rehabilitation of NDH symbols in Croatian nationalism prevented him performing in Sarajevo in 2011, Maribor in 2017, and, inside Croatia, at the prestigious Pula Arena in 2008.[79] In 2017, police in Karlovac charged him with a public order offence for shouting 'Za dom spremni' at that year's Oluja concert in Slunj, leading to a criminal trial at which he was acquitted in April 2018.[80]

While now excludes Thompson and his songs are rarely played on the state broadcaster, they receive regular airplay on Croatia's largest private music radio station (Narodni radio, where Thompson bought a 20% stake in 2004),[81] sympathetic mayors book him for commemorative concerts, the Croatian Football Association has played his song 'Lijepa li si' ('How Beautiful You Are') before international matches since at least 2012,[82] and state commemorations of Oluja at Knin in 2015–16 incorporated what is normally his annual concert at Čavoglave.[83] Thompson is thus simultaneously institutionalised and rejected as a celebrity and mediator of historical memory, exemplifying Croatia's politicised struggles over World War II memory, which are publicly mapped on to competing attitudes towards silencing or promoting critical attitudes towards Croatian conduct in the Homeland War.[84] Throughout these struggles, both centrist mainstream media and alternative/anti-nationalist journalists have framed Thompson's music and his concerts' permissive atmosphere towards NDH-themed clothing, flags and salutes as a social problem, at the root of which is Thompson's appeal *to youth*.[85] In this context, songs like 'Prijatelji' continue to produce meaning two decades or more after they were recorded as sonic and audiovisual artefacts.

---

[78] Pletenac, 'Accidental Celebrity?', 35.
[79] Raif Okić, 'Zabranjeni Thompson: odbili ga od Sarajeva do Rotterdama', *Express*, May 17, 2017, https://www.express.hr/kultura/zabranjeni-thompson-odbili-ga-od-sarajeva-do-rotterdama-10475# (accessed May 20, 2018).
[80] 'U Slunju završeno suđenje Thompsonu zbog poklića "Za dom spremni"', *Dnevnik*, April 25, 2018, https://dnevnik.hr/vijesti/hrvatska/u-slunju-zavrseno-sudjenje-thompsonu-zbog-poklica-za-dom-spremni—514984.html (accessed May 20, 2018).
[81] 'Thompson kupio 20% Narodnog radija za 4000 kuna', *Index*, April 14, 2004, http://www.index.hr/vijesti/clanak/thompson-kupio-20-narodnog-radija-za-4000-kuna/196676.aspx (accessed May 17, 2018).
[82] Aleksandar Holiga, 'Euro 2012: the Problem with Croatia's Nationalistic Fans Starts at the Top', *The Guardian*, June 26, 2012, https://www.theguardian.com/football/blog/2012/jun/26/euro-2012-croatia-racism-uefa (accessed May 19, 2018). The song describes the beauty and comradeship of each Croatian region, including 'Herceg-Bosna' on equal terms with regions of the Republic of Croatia.
[83] Space precludes a full overview of Thompson's career. See Baker, *Sounds of the Borderland*, 36–40, 95–132 (commenting on many of his songs about historical memory and/or veterans not analysed here); Stojanovska Rupčić, 'Songs That Sound "Right"'.
[84] See Tamara Banjeglav, 'Conflicting Memories, Competing Narratives and Contested Histories in Croatia's Post-War Commemorative Practices', *Politička misao* 49, no. 5 (2012): 7–31.
[85] E.g., after Thompson's 2002 stadium concert in Split, the newspaper *Slobodna Dalmacija* asked sociologists why Thompson and NDH symbols appealed to youth: Tomislav Klauški, 'Anti Pavelicu?', *Slobodna Dalmacija*, October 12, 2002. The alternative magazine *Feral tribune* described young people chanting NDH slogans at Thompson's concerts as symptomatic of Croatian historical revisionism: Toni Gabrić, 'Jasenovac i Bleiburg nisu isto', *Feral tribune*, May 10, 2003. The framing continues: e.g. the left-wing regionalist MEP Ivan Jakovčić accused Thompson and others of 'want[ing] to turn young people into neo-Ustašas' after the World Cup incident: 'Thompson treba dobiti sve moguće kazne, on to namjerno radi', *N1*, August 9, 2018, http://hr.n1info.com/a323043/Vijesti/Ivan-Jakovcic-o-Thompsonu-i-pozdravu-Za-dom-spremni.html (accessed October 8, 2018).

Youth identifications with veteran masculinities and the wartime past

Framings of Thompson's celebrity and the popularity of his music as a social problem that is likely to impede young people 'reckoning with' or 'confronting' the wartime past rest on an argument (not necessarily accepted in critical PCS) that public 'coming to terms with the past' after ethnopolitical violence is essential for preventing it breaking out again, and on assumptions that popular stars will persuade their audiences to share their ideology.[86] The pleasures of listening to and watching Thompson's music and performance, especially as part of a live crowd, appear to be thought to make it more attractive for young people to identify with historical narratives about the nation's recent and more distant military past which the left considers problematic for democracy and peace. Reactions to Thompson's popularity among young people, and to some young people's display of NDH symbols and/or integralist coats of arms at his live performances, occur in the context of long-running campaigns in civil society against the uncritical attitude towards the NDH that activists argue state education has promoted since Tuđman's presidency. The rehabilitation of NDH symbols and 'Za dom spremni', they contend, makes Serbs feel more insecure, legitimises other chauvinist behaviour and therefore works against peace.

Resisting the 'normalisation' of 'Za dom spremni', or indeed of Thompson, is thus part of anti-nationalist human rights groups' wider peace activism in the culture and education field. In 2016–17, the Center for Civil Courage (CCC), a 'feminist and freethinking' NGO founded in Zagreb in 2011, organised a complaints campaign against the Ministry of Education's sixth-grade literature curriculum, which included the Homeland-War-themed children's book *Moj tata spava s anđelima: mali ratni dnevnik* (*My Daddy is Sleeping With the Angels: a Little War Diary*) by Stjepan Tomas, set in 1991 and published in 1992–3.[87] The extracts on the specimen complaint form included one where the nine-year-old girl narrator witnesses her mother being excited to hear the introduction of 'Čavoglave' on the radio, and another scene from their refugee camp schoolroom in Austria where the children write 'Za dom spremni' as a patriotic slogan, plus seven other extracts sympathetic to a Catholic patriotic ideology of national victimhood as martyrdom or to wartime suspicion against Serbs.[88] While the children's ombudsman had been receiving individual complaints about the book since it was added to the literature curriculum in 2006 (a year after HDZ came back into power), this more sustained campaign let the CCC claim 'victory' when the ministry reformed its literature curriculum and withdrew the book in September 2017.[89]

Such contestations occur at curriculum level but also on the level of everyday behaviour, becoming more public during high-school graduation season ('norijada'). This custom gives graduating students ('maturanti') social sanction to

---

[86]See Jelena Obradović-Wochnik, 'The "Silent Dilemma" of Transitional Justice: Silencing and Coming to Terms with the Past in Serbia', *International Journal of Transitional Justice* 7, no. 2 (2013): 328–47.
[87]See Dubravka Zima, 'Hrvatska dječja književnost o ratu', *Polemos* 4, no. 2 (2001): 102–3.
[88]'Pritužba', Center for Civil Courage, May 2016, http://www.civilcourage.hr/wp-content/uploads/2016/05/PRITUZBA-spranca.docx (accessed May 17, 2018).
[89]Center for Civil Courage, 'Pobjeda! Hvala svim roditeljima i ucenicima koji su reagirali', Facebook, https://www.facebook.com/CenterForCivilCourage/photos/a.676213875734360.1073741828.330223803666704/1546658092023263/?type=3&theater (accessed May 17, 2018).

behave raucously in public streets and squares, and larger cities organise joint public celebrations for schools. In May 2017, the left-wing portal Lupiga, which often reports on political, social and cultural rehabilitations of the NDH, recorded two dozen students from three Zagreb schools giving right-fisted salutes and chanting 'Za dom spremni' during their customarily unruly procession to the city celebration at Bundek park, pointing this out as characteristic of a nationwide trend.[90] Cases in 2016 had included a group of students giving Ustaša salutes outside their school in Rijeka, and girls from a Zagreb school designing their class t-shirt in camouflage print with the slogan 'Za Domac spremni', punning on a teacher's name (Thompson's embodied public image routinely conveys his veteran identity through camouflage t-shirts and other details of 'military-inspired fashion').[91] The headline 'Maturanti from Kvarner gave fascist salutes during norijada then apologised: "We were joking"' typifies how mainstream press usually write off such behaviour as youthful misdemeanour.[92]

Indeed, patriotic popular music is present enough in everyday youth consciousness to be the subject of parody and play. A cameraphone video that YouTube's autoplay algorithm loaded after the Lupiga video in May 2017, for instance, showed six young women from another Zagreb school singing Thompson's 'Prijatelji' before the same norijada procession, drinking from plastic cups and parodying the comradely singing of male wedding guests. Exaggerating the chorus's extended vowels, an embodied sonic practice which in Croatia marks such ornamented singing as 'Dinaric' and 'Balkan', they appeared to perform a reversal of the everyday gender order and class order at once. The meanings behind their joking reappropriation of Thompson's address to veterans cannot be inferred without contextual, ethnographic knowledge. Yet even the fact they *were* mapping Thompson's lyrics about veterans' marginalisation and political betrayal in the late 1990s on to their own situation as young women graduating high school in the late 2010s draws attention to the frameworks of post-conflict militarised masculinity that made that reversal conceivable, culturally intelligible, and pleasurable.[93] Popular music expressing the veterans' movement's self-appointed role as guardians of wartime memory still has an everyday and commonsensical place in Croatian popular culture, creating an affective politics that makes it harder for human rights activists to tackle the banalisation of chauvinistic ethnonationalism and apparent sympathy for fascism among youth.

---

[90]Igor Fuka, 'Desnice u zraku (video): maturanti pokazuju kakve vrijednosti poštuju', *Lupiga*, May 19, 2017, https://www.lupiga.com/vijesti/desnice-u-zraku-video-maturanti-pokazuju-kakve-vrijednosti-postuju (accessed May 17, 2018).
[91]See Jane Tynan, 'Military Chic: Fashioning Civilian Bodies for War', in *War and the Body: Militarisation, Practice and Experience*, ed. Kevin McSorley (London: Routledge, 2013), 78–90.
[92]'Maturanti u Rijeci obilježili kraj škole nacističkim pozdravom', *Index*, May 17, 2016, http://www.index.hr/vijesti/clanak/maturanti-u-rijeci-obiljezili-kraj-skole-nacistickim-pozdravom/893878.aspx (accessed May 20, 2018); 'Zagrebačke maturantice na norijadi nosile majicu "Za Domac spremni"', *Index*, May 17, 2016, http://www.index.hr/black/clanak/zagrebacke-maturantice-na-norijadi-nosile-majicu-za-domac-spremni/893876.aspx (accessed May 20, 2018); and 'Maturanti s Kvarnera tijekom norijade fašistički salutirali pa se pokajali: "zezali smo se"', *Jutarnji list*, May 17, 2016, https://www.jutarnji.hr/vijesti/hrvatska/maturanti-s-kvarnera-tijekom-norijade-fasisticki-salutirali-pa-se-pokajali-zezali-smo-se/4056081/ (accessed May 20, 2018).
[93]Compare Partis-Jennings, this issue.

Conclusion

The translation of veteran (hyper)masculinity into entertainment stardom in post-conflict Croatia illustrates an underappreciated site of everyday peace contestation: popular music and youth engagement with it. Today's Croatian youth, born after the war, depend on family, school and media for narratives about the wartime past, informing their perspectives on present-day inter-ethnic relations. The sociologist Tanja Vuckovic Juros argues that young people find socially-mediated narratives of the Yugoslav past (and thus the war) more credible when they have emotional bonds with the source, meaning youth trust family members' more than teachers', journalists' or historians' accounts of the past.[94] Yet media, especially popular music, create their own emotional bonds. The pleasures of identifying with stars that inform popular-cultural spectatorship and fandom, and the ways that popular music stardom in particular harnesses the biographical authenticity performers embody, means young people's relationships with historical narratives mediated and embodied by musicians can also be affectively charged. In Croatia, Thompson's twenty-five-year-long career means his wartime and early post-war songs are still part of everyday youth consciousness.

If popular music is indeed a site where the gendered meanings of peace and conflict are contested, understanding *where* and *how* they are contested should acknowledge there is much more to musical meaning than lyrics, and more senses involved than sound. Even live music is an embodied performance; videos, which most singles have had since the 1980s, make songs audiovisual as well as aural texts. This paper's audiovisual analysis of Thompson's song 'Prijatelji', for instance, shows it was the video which fixed its lyrics to the Blaškić case as well as everyday male veterans' social exclusion, tying them together to suggest that unemployed and depressed veteran men were victims of anti-Croatian political forces that had also victimised Blaškić. Popular music's 'audiovisuality', not just its sound and performance, helps constitute everyday understandings of the post-conflict nation. Indeed, this paper shows music video can blend historical and political mythology in apparently 'natural' ways, creating spaces for viewers to remember or imagine personal emotional connections to the war.

Yet these affective politics enter the everyday even more concretely in interpersonal encounters. Arguments within schools over whether students should be allowed to sing Thompson's songs, wear his t-shirts and symbols, or play his music aloud are likely to be everyday occurrences in Croatia (and BiH). So are the inferences Serb, left-wing and LGBTQ students draw about their everyday (in)security from environments where slogans and symbols they associate with militant Croatian nationalism are present and sanctioned. Here, spectatorship of audiovisual material and live performance seeps into the micro-political level where young people exert agency through 'practices of resistance, rebellion and socio-political intervention' that build but also contest everyday peace.[95] Feminist insights explain why this matters in PCS. Firstly, they show how the prominent representation of politicised veteran masculinities contributes to post-conflict militarisation, including a problematic conflation of the veteran figure *with* masculinity. Secondly, they highlight how veteran masculinities embodied in popular culture can become points of identification

---

[94]Vuckovic Juros, '"Things"', 1.
[95]See Berents and McEvoy-Levy, 'Theorising Youth', 119.

for youth through the dynamics of spectatorship and stardom, affecting how young people who did not live through the war remember it. The struggles over how far mythologised veterans and the war memory they represent should define masculinity, and identification with the nation, in today's Croatia may be expressed about popular culture but are in fact part of the gender politics of negotiating and contesting peace in the everyday. A feminist aesthetic consciousness is necessary to understand, or even notice, what such struggles have to do with peace.

Disclosure statement

No potential conflict of interest was reported by the author.

Funding

This work was not supported by any particular funding agency.

ORCID

Catherine Baker http://orcid.org/0000-0002-3991-7946

Index

Tables are shown in bold type. Footnotes are indicated by the page number followed by "n" and the footnote number e.g., 107n61 refers to footnote 61 on page 107. "PCS" refers to "peace and conflict studies".

accountability 26, 30, 33
Aceh, Indonesia 67, 69, 72–4, 80
acknowledgement 26, 30, 32, 33
action manifesto 17–19
activism 9, 24n18, 99, 101, 106, 110, 112
aesthetic consciousness 99, 100, 101, 115
aesthetic turn, of international theory 99, 101
affective politics 14, 99, 100, 101, 106, 113, 114
agency 4, 11, 16, 24, 28, 30, 90, 91; and contested everyday peace 102, 104, 108, 114; and hybridity 56, 58, 60, 62; and intersectionality of peace 37, 39, 44
aid 51n1, 64, 84, 87, 91
apartheid 45, 48
Arakanese 93, 94, 95
armed conflict 6, 9, 12
armed violence 73
arts-based methods 14, 95–6
arts-based peacebuilding 102
attachment 36
audiovisual analysis 101, 114
audiovisual popular music, in post-conflict Croatia 13, 14–15, 99–115, **109**
audiovisuality 108, 114
auto-ethnography 50

being in the world 22, 26, 30, 31
'betrayal' narrative, of Croatian war of independence 104–5, 108, 110, 113
BiH (Bosnia-Herzegovina) 104, 105, 107n61, 114
binaries 13, 15–16, 52n6, 55, 57, 59; power-blind 34, 35, 36, 37, 38, 40, 43, 44, 45, 48, 49
biopower 28–9, 28n36, 29
Blaškić, Tihomir 107, **109**, 110, 114
Bojna Čavoglave 101, 107, 111
Bosnia-Herzegovina (BiH) 104, 105, 107n61, 114
Boulding, Elise 25–6, 27, 39
boundaries, between feminist and critical PCS 17
Buddhism 75, 93, 94, 95

Burmans 94
Burmese research associates, working with 92–3, 93–4n47

care 26–7, 93; as community-building 71–2; as everyday peacebuilding 15, 67–81
care ethics: feminist 68, 70, 72, 78, 81; Kashmiri 77
care needs 67, 68, 70, 71, 72, 81
care relations 70, 74, 76, 80–1
Čavoglave platoon, The 101, 107, 111
choreography 20, 31–2
citizenship 40, 44, 57, 58, 59
class 2, 16, 43, 44, 45, 46, 47, 48, 50, 55, 61, 64
co-being, event of 31
conflict: analysis of 8, 83, 84–8, 89, 92; armed 6, 9, 12; management of 4, 6–7, 9, 69, 70, 74; resolution of 4, 6, 7–8, 80; sensory perception of 1, 3; transformation of 4, 68, 69, 84, 85, 90, 100–1; violent 6, 77, 83–97
Confortini, Catia 27, 71
control, mechanisms of 8, 28n36, 29
corporeality 15, 20, 21, 22, 24, 25, 27, 32
Crenshaw, Kimberlé 42, 43
critical peacebuilding research 34, 35, 101–2
critical scholarship 1, 2, 4, 5, 11, 12, 12n83, 15–16, 84, 103, 110
Croat Defence Council 106, 107, 110
Croatia, post-conflict 13, 14–15, 99–115, **109**
Croatian Democratic Union 104, 107, 112
Croatian nationalism 100, 105, 110, 111, 114
Croatian war of independence 99, 100–1, 104, 105, 107, 108, 110, 111, 112
cultural figures 73
cultural violence 7, 70, 102
curiosity 2, 22–3, 103

decision-making 40, 93
decolonisation, of PCS 12, 15–17
deprivation 71, 81
detachment 36

dichotomies 35, 37–42, 57
difference 22, 40–1, 43, 52, 53, 55–6, 57, 60, 65
diffractive reading 22, 23, 33
diplomacy 6, 7–8, 68
direct violence 7, 70, 77
disarmament 86, 100–1
discrimination 30, 35–6, 42, 48, 49, 57, 64
disempowerment 64, 108
diversity 17, 18, 38, 45, 46, 53, 75, 87, 90, 94
domination 6, 8, 13, 44, 61
drawing workshops 93, 95, 97
DrawingOut method 95

emancipation 13, 25, 26, 35, 37, 63, 91
embodied data 23, 32, 33
embodied ethics 70
embodied experiences 14, 15, 16, 21, 25, 53–4, 55, 101
embodied hybridity 56
embodied identities 56
embodied knowledge 87, 89
embodied performance 101, 113, 114
embodied personas 100, 113
embodied turn, of international relations 104
embodiment 3, 12, 14–15, 22, 26, 27, 29, 30, 54
emotions 29, 33, 40, 41, 80, 91; and contested everyday peace 101–2, 104, 107, 110, 114
empathy 12, 70, 87, 102, 103n35
empowerment 39, 45, 64, 90, 91, 97, 107–8
Enloe, Cynthia 1–2, 100
EPI (Everyday Peace Indicators) project 68
epistemology: Burmese research associates 92; corporeal 27; everyday 27; feminist *see* feminist epistemology; participatory 27; PCS 18, 35, 41; peace 25
equality 40, 58, 66, 95; gender 9, 10, 11, 56, 61, 63
ethics 13, 16, 22, 26; embodied 70; feminist care 68, 70, 72, 77, 78, 81
ethnic cleansing 105–6
ethnography 11, 12, 17–18, 50, 89, 90, 113
ethnopolitics 106, 107, 112
EU (European Union) 105, 108
Eurocentrism 16, 17, 18
European Union (EU) 105, 108
eventness, of peace 20, 22, 30–2
everyday, the 55, 64, 74, 84, 88, 89, 96; and contested everyday peace 101–4, 114, 115; and feminist interventions 3, 4, 10, 12, 13, 15, 16; and feminist research agenda 20, 21, 22, 23, 24, 25, 26, 27, 29, 30, 32; and intersectionality of peace 34, 35, 36, 37, 39–41, 43, 47, 48, 49
everyday epistemology 27
everyday peace 11, 15, 17, 90; in post-conflict Croatia 13, 14–15, 99–115, **109**
Everyday Peace Indicators (EPI) project 68
everyday peace literature 68, 69–70
everyday peacebuilding, care as 67–81
everyday praxis of peacebuilding 53
everydayness 21, 32

exclusion: of Croatian veterans 107, 114; of feminist scholarship 2, 5; and intersectionality 36, 44; and 'the local' 86; and peacebuilding 10, 35; of socially marginalised groups 88; of women 104
experiences: gendered 51–66; lived *see* lived experiences; local 83–97; personal 11, 88, 89, 94
experiential knowledge 14, 83, 84, 87, 88–96, 97, 103
expert knowledge 83, 84–8, 90, 92

family, the 18, 39
femininity 3, 48, 56, 57, 59, 60–1, 64
feminism 1, 3–4; and critical PCS 4, 5, 8, 12, 14, 34–50
feminist aesthetic consciousness 115
feminist care ethics 68, 70, 72, 77, 78, 81
feminist consciousness 99, 115
feminist engagement, with hybridity 59, 66
feminist epistemology 1, 3, 12, 13–14, 83, 84, 88–92, 96, 97
feminist genealogical analysis 1
feminist interventions, in critical PCS 1–19
feminist marginalisation 1, 2, 3, 4–5, 17–18
feminist methodologies 2, 3, 13–14, 35, 35n7, 36, 89
feminist peace and conflict studies 21, 22, 25–7, 53, 99
feminist peace research 1, 2, 12, 16, 17, 69, 70–1, 80, 81
feminist theory 2, 3, 12, 13–14, 20, 25
fieldwork 11, 36, 69n13, 71n27, 74n45, 92
first generation, of PCS scholarship 6–7
foreign womanhood 58–9
four generations, of PCS scholarship 1, 2, 4–5, 6–12
fourth generation, of PCS scholarship 2, 5, 11–12
Free Aceh Movement 73–4, 73n41, 74n44
friction 4, 11; and hybridity 51, 52, 53–4, 56, 58, 59, 60, 62, 64, 65
Friends 107–8, **109**, 110, 111, 113, 114

GAM (Gerakan Aceh Merdeka) 73–4, 73n41, 74n44
gender analysis 12, 16
gender dynamics 15, 53, 65, 71, 103
gender equality 9, 10, 11, 56, 61, 63
gender identity 8, 55–6, 58–9, 59–60, 63, 64
gender justice 9–10, 104
gender norms 8, 52, 59
gender order 10, 52, 59, 61, 65, 113
gendered expectations 56, 59, 60, 64
gendered experience 51–66
gendered hybridity 15, 53
gendered power relations 4, 11, 13, 15, 55, 69, 74
genealogical analysis, feminist 1
George, Nicole 38
Gerakan Aceh Merdeka (GAM) 73–4, 73n41, 74n44

ghettoization, of 'gender issues' 1, 5
global justice 70
Global North 16, 17, 90
Global South 17, 18, 19
Goodwin, Andrew 101
governance 9, 38, 52, 80, 85; and feminist research agenda 23, 24, 27–8, 29, 29n42
guesthouse, of South Africa 34, 36, 37, 44, 45–9

HDZ (Hrvatska Demokratska Zajednica) 104, 107, 112
healing 72, 73
Homeland War 99, 100–1, 104, 105, 107, 108, 110, 111, 112
Hrvatska Demokratska Zajednica (HDZ) 104, 107, 112
Hrvatsko Vijeće Obrane (HVO) 106, 107, 110
human needs, fulfilment of 7–8
HVO (Hrvatsko Vijeće Obrane) 106, 107, 110
hybrid identities 13, 34, 40, 41, 42, 43, 44, 47–8
hybridity 4, 11, 12; as a gendered experience 15, 51–66; and PCS 13, 34, 35, 36, 37–9, 40, 42, 43, 44, 46, 47–8, 49
hypermasculinity 110, 114

Iceland, women's collective in post-crash 77–80, 81
ICTY (International Criminal Tribunal for the Former Yugoslavia) 105, 107, 108, 110
identity: categories of 42, 43, 49, 50, 60; embodied 56; ethnopolitical 106; formation of 36, 41, 44, 50; gender 8, 55–6, 58–9, 59–60, 63, 64; hybrid 13, 34, 40, 41, 42, 43, 44, 47–8; intersectional 44, 49, 50; Kashmiri 76; local-international 35, 46; multidirectional nature of 50; multiple 13, 34, 40, 41, 42, 43, 44, 47–8; Muslim 75; in Myanmar 94; national 79, 100, 106; politics of 3, 43; post-conflict 39; religious 75, 77; social 41, 101, 106; transversal nature of 50; veteran 101, 108, 113
illiberality 52, 56, 58, 61, 64, 65, 66
inclusion 18, 23, 36, 63; of local experiences 83–97
Independent State of Croatia (NDH) 100, 107, 111, 111n85, 112, 113
Indian state 74–5, 74n45, 76, 77
Indonesia 72–3, 73n41
inequality 4, 8, 50, 61; and intersectionality of peace 40, 42, 44, 45, 46, 47, 48, 49
inter-communal care, and everyday peace 74–7
international, the 23, 35, 38, 40, 86
International Criminal Tribunal for the Former Yugoslavia (ICTY) 105, 107, 108, 110
international organisations (IOs) 51n1, 52, 54, 59–60, 63, 87, 90
international politics 86, 88, 108
International Relations (IR) 4, 12, 21, 37, 39, 41, 103, 110
International Security Assistance Force (ISAF) 54, 58, 59, 61, 62, 63

International Studies Association (ISA) 17
international theory, aesthetic and visual turns of 99, 101
intersectional identity 44, 49, 50
intersectionality: feminist approaches to investigating 42–5, 49, 50; of peace 13, 34, 36–7, 39, 41, 46, 48–9
interventions, feminist 1–19
intra-communal care, and everyday peace 74–7
IOs (international organisations) 51n1, 52, 54, 59–60, 63, 87, 90
IR (International Relations) 4, 12, 21, 37, 39, 41, 103, 110
ISA (International Studies Association) 17
ISAF (International Security Assistance Force) 54, 58, 59, 61, 62, 63
Islam 63, 73, 74n45, 75–7, 75n50, 94

justice 6, 7; gender 9–10, 104; global 70; transitional 43, 45, 110

Kachin state, Myanmar 83, 93, 95, 96
Kaisu 28, 29, 30, 31
Kashmir 67, 69, 74–7, 80–1
Kashmiriyat 75, 76, 77, 80–1
Keuchik 73
kindness 70, 72–4
knowledge: embodied 87, 89; experiential 14, 83, 84, 87, 88–96, 97, 103; expert 83, 84–8, 90, 92; local 85, 86, 88, 94n48; production of 3, 16, 17, 27, 83–4, 87, 88, 89–90, 92

Lederach, John Paul 91
liberal citizenship 58, 59
liberal peace 8–11, 23, 24, 34, 85, 100, 102; building of 4, 9, 10, 16, 24, 38, 52, 65, 69, 70; and hybridity 52, 53, 54, 56, 59, 62, 64, 65–6
liberalism 56
listening 84, 85, 91, 92, 104, 112
lived experiences 2, 17, 46, 48, 52, 54, 62, 68, 103; and feminist research agenda 21, 22, 26, 27; of violence in conflict 84, 89, 95, 96
local, the 3, 4, 11, 16, 20, 23, 25; and intersectionality of peace 34, 35, 39, 40; and violence in conflict 83–4, 84–8, 95, 96
local actors 11, 37, 38, 55; and violence in conflict 85, 86, 87, 88, 91, 92, 93, 96
local elites 89, 96
local experiences, and violence in conflict 83–97
local knowledge 85, 86, 88, 94n48
local turn, within critical scholarship 12, 12n86, 24–5, 33, 34
local-international identity 35, 46
Luise 58–9, 61, 62, 63–4

Mac Ginty, Roger 23, 24n18, 68
McEvoy-Levy, Siobhan 102, 103
McLeod, Laura 38, 52
marginalisation, of feminism 1, 2, 3, 4–5, 17–18

masculinities 3, 7, 52, 56, 57, 63, 64; veteran *see* veteran masculinities
Maternal Thinking 70
mediation (dispute resolution) 6, 7, 8, 9, 73
mediation (intermediate mechanism) 22, 71, 102, 107, 111, 114
Merleau-Ponty, Maurice 22, 26
methodology 54; for conflict analysis 84, 88, 90, 92–6; diffractive reading 22, 23, 33; experiential knowledge 84, 88, 90, 92–6; feminist 2, 3, 13–14, 35, 35n7, 36, 89; for gendered narratives 101, 108; and intersectionality 44
militarism 7, 70, 102
misogyny 4, 61
mothering 27, 70, 76
multidirectional nature, of identities 50
multiple identities 13, 34, 40, 41, 42, 43, 44, 47–8
mundane peace 20–33
mundane practices: of conflict management 70; of peace 20, 21, 22, 24, 27–8, 31, 32, 33
music, popular 13, 14–15, 99–115, **109**
Muslims 63, 73, 74n45, 75–7, 75n50, 94
Myanmar, silenced voices in 13, 14, 83, 84, 87, 92–6
mythology, of Croatian war of independence 100, 104, 107, 110, 114, 115

Nan 26, 27
narrative studies 36, 37, 44
narratives: intersectional 34, 43, 44, 49; and local realities 41–2
national identity 79, 100, 106
national regeneration 105, 107
nationalism 100, 101n9, 102, 105, 106; Croatian 100, 105, 110, 111, 114
NDH (Independent State of Croatia) 100, 107, 111, 111n85, 112, 113
negative peace 6–7, 21, 68
neo-liberalism 9, 23, 24
Nezavisna Država Hrvatska *see* NDH (Independent State of Croatia)
Ngcoya, Mvuselelo 46–7
non-governmental organisations (NGOs) 51n1, 52, 54, 94
non-standard entry point, to the field 94
Nonviolent Peaceforce (NP) 90n33, 91n43, 92–3
Northern Ireland, peacebuilding in 67, 69, 71–2, 74, 80
NP (Nonviolent Peaceforce) 90n33, 91n43, 92–3

oppression 42, 43, 44, 47, 48, 49, 62, 76
ordinary people 14, 16, 20, 24, 32; and violence in conflict 83, 89, 91–2, 97
other, the 24, 30–1, 65, 71, 72, 85–6

participatory epistemology 27
patriarchy 4, 7, 48, 74; *see also* structural violence 7, 77, 81
patriotic music 99, 101, 106, 107, 113

PCS epistemology 18, 35, 41
peace: eventness of 20, 22, 30–2; everyday 11, 13, 14–15, 17, 90, 99–115, **109**; inclusive 63; intersectionality of 13, 34, 36–7, 39, 41, 46, 48–9; mundane 20–33; negative 6–7, 21, 68; politics of 102, 103, 106; post-liberal 11–12, 15, 70, 101–2; sensory perception of 1, 3; sustainable 6, 106
peace activism 112
peace agreements 10, 43, 73
peace epistemology 25
peace negotiations 7, 7n29
peace research 7, 55, 83, 86; feminist 12, 16, 17, 69, 70–1, 80, 81
peace theory, feminist 20, 25
peacebuilding: arts-based 102; care as 69–77; liberal *see* liberal peacebuilding; post-liberal 4, 67–8
Peacebuilding Commission (UN) 5
peacebuilding missions 6, 9, 34
peacebuilding policy 3, 4
peacebuilding practice 4, 13, 41
peacebuilding studies 48, 90, 103
peaceful transformation 67, 69, 72, 80, 81
peacekeeping missions 6, 9, 34
peacemaking 27, 84–5
Perković, Marko 101, 106–11, **109**, 112
personal, the 3, 14, 25–6, 38
personal experiences 11, 88, 89, 94
phenomenology 21, 22, 26, 32
political, the 30, 38
politics: affective 14, 99, 100, 101, 106, 113, 114; identity 3, 43; international 86, 88, 108; of peace 102, 103, 106; of vulnerability 15, 20–33
popular music 13, 14–15, 99–115, **109**
positionalities 16, 46, 55
positivism 2, 87
post-colonialism 20, 21–2, 27, 33, 38
post-conflict Croatia 13, 14–15, 99–115, **109**
post-conflict identity 39
post-liberal peace 11–12, 15, 70, 101–2
post-liberal peacebuilding 4, 67–8
power dynamics 13, 36, 45, 49, 88
power relations 55, 70, 72, 81, 91; and feminist interventions 5, 8, 10, 13, 14, 16; gendered 4, 11, 13, 15, 55, 69, 74; and intersectionality of peace 35, 37, 38, 39, 44, 47–8, 49, 50; between researcher and researched 88, 91
power-blind binaries 34–50
practices of care 27, 67, 68, 69, 70, 71, 73, 77, 80, 81
praxis of peace 26, 52, 53, 56
Prijatelji 107–8, **109**, 110, 111, 113, 114
private, the 11, 40, 55
privilege 16, 53, 55, 59, 83, 86, 87; and intersectionality of peace 35, 36, 44, 45, 46, 48, 49, 50
protection 28–9, 28n36, 84, 89, 90, 92, 97
public, the 36, 40
public myths 104–6

race 2; and hybridity 53, 55, 56, 57, 58, 59, 60, 61, 64; and intersectionality of peace 43, 45, 46, 48, 50
racialisation 5, 14, 54, 56, 57, 58, 60–1, 62, 65
'Raising Silent Voices' project 14, 83, 84, 89, 92–6
Rakhine state, Myanmar 83, 93, 94, 95
Read, Róisín 51–2, 64
Ready for the Home 111, 112, 113
recognition 26, 30, 32, 33
reconciliation 6, 31, 73, 74, 104, 105
reintegration 74, 86, 100, 105
relatedness 20, 70–1, 81
relationality 21, 22, 26, 27–8, 81
relations of power *see* power relations
religion 24; and care as everyday peacebuilding 73–4, 75, 76, 77; and contested everyday peace 100, 101n9, 105, 106
resistance 11, 28, 29, 75, 102, 103, 104, 114
Resolution 1325 on Women, Peace and Security (UN) 9
respect 9, 61, 62, 65, 76, 78
Reykjavik, Iceland 67, 78
Richmond, Oliver P. 4, 23, 53, 101–2
root causes, of conflict 8, 83
Ruane, Abigail 27, 71
Ruddick, Sara 25, 26–7, 39–40, 70

Safia 59–60, 63
second generation, of PCS scholarship 7–8
sectarianism 102
Security Council (UN) 9
sensory perceptions 1, 3, 12, 14–15
sexuality 2, 43, 54, 57
Shepherd, Laura J. 65, 101
Sikh community, in Kashmir 76–7
social identities 41, 101, 106
social relations 27, 29, 40, 46, 48, 67, 69, 70, 72, 74
societal healing 72
solidarity 24, 24n18, 26, 27, 75, 110
South African guest house 34, 36, 37, 44, 45–9
Srinagar, Kashmir 76, 77
structural inequalities 13, 18, 43, 49
structural violence 7, 77, 81; *see also* patriarchy
subaltern, the 17, 24–5
subjectivity 16, 61, 64, 70
subordination 61, 62, 73
suffering 14, 31, 71, 81, 102, 107
sustainable peace 6, 106
Sylvester, Christine 6, 40

taboos 76, 91
Tengku 73–4

theory: feminist 2, 3, 12, 13–14, 20, 25; international 99, 101
therapy 96, 105
third gender, in Afghanistan 13, 15, 51–66
third generation, of PCS scholarship 8–11
third sex 54, 57, 58
Thompson, Marko Perković 101, 106–11, **109**, 112
transformation: conflict 4, 68, 69, 84, 85, 90, 100–1; peaceful 67, 69, 72, 80, 81
transitional justice 43, 45, 110
transversal nature, of identities 50
Troubles, the 69, 71, 72
trust 69, 72, 73, 74, 76, 77, 80, 81, 91, 95, 97, 114
Tuđman, President Franjo 104, 107, 110
Tuhapeut 73

uncertainty 58, 65, 66, 77, 78, 79
United Nations 5, 9

values 61, 62, 78, 79, 93, 105
veterans 99, 100–1, 105, 106–11, **109**, 113, 114; identity of 101, 108, 113; masculinities of 99, 100, 101, 101n9, 103, 104, 106, 112–13, 114–15
victimhood 61, 73, 100, 112
village chiefs 73
violence: armed 73; in conflict 6, 77, 83–97; cultural 7, 70, 102; direct 7, 70, 77; ethnopolitical 106, 112; structural 7, 77, 81
visual turn, of international theory 99
vulnerability 70; politics of 15, 20–33

war 40, 44, 52, 70, 77, 85, 88, 96; of Croatian independence 99, 100–1, 104, 105, 107, 108, 110, 111, 112; and feminist interventions 8, 11, 12, 14, 18; and feminist research agenda 21, 26, 27, 28, 29, 31; memories of 101, 103, 105, 107, 115
wartime past 99–100, 112–13, 114
white female researcher (WFR) 46, 47, 48
womanhood 58, 59, 63, 64, 65
women, definition of 3
Women, Peace and Security (WPS) 5, 9, 16
women's collective 77–80
women's rights 9, 52
WPS (Women, Peace and Security) 5, 9, 16

youth engagement, with popular music in post-conflict Croatia 13, 14–15, 99–115, **109**

Za dom spremni 111, 112, 113